ORLANDO
—BLOOM—

Wherever It May Lead

Robert Steele

Plexus, London

Published by Plexus Publishing Limited
55a Clapham Common Southside
London SW4 9BX
www.plexusbooks.com
First printing 2004

British Library Cataloguing in Publication Data

Steele, Robert
    Orlando Bloom : wherever it may lead
    1. Bloom, Orlando 2. Motion picture actors and
    actresses - Great Britain - Biography
    I. Title
    791.4'3'028'092

    ISBN 0 85965 354 4

Cover design by Brian Flynn
Book design by Brian Flynn and Rebecca Martin
Cover photograph by Armando Gallo/Retna
Printed by Scotprint, Haddington

Acknowledgements
We would like to thank the following journalists, newspapers, magazines
and websites, whose interviews and articles on Orlando were invaluable:
'How my Orlando Bloomed: An Interview with Sonia Copeland Bloom'
by Grant Rollings, the Sun, August 2003; 'Bloom or Bust?' by Lesley
O'Toole, Metro Life, December 2003; 'Full Bloom' by Emily Bearn, the
Sunday Telegraph Magazine, April 2004; 'Return of the swashbucklers'
by Helen Barlow, the New Zealand Herald, June 2004; 'Take your
clothes off, Orlando!' in Frida Magazine, January 2003; 'Elf Assassin' by
Ian Spelling, Starlog Magazine, May 2002; 'Heath of the Moment' by
Claire Sutherland, Herald Sun Weekend Magazine, May 2002; 'Hot Elf
Orlando Bloom', Rolling Stone, October 2002; 'True Brit' by Richard
Alleman, Vogue Magazine, (USA), December 2002; 'The Heroes: Stardom
is good for your elf' by David Matthews, the Mirror, December 2002;
'Boy Wonder' by Angus Fontaine, HQ magazine, March/April 2003;
'Back into the Ring' by Aaron Langmaid, icTheWharf.co.uk, September
2002; 'British Actor Bloom Cuts Swath through Epic Flicks' by Betsy
Pickle, Knoxville News Sentinel, July 2003; 'A Superstar in Bloom' by
Brian Truitt, the Journal, July 2003; 'Orlando Magic' by Mona Gable, the
Los Angeles Times, July 2003; 'The Budding of a Heartthrob' by Kate
Stroup, Newsweek Magazine, July 2003; 'Orlando Bloom: Is He the Next
Brad Pitt?' by Jenny Sundel, US Weekly, July 2003; 'In Full Bloom' by Ian
Nathan, the Times, July 2003; 'Why heartbreak has made me stronger' by
Alison Begbie, Sneak, July/August 2003; 'Fantastic Voyage…' by Jonathan
Heaf, the Face, August 2003; 'The Moon and Stars Came Out Tonight'
by Zoe Williams, Elle, August 2003; 'Tangled Up In Bloom' by Ian
Nathan, FHM Collections, Spring/Summer #6 2003; 'Gotta Lotta Bottle'
by Anwar Brett, Film Review, April 2004; 'The Incredible Hunk' by
Derek O'Connor, the Irish Times, August 2003; 'Next Stop Hollywood'
by Henry Fitzherbert, the Sunday Express, August 2003; 'Swashbuckling
Orlando…' by Helen Hanley, the Irish Independent, August 2003;
'Orlando Just Loves Playing at Pirates' by Andy Dougan, the Sunday
Herald, August 2003; 'Ship Shape and No Mistake' by Gavin Miller, the
Lincolnshire Echo, August 2003; 'Making Waves' by Rob Driscoll,
Western Mail, August 2003; 'In the Hot Seat' by John Millar, New!,
August 2003; 'A British Star in Full Bloom' by Jeff Chu, Time Magazine
Europe, August 2003; 'Depp Blue Sea' by Nick Setchfield, SFX Magazine,
September 2003; 'From the historic elf warrior to the romantic bucca-
neer…' by Heiko Rosner, Cinema, September 2003; 'Full Bloom' by Nick
Compton, Details, June/July 2003; 'Beautiful Creatures' by Chloe Fox,
British Vogue, July 2003; 'Early Bloomer' by Tami Mnoian, Fluant
Magazine, July 2003; 'Career in Full Bloom' by Steve Tilley, Toronto Sun,
July 2003; 'En garde!' by Amy Longsdorf, the Record, July 2003; 'Yo-ho,
yo-ho, a 'Pirates' film for Orlando Bloom' by Stephen Schaefer, the
Boston Herald, July 2003; 'Bloom and Doom' by David Eimer, the Times,
May 2004; Interview by Christian Henning, YAM!, September 2003;
Interview by Antonia Steffens, Maedchen, August 2003; Interview by
David Holscher, Sugar (Germany), September 2003; Interview by Robin
Lynch, Sugar (UK), September 2003; Interview by Andreas Renner, Petra,
September 2003; Interview in JOY, September 2003; Interview by Markus
Tschiedert, MovieStar, September/October 2003; 'Orlando Bloom' by
Alex Bilmes, GQ, October 2003.

We would like to thank the following magazines, newspapers and
websites for their coverage of Orlando: USA Today; the Guardian; the
Observer; the Evening Standard; the Daily Mail; the Sun Herald;
Entertainment Weekly; Minneapolis Star-Tribune; the Wall Street Journal;
the Courier; Teen People; Who Magazine; Newsweek; the Mirror; the
Daily Telegraph (Sydney); the Sunday Telegraph (Australia); Daily
Variety; YM Magazine; Empire Magazine; Los Angeles Daily News;
CosmoGIRL magazine; Dolly Magazine; NW Magazine; Premiere; the
Sunday Times; Bravo; the Houston Chronicle; the New York Observer;
the Sunday Herald; the Telegraph; the Times; Hollywood Reporter; Time;
the Daily Express; the Daily Mail; Movie Idols; Uncut Magazine; full-
bloom.net; angelfire.com; orlandocentral.net; orlandomultimedia.net; rot-
tentomatoes.com; imdb.com; celebstation.org; culturevulture.net; flipside-
movies.com; ka-bloom.org; boston.com; nypost.com; thisislondon.co.uk;
moviecompound.com; pachome1.pacific.net; oscar.com; hollywood.com;
thezreview.co.uk; amazon.co.uk; salon.com; efilmcritic.com;
teenmag.com; angeltowns.com; joblo.com; dailynews.com; usatoday.com;
guidelive.com; hollywoodreporter.com; nydailynews.com; bbc.co.uk;
ananova.com; theorlandobloomfiles.com; filmthreat.com; cinescape.com;
movies.yahoo.com; funny.co.uk; variety.com; orlandobloomweb.com.

Thanks are due to the following photographers, photo libraries, maga-
zines and film companies: Luis Martinez/Retna; Wendy Idele/Retna;
Armando Gallo/Retna; Grayson Alexander/Retna (Retna.com); Sneak
magazine; Big Pictures; Gig/Big Pictures; Todd Plitt/ Big Pictures; The
Lord of the Rings film stills copyright New Line Cinema courtesy Big
Pictures/Gig (Bigpicturesphoto.com); The Lord of the Rings film posters
copyright New Line Cinema/New Line Productions, Inc; Doug Benc/Getty
Images; Dave Hogan/Getty Images; Dean Treml/Getty Images; Ande
Mertl/AFP/Getty Images; Mark Mainz/Getty Images (Gettyimages.com);
Anthony Phelps/Reuters/Corbis; Pictures/ZUMA/Corbis; Neal
Preston/Corbis (Corbis.com); Paul Smith/All Action (Allaction.co.uk);
Empire; Cosmo Girl; Arena; The Telegraph Magazine; The Face; GQ; John
Frost Newspapers; BFI Stills, Posters and Designs; Teen People; People;
Sunday Times Culture; HQ; Kinema; Premier; YM; Esquire; Flaunt.

Films Stills courtesy of: Bentley Productions/ITV; New Line
Cinema/WingNut Films/Lord Zweite Productions Deutschland
Filmproduktion GmbH & Co. KG/The Saul Zaentz Company; New Line
Cinema/Warner Bros; Working Title Australia/Working Title Films; Focus
Features/United International Pictures; Universal Pictures/Working Title
Films; Universal Pictures; First Mate Productions Inc/ Jerry Bruckheimer
Films/ Walt Disney Pictures; The Walt Disney Company/ Buena Vista
Pictures/Buena Vista International; Columbia Pictures Corporation/
Revolution Studios/Jerry Bruckheimer Films/Scott Free Productions;
Columbia Pictures/Revolution Studios/Sony Pictures Entertainment; Plan B
Productions Inc/Radiant Productions/Warner Bros; Warner Bros; 20th
Century Fox/Scott Free Productions; 20th Century Fox Pictures.

It has not been possible in all cases to trace the copyright sources,
and the publishers would be glad to hear from any such unacknowledged
copyright holders.

CONTENTS

INTRODUCTION

'I think I'm incredibly lucky to be doing what I do.' – *Orlando*

Orlando Bloom is a 21st century movie star. Combined with a spiritual, intuitive side that seems strangely in tune with the character of Legolas Greenleaf, the warrior-elf character who put Orlando on the map, he is a star of the New Age.

No one could have anticipated how *The Lord of the Rings*, in its equally exciting component episodes, would make an icon of its elven archer. In the early days of the grass-roots eruption that is Bloom-mania, Orlando Bloom was Legolas. The actor and his character were interchangeable. As Orlando (or 'Orly', as the fans familiarly refer to him) was non-egotistic enough to recognise, 'There's absolutely nothing sexually threatening about an Elf. Legolas is a good, safe guy for girls to pin their dreams on.'

It seemed like the happy continuation of a seemingly charmed life. This, after all, was the young guy who could break his back in a freak accident and later claim that the ordeal was 'the making of [me]'. With his indomitable positive outlook and lust for life, he wouldn't let a little matter like a damaged spine prevent him indulging in bungee jumping, sky-diving or surfing.

'There's absolutely nothing sexually threatening about an Elf. Legolas is a good, safe guy for girls to pin their dreams on.'

'It's an unusual story,' Orlando admits of his early life, '[but] if you didn't have those things in your life, you'd be so bland.' But he wouldn't be typecast as an otherworldly being with a bow and arrow forever. After effortlessly stealing scenes in the underrated (and little-seen) Ned Kelly, the release of Pirates of the Caribbean: The Curse of the Black Pearl made the charismatic Bloom a recognisable star in every sense. The near-hysteria that would break out when he was spotted in public was on account of being recognised as himself, not on account of being mistaken for a mythical being from a movie.

There is no doubt that Orlando is among the most powerful, hypnotic screen presences of the modern age. He is, in that effortless, indefinable way, a true Star. But still, the path of his early career has led to the odd, recent explosion of discontent: 'I've had enough of being the cool, clean-shaven Elf; the cool, wholesome pirate slayer. Do I want to be a pin-up? Do I want to just be a poster boy?'

The second stage of his career, now well underway, will determine whether Orlando Bloom can transcend merely being a great Star, and fulfil his ambition to be a great Actor.

CANTERBURY TALES
The Early Years

'I always really loved performing as a kid.' – *Orlando Bloom*

Orlando Bloom first saw the light of day in the fabled English cathedral city of Canterbury, Kent, on 13 January 1977. Born to Harry Bloom, a Jewish South African, and his wife, Sonia, he was the second of two children – his sister, Samantha, being two years older. Orlando's family background was at once unusual and distinguished. Harry had been a prominent lawyer in his native South Africa. To his great credit, he had also been an active campaigner against Apartheid, the old system of racial inequality and white supremacy.

As a lawyer, he defended black activists from the African National Congress (ANC), the then outlawed political liberation movement led by future SA president Nelson Mandela, who Harry also got to know. As a writer, he published a 1956 novel entitled *Episode* (later retitled *Transvaal Episode*, referring to the region in which the book is set), that describes an uprising in a black township during an ANC campaign of political defiance in the early 1950s. Serving a three-month prison sentence on charges of political sedition, living under continual threats of violence from the security service and their lackeys, it's little wonder that, in 1963, Harry would exile himself to the more tolerant climate of Great Britain.

On resettling in Canterbury, Harry took the post of Professor of Law at the University of Kent. It was in the same locality that he met his future wife, Sonia Copeland, who had a dual background in business and as a writer. Sonia would start her own English language school for foreign students, Concorde International, which has continued to the present day.

Harry, who was some years his wife's senior, suffered a stroke in the early 1980s. From thereon, his condition deteriorated rapidly. He died, aged 68, on 28 July 1981. 'I was four when Harry died,' says Orlando, 'so what do you remember when you are four? My mother has always spoken highly of him. He's been a role model for me in my head.' Looking back on his influence, Orlando acclaims, 'Harry was a great man. It was as though he'd done his job and he'd left the world.'

Soon after Harry's passing, a family friend named Colin Stone was appointed as Samantha and Orlando's legal guardian. As a work colleague and very close friend of Sonia Copeland Bloom, Stone, then 30 years old, had already moved into the family home to help Sonia nurse her gravely ill husband. Colin would soon become the classic 'uncle' figure, to evoke the quaint English euphemism, to Samantha and Orlando, and would eventually take over as director of Concorde International when Sonia retired.

But it was Sonia Bloom who was the most formative influence upon her son's life. Given his name by Sonia, Orlando was not, as fanciful journalists have claimed, named after the androgynous title character of Virginia Woolf's novel, *Orlando*. In fact, his mother once informed him that his name meant 'famous throughout the land' – 'a hard one to live up to,' he claims, though it displays the admirable faith in her son that she maintains to this day. His name was also inspired by Orlando Gibbons, a sixteenth century composer who was buried in Canterbury Cathedral. As Orlando explains, 'The name Orlando Gibbons was floating around when I was younger.'

The choice of name displayed both Sonia's spiritual and artistic bent. She had always been enamoured of the arts – whether fine art, the visual arts and photography (interests which were inherited by her son) or the classical performing arts and literature. Throughout their childhood and their early youth, she would always encourage Samantha and Orlando to participate in performance events. '[My mother] was quite interested in both my sister and me being creative,' acknowledges Orlando. 'She was always taking us to the theatre to see plays and musicals, and she'd do things like enter us into the Canterbury Festival, which was good because it got both of us used to being in front of an audience.' Ultimately, both Samantha and Orlando would harbour ambitions to become actors, gaining their first experiences of reciting poetry, prose and passages from the Bible at the annual Canterbury Festival – winning prizes for their performance on more than one occasion.

'I was an adventuresome baby. As a child I was in and out of hospital so many times that the staff worried I was being beaten. Obviously, I wasn't.'

'We used to win first prize,' says the younger sibling, still obviously retaining a sense of pride, before reciting from the poet Robert Frost's 'Stopping by Woods on a Snowy Evening': '"The woods are lovely, dark and deep / And I have promises to keep / And miles to go before I sleep . . ."' Not bad for a ten-year-old memory. I think those experiences are what inspired me to be an actor.

'It gave me a sensitivity to language in terms of vocalising it,' he continues. 'I always used to get involved with the school plays. My teacher at school, who would take drama, would always give me interesting roles as a kid. My mum would take us to the theatre, and watching these larger-than-life characters I decided I wanted to become an actor.' There were frequent visits to the celebrated Marlowe Theatre – named after Canterbury's most infamous son, Elizabethan playwright, spy, *agent provocateur* and gay rogue Christopher Marlowe. 'I don't know why she wanted us to do it. But it was great. I loved it. My mum always encouraged us to be creative. And she would have people come around and teach us art and pottery and stuff like that.'

Orlando caught his own strain of the acting bug as he was first starting primary school. 'I always really loved performing as a kid,' he confirms. 'My first performance was a little embarrassing because I was doing a play at a local theatre and it was quite a big deal because the whole of Canterbury was there, and I was a monkey. Dressed in a monkey suit. There were three of us. And this monkey suit was really hot, you know? It was like one of those sort of synthetic suits, and I was only four, and I'll never forget it. I think it's lived with me ever since. I've been really paranoid about making the same mistake, but I, um, itched my butt on stage but it was like, I had this terrible itch, and of course the audience went mad with laughter. But I was a monkey, so it was sort of what a monkey would do! But I was like, "what did I do?" because I'd sort of broken the routine out of what I was supposed to be doing, so I was like, Uh! So it was sort of stage fright.'

In terms of his general education, Sonia was also prepared to give Orlando nothing but the

best. As he reached his early high-school years, she would pay £9,000 a year for him to attend the local public school, St Edmund's in Canterbury – granting him a first-rate education as well as allowing him to live at home with his adoring family. It was fortunate, perhaps, that his family had the funds to pay for a private education. For Orlando had been diagnosed early in his school life as severely dyslexic, a condition that leaves many state-school pupils floundering without educational assistance, and made school, by his own admission, into 'hard graft'. But once again, there was the invaluable help and encouragement of his mother, herself adept in training the unfamiliar eye to new words and language. Despite his later, tongue-in-cheek protestation, 'I'm a pikey boy from Kent at the end of the day,' he and his family had a lot less in common with the 'pikey' travellers or gypsies of the region than with Virginia Woolf's well-heeled Bloomsbury bohemians.

Wherever life would lead Orlando Bloom, his mother was determined he would not be held back. As he later said of her influence, 'My mum pretty much did what the hell she wanted in life, and I intend to do the same.' Indeed, Sonia Copeland Bloom's adventurousness extended beyond her marriage to an acclaimed writer and courageous human rights campaigner, and taking a younger man as her lover. At various times, she had ridden across Mexico on a mule, or been one of the organisers of the first Junior Golf Championships competition in Russia. Whatever captured her imagination became, to her, a practical possibility. It was a positive outlook she communicated to her children.

'My mum would take us to the theatre, and watching these larger-than-life characters I decided I wanted to become an actor.'

And then, of course, their immersion in the performing arts was becoming a constant theme. 'I loved joining in with school plays at the place in Canterbury where I used to go,' recalls Orlando. 'I was a pretty good "sergeant of police" in Gilbert and Sullivan's *Pirates of Penzance*. At least, I thought that I was!' Other parts included a lecherous old man in the musical pastiche *The Boy Friend*, once filmed with 1960s model Twiggy. As he'd later complain, 'I never got a dashing lead, not once, although I always wanted those. I got to be the old man, the police officer – the character stuff.' Quite possibly, given his innate charms, his drama teachers were trying to cast against type and give the other boys a chance.

But his early grounding in life was not any kind of hothouse flower cultivation. On the contrary, Sonia taught her children not just to appreciate and participate, but to *live*. Besides his interests in acting and visual art, Orlando became enamoured of the outdoor life. Always physically extrovert and impulsive, 'I'd be the first to jump off the wall or go into the woods. I like to do things as a group, but I think I'm more of a leader than a follower.' It was also this adventurousness and impetuousness that led him into danger, at certain points of his young life.

His incredible tally of personal injuries began when Orlando was only a small baby, less than a year old, and his mother accidentally fractured his skull against a tree. 'It's not nearly as terrible as it sounds,' he laughs. 'She was gathering wood and holding me, and she bent over and knocked my head.' From thereon, most of the injuries suffered by the young Orlando would be self-inflicted. Several months later, the small child would fall off a kitchen stool and fracture his skull all over again. In an early introduction to horses, to which he developed a lifelong affection, the little boy's toe was crushed beneath a horse's hoof. 'I was an adventuresome baby. As a child I was in and out of hospital so many times that the staff worried I was being beaten. Obviously, I wasn't,' he stresses.

Orlando became a keen horse rider from an early age. It's one of those rare omens of things-to-come that he believes run through his life, like fragments of the future fallen fortuitously into place. His first part-time job also made good use of the beautiful Kent countryside. He became a clay trapper: 'You know when you go shooting and the ceramic discs fly out and you shoot them? I was the guy who pulled the trap and let it go . . . I always wanted to be the shooter.' Orlando was also a keen sportsman at school, playing rugby and hockey, and learning how to fence – a skill that would become more useful in his later career than he could have possibly imagined.

As he grew older and became ever more active, so his accidental injuries grew more severe. Aged eleven, he broke his right leg whilst skiing. At twelve, he broke his nose playing rugby. 'I broke my finger in rugby as well,' Orlando remembers. 'It was part of growing up.' At thirteen, he broke his wrist whilst snowboarding – 'It was my first time and I kind of went at it a bit hard,' he acknowledged with a smile. 'You could say that I'm accident prone.

'I think I was quite loud then,' he says of himself as a child, 'which is kind of bizarre. I was quite kind of outgoing in a whole different way. I was like, nothing is stopping me. Had my life in the goal and I was going for it.'

But those early goals, which have remained amazingly consistent, were just taking shape. In a safer imaginary world, Orlando's growing love of films and TV shows was crystallising into something as yet unformed. As the nascent action man would later acknowledge, 'a huge part of my life is spent watching movies.'

His absorption in the performing arts did not seem to extend to music. As Orlando readily admits, he was never very familiar with the pop music charts or the Top Ten. 'I never knew who the Spice Girls were or anyone like that.' Orlando's musical tastes were mostly of a quiet, introspective folk-rock style (despite his first record purchase being Michael Jackson's 'Thriller' and his first gig being a Jamiroquai concert). The first CD album he ever bought was by Edie Brickell and the New Bohemians, led by the eclectic female vocalist-lyricist, who became the wife of singer-songwriter icon, Paul Simon. Orlando's preference for acoustic guitar sounds and lyrical introspection continues to develop throughout his adulthood.

'I always used to get involved with the school plays . . . I always loved performing as a kid.'

As a boy though, despite his relatively cultured upbringing, 'I used to get *The Beano* every week and I used to read a lot of *Garfield*, watch a lot of trashy American TV.' As he later admitted, he had a precocious schoolboy crush on Linda Evans, the star of 1980s US soap opera *Dynasty*. Whatever the undoubted appeal of the blonde Ms. Evans, she was still much closer to his mother's age than his own. But that doesn't deter a little boy in love. 'My aunt works in publicity in New York,' he explained, 'so I got the chance to meet her [Linda Evans] when she went to shoot a commercial there. She signed a photo for me. I was so excited. I still have it.'

As for the male idols he followed religiously on the small screen as a child, 'When I realised the heroes on *The A-Team*, *The Fall Guy* and *Knight Rider* weren't real, I decided I wanted to act because I thought I'd love to be any number of those guys.' Then there was *Superman*, the 1978 comic-book adaptation. When Orlando first saw *Superman* on TV as a boy, he was smitten. And not just by Christopher Reeve in his blue and red tights either: 'Aged nine, I had this girlfriend, and we used to have running races in the park to see who would be her boyfriend for the day. I wanted to be like Superman and fly in and rescue her. Once I realised Superman was an actor, I thought, "That's for me." I got into acting for the women.'

The potentially liberating scope of an actor's life really began to hit home three years later. Over the Christmas period of 1989, the Blooms were spending the holiday with family members in Boston, USA. Orlando distinctly remembers how his older cousin, an art director then working in Los Angeles, rented a whole bunch of videos to watch over the festive period. Two of them, in particular, proved to be potentially life-changing experiences: 'one of them was *The Hustler*, with Paul Newman. It was a black-and-white film, and at first I thought, "Ugh – I don't know if I'm going to be impressed by this." And, of course, Paul Newman was so cool in that, that I was incredibly impressed by him, and still am.' For this, Newman entered the pantheon of Orlando's coolest actor-icons – alongside Steve McQueen and Johnny Depp. Orlando says of *The Hustler*, 'I just loved it, man. From then on, it [an acting career] was a done deal.'

His cousin's other choice, *Stand By Me*, was an adolescent rites-of-passage movie. Starring the blessed and doomed River Phoenix as a troubled twelve-year-old, it is a classic coming-of-age movie. As Orlando says, *Superman* may have been his first film, 'but *Stand By Me* really got me into acting.'

From the late 1980s and all through the ensuing decade, acting, and its potential versatility, would grow into an obsession. 'The reason I got into acting was because when I was younger, I had an incredible imagination, like most kids, and I was always drawn to these larger-than-life characters that I would see either at the theatre, on TV or at the cinema. Once I was old enough to realise that those characters weren't real, they were actors – once I realised I could be Superman or I could be *The Hustler* or I could be Daniel Day-Lewis's character in *The Last of the Mohicans* – I was like, "Man, I can become an actor and be all of those things."'

For an actor, it was now abundantly clear to him, these disparate roles were all in a day's work. The anti-hero was as compelling a screen icon as the action hero. 'I used to watch *Taxi Driver* and see [Robert De Niro's] Travis Bickle,' says Orlando. 'I'd

Orlando with his cousin, art director Sebastian Copeland, who introduced his younger relative to American popular cinema.

go, "Wow, see that character?" . . . You sit in a movie cinema and you sort of transcend, don't you? You sort of project yourself into a character.'

From this point on, Orlando would take his thespian ambitions more seriously, with a move into local community theatre productions on his family's return home from the US. To this day, it's the versatility and unpredictability of his profession that he continues to thrive on – even though many have stereotyped him as an action man who only appears in epic adventure films. 'I realised those larger-than-life actors that I saw on TV, in the movies, in the theatre, even street performers, could be multiple characters, and I thought that was just great. You can be an action hero, you can be a Jimmy Dean, you can be those characters.' Orlando is still seeking to resolve this contradiction in his present-day career choices.

'My mum pretty much did what the hell she wanted in life, and I intend to do the same.'

For all the appealing unconventionality of their background, neither Orlando nor his sister seem to have been marked by negative experiences or childhood traumas. Not even, it seems, when Orlando reached the age of thirteen, and was given a mild shock that might have undermined a weaker personality. It was on a family holiday in 1990 that it was revealed to him that Harry Bloom, the man who had given him his name and had brought him up as a small boy, was not his natural father. Orlando belatedly discovered that his real father had always been close at hand, unbeknownst to himself. 'When my father died, Colin was made my legal guardian,' he calmly explains. 'He was always a close family friend, but I always thought Harry was my biological father . . . [then] I found out that Colin was my real father. Not Harry. But Colin.' It was revealed,

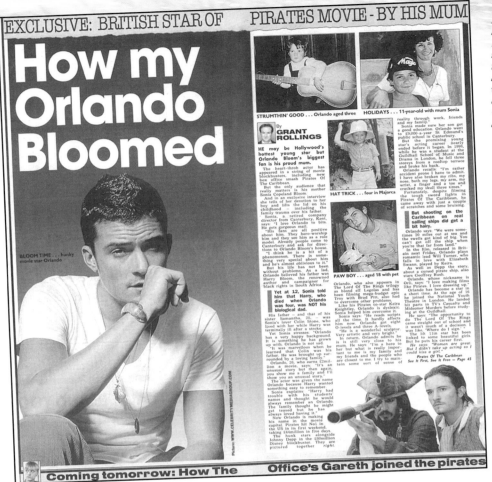

A mother's pride: Sonia Copeland Bloom gave this interview to UK tabloid The Sun, *after* Pirates of the Caribbean *established Orlando as a star.*

all in the space of one day, that not only had Colin Stone been his mother's longterm lover, but he was also the man that Orlando might have called 'Dad'.

'My mum was married to one man, but I was fathered by a second. I think she was waiting for me to be old enough to understand it. But when would you tell a kid about that stuff? It's very difficult.' Indeed, if Orlando had been brought up in California, it might have been the cue for expensive therapy sessions. But, with his down-to-earth, phlegmatic Englishness, he wears it lightly. 'It's an unusual story but then, you show me a family and I'll show you an unusual story.' Besides, he asserts, 'if you didn't have those things in your life, you'd be so bland.'

'I like to do things as a group, but I think I'm more of a leader than a follower.'

'Orlando has a very happy background. It is something he has grown up with. Orlando is not sad,' defended Sonia, when this very minor hint of scandal was seized on by the UK tabloids. 'It was marvellous when he learned that Colin was his father. He was brought up surrounded by a loving family.' It was a sentiment echoed by Colin himself, in response to an 'expose' in the *Sunday Mirror*: 'Orlando and Samantha have . . . had a lot of love, a very happy upbringing, and they've grown up to be very well-balanced, happy people.' As Orlando himself so plainly puts it, 'I was lucky, I had two dads.' Just as his mother's memories of the late Harry Bloom remained a role model for him, so Orlando would acknowledge Colin Stone as 'a great guide' in his life. As a tribute to the older man who saw him through the earliest years of his life, however, Orlando seems never to have contemplated a change of surname from 'Bloom' to 'Stone' – just as his mother has remained posthumously faithful in that respect.

In his high school years, though Orlando has claimed, 'I was a rebel. I still am!', his background actually gave him very little to rebel against. Still, the young teen was displaying the confidence and independent spirit his mother had instilled in him. At fifteen, he was technically underage to have part of his body permanently tattooed. As he later said, 'You have to be quite serious about tattoos . . . they're there forever.' Nonetheless, in reflection of his optimistic nature, he had a small tattoo of the sun etched permanently into his abdomen, very close to his navel. 'I sort of lied and told my mum, "Oh, it's only going to last for a couple of years,"' recollects Orlando, who would adopt a much more famous tattoo design eight years later.

He had also developed a flamboyantly romantic, even Byronic, sartorial style, by wearing original 1960s hippie and mod clothes. The impact on the young women of Kent, seeing dark-haired, olive-skinned 'Orly' in glamorous vintage designs, can only be guessed at. Though these clothes, it has to be said, were borrowed from the collection of a friend's mother: 'My best friend, Chris, his mum had a whole load of sixties clothes, so we used to get dressed up in that stuff.'

And then, of course, there were girls. As with most other adolescent boys, they became a constant preoccupation. 'I've had quite a few girlfriends,' he admits, almost bashfully self-conscious of his image. 'My mum ran a language school and I met lots of European girls there.' But Orlando is also candid enough to admit, 'when I was trying to snog my first girlfriend, I didn't know what word to use, so I was going: "Can I, er, can I, er kiss you? Er, can I get off with you?" I felt like such an idiot. And then when I did do it, I didn't know what to do with my teeth. It was awful.'

'Once I realised I could be Superman or I could be The Hustler or I could be Daniel Day-Lewis's character in The Last of the Mohicans – I was like, "Man, I can become an actor and be all of those things."'

But, despite the customary pubescent gaucheness, it's difficult to believe that attracting female attention wasn't indecently easy. Plus, of course, there was the added luxury of Mum's language school. 'There were always cute girls from all over, especially French,' he reminisces. But, when it came to the big moment, Orly got together with an 'English rose'. 'When I was fourteen, I met this very special girl. I lost my virginity to her.' This particular encounter was not a mere blip on the chart. 'Let's just say that my interest in women grew more then!' But, characteristically, Orlando remains ever the gentleman – refusing to name the girl who granted him his first time, or any of the other teen conquests who followed.

Despite the problems with dyslexia that Sonia had done her best to help him combat, he would go on to pass eight GCSE exams at St Edmund's. Orlando claims, however, 'I never responded to teaching. I was more interested in what was happening on the playing fields.' Clearly, his interests didn't lay in the field of academia. So, Orlando made a major lifestyle choice: in 1993, aged sixteen, he decided to move approximately 50 miles north of Canterbury to the English capital to continue his education. Though most of his culturally formative experiences had taken place in his native Kent, it wasn't unknown for Sonia to take Samantha and Orlando to visit the theatres of London. And it was there, he asserted, with the confidence and determination she'd instilled in him, that he wanted to take acting courses with the National Youth Theatre and do his A-levels. He may have been only touching on the adult age of consent, but this was no deterrent. 'I felt good about it,' testifies Orlando. 'I've always been a bit ahead of myself and I was ready to leave. I felt like London was the place to be.'

WILDE
AT HEART

'I feel really privileged to be an actor, to be paid to do something I love.' – *Orlando Bloom*

Orlando Bloom would go on to study photography and sculpture at A-level (for which he gained A grades), as well as adding theatre studies to his personal curriculum. 'I did better in sculpture exams for A-levels than I did in theatre studies,' he admits. In fact, Orlando would barely scrape through with an 'E' pass in theatre studies, which proves how far his performing ability outstrips any theoretical knowledge. 'My mum is always going, "Just keep up the sculptures, darling" – she's convinced she's gonna have a little shop somewhere and sell my sculptures someday,' he acknowledges, with only mild embarrassment.

Orlando also spent two seasons training at London's National Youth Theatre (NYT). Winning a variety of parts, he came to the attention of the NYT's artistic director, Ed Wilson, who called Orlando 'one of the finest young performers we've ever had in our companies, in all of the fifteen years I've been in post.' The prodigal young talent also had the advantage of knowing 'what I wanted to do from a very young age, because as I was growing up, I was able to make a beeline straight for it.' But there would be some dramatic diversions along the way.

This time was also, precociously, the start of his adult social life. 'That was a big growth period for me. Me and my friends, who were mostly older, used to go clubbing, and I experienced a lot of life at a young age because of that.' He had found himself a flat in the Camden district of central London, where cosmopolitan affluence and urban street life exist side by side.

Although he was only sixteen, and technically underage, Orlando would hang out with the older students and attend the same clubs and bars they did. 'I moved to London expecting to meet a whole load of new mates instantly,' he recalls. 'But London can be such a lonely city at first. But soon I got a place just behind the BT [British Telecom] Tower and found my niche: clubbing and clothes!' It granted him an exposure to metropolitan life, in all its excitement and its seediness, that would have been off-limits to most provincial teenagers. This was the heyday of the post-acid house London club scene, where dance music and rock, straight patrons and gay people, would all intermingle at clubs with a distinctly decadent glam appeal.

'I used to go to all these clubs with great names like Kooky, Hollywood Babylon and Billion Dollar Babes. It was an amazing party scene with even more amazingly beautiful women. It was a mixed gay crowd, transvestites, go-go girls . . . just a whole load of night creatures. Everyone forgot about their job and became models or movie stars for the night . . . yeah, ironic, huh? Trust me, it's much easier faking it.'

It was one more aspect that would grant him a wider education in the human condition. 'That's the way most actors are,' says Orlando. 'I watch people and observe what they do.' Not that he was so far removed from the funky but chic 'Notting hillbillies' he sometimes found himself among. As a relatively privileged upper-middle class boy, there was never any 'starving artist' period. However, as an acting student, his life wasn't awash with material comforts, and he often had to take part-time jobs in mainstream fashion stores like Boxfresh to make ends meet.

As for the latest hip sportswear or footwear, it was beyond his price range. He would often windowshop at Soho stores for the latest imported sneakers from Japan, for example. 'I could never afford them mind. I used to go in and stare them out. I mean I used to work in Paul Smith, and Boxfresh, so I do like fashion. But it was my sister who used to drag me to [charity thrift-store] Oxfam and throw suede jackets and flared trousers on me.'

Despite living the frenetic life of a young adoptive Londoner, Orlando still seemed to belong to a more romantic, thoughtful age. He's always admitted that he 'can't stand computers', and, while claiming to enjoy 'all sorts of music', he's always leaned away from the ecstasy-suffused house, techno and garage sounds of that era, and toward 'the Ben Harper, the David Gray, and the Bob Dylan type of folk music', as well as the introspective tones of the late Jeff Buckley.

He also maintained at the time a level of personal and creative balance in his life: 'It is important to exercise different creative areas of your brain. It balances you.' In his case, it would be sculpture that kept his inclination toward fine art and extra-thespian activity alive – up to the point of a successful A-level exam.

'One of the finest young performers we've ever had in our companies, in all of the fifteen years I've been in post.' – *Ed Wilson, Artistic Director, NYT on Orlando*

Orlando's first screen appearance would also take place in his days as an NYT student, on British TV in 1994. BBC1's *Casualty* was referred to by him as 'a cheaper version of *ER*'. 'That was my first-ever job,' he remembers, 'playing a self-mutilator – a guy who cuts himself for attention. He was quite a dark character. I had a skinhead, it was cool. It gave me a bit of experience. I remember shooting it in Bristol, having a right laugh.'

At the very end of his NYT period, in 1995, he was offered a one-year scholarship to train with the British American Drama Academy (BADA). It was via BADA that he won a role in their production of *A Walk in the Vienna Woods*, staged at the Tricycle Theatre in Kilburn, north-west London. Based on Odon Von Horvath's *Tales from the Vienna Woods*, the play centres on a group of picnickers and a love triangle. In the first glimmering of the good fortune that has followed him ever since, Orlando was talent-spotted by the casting agency Hubbards for his role.

It would be two years later, at the end of his BADA period, that Hubbards would win him his first small role in a film. As Orlando later said of how he became noticed at age twenty, 'I think I put in the legwork at quite a young age in terms of trying to make sure that I was in the right place at the right time. I moved to London to go to drama school when I was sixteen, so I kind of geared myself up at a young age to put myself in the right arena to become an actor and get work. I think the biggest compliment for me was just getting work.'

Wilde, released in 1997, was a biography of the notoriously brilliant and brilliantly notorious Irish playwright, poet and author Oscar Wilde, poignantly portrayed by Stephen Fry. The film focused on Wilde's homosexual activites and featured a fine supporting cast including a young Jude Law as Bosie and Orlando Bloom in a one-line part as a 'rent boy' (male prostitute), who propositions Fry's Wilde when Bosie introduces him to the gay Victorian underworld.

The rent boy's one-line come-on was enough to get him noticed, and to elicit numerous offers to his agent for film and TV roles. *Wilde* may also have briefly supplemented his income enough to indulge an endlessly romantic heart. 'I flew all the way to Dubai once to be with a girl that I dated at the time,' he later admitted. 'And when I was in love with an Irish girl, I sent her plane tickets and asked her to come and visit me in London.' Unsurprisingly, she came. Characteristically, however, Orlando has refused to name exactly who the young women were, and when exactly they took first place in his heart.

Perhaps more surprisingly, Orlando refused all further acting roles in favour of continuing his thespian training. 'I wasn't influenced. I always planned to go to drama school. I suppose I could have trained in the industry more. But, instead, I chose an environment that would be more conducive to experimenting.' This time, the venue was to be the prestigious Guildhall School of Music and Drama.

'I had an agent before I went in, but I wanted to train,' acknowledges Orlando. 'I needed fine-tuning and to know more about the playwrights and poets.' He signed up for a three-year course in 1997, close to the release of *Wilde*, and would appear in many Guildhall productions over the several seasons that he attended. It was, he would later recall, 'hard work, good but hard.'

'I needed it,' he underlines. 'I needed grounding. I needed an education in an industry that I wanted to be working in. I learned to work with a company of actors and to work with a bit more, I hope, integrity, than I would have done otherwise. That's probably what kept me sound in the head, getting the chance to mess it up in the safety of an environment where it's all about education and growing and learning.'

The school's famous alumni included Ewan McGregor, Joseph Fiennes and David Thewlis. A mere three years later, Orlando would recall, 'They've got a board somewhere with photos of different people. My sister, who's training there now, says I'm up there next to Ewan McGregor!'

The roles Orlando took over those three years could not have been more different from the current screen image of him. In the very earliest part of the curriculum, as he describes it, 'For one of my first exercises, we went to the zoo to study animals and the teacher asked, "What animal do you want to be?" I think I wanted to be an ape, but she said, "No, you're going to be a lizard because you need to learn to be still and find that stillness."' Cast largely in character roles during his time at Guildhall, very few of them would rely on any physical derring-do on Orlando's part, all depending entirely on his ability to act.

To echo Orlando himself, 'Man, I can become an actor and be all of those things.' The sheer diversity of an actor's life seemed to be in his grasp – albeit not yet on a professional level. Acting in theatrical and literary classics also helped him to further overcome his educational impediment, to the extent where he now describes himself as only 'mildly dyslexic'. His long-term ambition also seemed very clear-cut: 'I had every intention of going on the stage.' And, apart from walk-on parts in two TV comedy shows – Ben Elton's show in 1998, and female sketch revue *Smack the Pony* in 2000 – it looked as if that was where he was headed.

In the autumn 1997 and spring 1998 seasons at the Guildhall, Orlando's first acting roles would include a crucial part in *The Trojan Women* – the ancient Greek Euripides' tragic view of the aftermath of war, first produced in 415 BC. Orlando played Menelaus, husband of the Greek beauty Helen who caused the siege of Troy by eloping with the Trojan prince Paris. Orlando also appeared in Sophocles' *Antigone* in the crucial role of Prologue and Chorus, the narrative voice that used to comment upon the action in Greek drama.

In Russian playwright Anton Chekhov's *The Seagull*, perhaps the bleakest play Orlando performed in his three seasons at the Guildhall, he played the idealistic young playwright Constantine Treplef, who becomes disillusioned when he is rejected by his muse, Nina, and commits suicide.

In a much lighter tone, Orlando took the title role in George Farquhar's 1706 Restoration drama *The Recruiting Officer*. Orlando played the part of a swashbuckling hero for the first time, as Captain Plume, an adventurous, womanising, but good-natured Grenadier Guard.

In complete contrast, his next role was in an adaptation of *A Night Out*, a 1960s radio-TV play by the British master of elliptical alienation, Harold Pinter. Orlando played the unlikeable role of a bully named Gidney, who encourages two girls to humiliate the main character, Albert.

In perhaps the ultimate turnaround, one of Orlando's major roles at the Guildhall was as far

removed from a petty-minded bully as it's possible to be. Orlando played Jesus Christ in a revival of the traditional English *Mystery Plays*, where the history of the world, as according to the Bible, was condensed into a number of vividly truncated cycles, culminating in the crucifixion and resurrection.

In 1998, in the middle of his tenure at the Guildhall, everything nearly came to an abrupt and dramatic halt for Orlando at the age of 21. When visiting a friend's flat for Sunday lunch, in the trendy West London neighbourhood of Notting Hill, the party tried to adjourn to the roof terrace. But, with the doorframe warped by the classically damp British weather, no one could exit onto the roof.

No matter. Orlando, as energetic and as physical as ever, and by all accounts sober ('shimmying down a drainpipe and I hadn't even been partying – there's just no excuse'), took charge. Stretching out his six-foot frame (which has often been variously measured at either five foot eleven or six foot one) to its full extent, he attempted to climb out of a window onto the level just below, and clamber up to kick the upper terrace door in from the outside – 'always the first on the ledge,' as he puts it. It must have seemed like a good idea at the time.

As he describes it, 'It was a Sunday afternoon and I'd just had a big roast lunch. I went round to a mate's house in Notting Hill – it had an apartment on the top floor but the door had been warped by the weather and needed kicking from the outside. There was a roof terrace on the landing below so, without even looking down, I thought I could jump across, but instead I landed on a piece of metal – lead flashing or something . . .' As soon as he tried to set his foot on it, the dilapidated guttering gave way. Orlando tried to hold onto a drainpipe, but stepped into space: 'I fell off the drain pipe. It gave way, actually, and I fell three floors.'

'I moved to London to go to drama school when I was sixteen, so I kind of geared myself up at a young age to put myself in the right arena to become an actor and get work.'

As he later acknowledged, 'I've broken both my legs, my wrist, my nose and all sorts of things, but breaking your back is a different thing. I didn't think I was going to get through that one. I was told I was going to be in a wheelchair – for four days they thought I'd never walk again.'

The damage done on that day eclipsed all of his other injuries. On being rushed to hospital it was discovered that he had one crushed vertebra, three fractured vertebrae and three broken ribs. 'I fell three floors, landed in between some bins and broke my back. Fucking awful. Imagine having four nurses to move you, wash you, do everything for you. My mum was so distraught.

'It was amazing that I didn't die,' Orlando would soberly reflect. Close to the concrete floor where he landed were an old, abandoned washing machine on one side, and iron railings on the other. Recuperating in hospital, Orlando was forced to face the full extent of his injuries. 'I've always been "act first think later". It can lead to an exciting spontaneity – but it was a big wake-up call. I was almost paralysed.' As he now recalls, 'I experienced all these weird moments where I was exploring really dark corners of my mind. I was lying there on my back, unable to do anything. You don't know how you're going to be under those circumstances.

'It was the biggest test of my life . . . I did, and do, consider myself a physical person, an outdoorsy type and I couldn't contemplate the idea of not living an active life.

'I was quite fearless as a kid. But I've had to realise I'm not invincible. That's what breaking your back does. It makes you grow up and reassess life.'

In all likelihood, his specialists told him, the prognosis was bleak. But still, an agonising operation that bolted metal plates to his damaged vertebrae would regain him the posture that, added to sheer willpower and optimism, would allow him to rise again. 'I had some sort of damage done to me and the doctors told me I might never walk again . . .' acknowledges Orlando. 'So, for about four days, I was contemplating that as a serious part of reality.' Then, after six hours of surgery, 'the bolts and plates were inserted [and] I was able to leave the hospital after twelve days with a neck brace. I had to wear it for the entire next year though.' He also had to re-learn, through intensive physiotherapy, the art of putting one foot in front of another: 'I couldn't remember how to walk. I literally couldn't remember whether to do toe, ball, heel or heel, ball, toe. It was bizarre.

'I definitely went through that "Why the fuck did this happen to me?" stuff. I'm not some saint. I was really depressed. I was in a lot of pain. I was on a lot of drugs. But I had this one great teacher who came to visit me and said to me, "This is going to be the making of you." And it was.'

Though his rate of recovery, after hobbling out of the ward on crutches, was remarkable, to some extent the pain and discomfort may always remain – alongside the inconvenience of setting off every airport metal detector that he passes through. That, however, casts only a small shadow over the charmed life of Orlando Bloom. The accident was, as he stresses, 'A wake-up call to life and responsibility and respect for myself. It made me go, "You fucking idiot. How could you even think of doing that? How could you not have thought that through?" For a while I wasn't going to be able to walk. I wasn't going to be able to finish my course. I may never have been able to act.'

Despite the physicality of his eventual screen roles, Orlando also admits, 'My back is a constant reminder of how lucky I am . . . . Now if I start to take on too much, my back goes, "Twang! Listen, man, remember who you are."'

While emphasising, 'I've tried to turn the accident into a positive thing because, otherwise, maybe I wouldn't keep fit in the way that I do,' Orlando still had to take on board that, on his return to Guildhall, the injury 'meant I was cast in a lot of parts requiring me to be still,' and that there was 'bureaucratic red tape and insurance bollocks that had to be dealt with' before he could perform again.

'I was quite fearless as a kid. But I've had to realise I'm not invincible. That's what breaking your back does. It makes you grow up and reassess life.'

As soon as the necessary cover was granted Orlando was back on stage for the autumn 1998 and spring/summer/autumn 1999 seasons – in roles that demanded thespian versatility, rather than physical demonstrativeness. In Shakespeare's Elizabethan comedy *Twelfth Night*, Orlando was at the centre of a complex love triangle, playing the love-struck Duke Orsinio. In the German play *Mephisto*, by Thomas Mann, Orlando played a small, but crucial supporting role of a character named Alex, who tells a haunting tale of encountering a night train of deportees to a Nazi concentration camp. In Henrik Ibsen's *Peer Gynt* Orlando was the Strange Passenger, one of the mythic-archetypal figures who populate the title character's surreal wanderings.

Rather more lightweight roles came in Ivan Turgenev's Russian comedy of manners, *A Month in the Country* – in which Orlando was Herr Schaaf, a bumbling German tutor who, like most of the characters in the play, nurses an affection for someone who pays no attention to him – and *Little Me*, an adaptation of the Broadway musical by Cy Coleman, in which Orlando took the part of Fred Poitrine, the hapless returning World War One soldier, making his musical debut singing 'Real Live Girl', one of the show's main numbers.

In the latter, more angst-ridden displays of his stagecraft, Orlando played crucial secondary roles in two more classic plays by the melancholic Chekhov. In *The Three Sisters*, an almost unbearably pessimistic story, he played the local bully, Solyony, who is seriously obsessed with one of the sisters of the title. In Chekhov's *Uncle Vanya*, the young actor found himself embroiled in another hopeless love triangle, playing a doctor named Astrov.

Playing three such intense dramatic roles (including *The Seagull*) was obviously a good experience for Orlando – particularly in that he was often playing characters a great deal older than himself. As he says, 'I started reading Milton and Chekhov and Shakespeare, and that definitely inspired me. What drew me to acting was an ability to be versatile and to be able to get under the skin of anybody.' But Chekhov's civilised yet pessimistic view of the human condition was the very antithesis of what Orlando's career would become: an ongoing tribute to heroism, and the indomitability of the

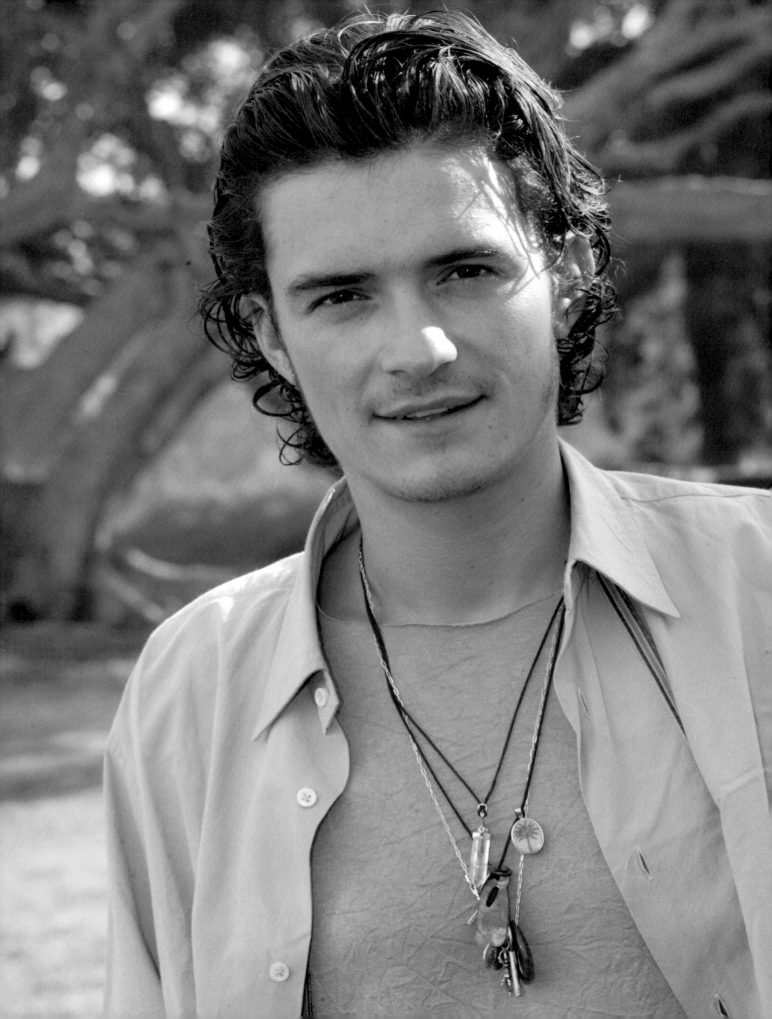

human spirit. Destiny, should such a capricious force truly exist, obviously had other plans for him.

Early in 1999, during the last year of his tenure at the Guildhall, a buzz was going around that infected all of the students. When word got around that New Zealand film director and industry maverick Peter Jackson was holding auditions for his adaptation of J. R. R. Tolkien's classic fantasy trilogy, *The Lord of the Rings*, everyone felt they were potentially up for a part. 'There was a huge casting process that went on with this project,' confirms Orlando. 'Everyone I knew went up for a role. I went on tape for it, probably like a hundred thousand other actors across the world.

'Obviously, *Lord of the Rings*, that's been around for a long time and it's very well known in England and most of the English-speaking countries of the world, but when I heard about the casting at that point I was drawn to it because it was out there and everyone was drawn to it.'

Prompted by his agent at Hubbards, Orlando made an audition by video. 'We weren't really meant to be auditioning for jobs while we were at Guildhall, but I had this great agent who kept pushing stuff for me. She kept the pot boiling, the interest going.

'Basically, there was a huge casting process. It was in all the English-speaking countries of the world. I went on tape for the role of Faramir initially in London and then I met Peter Jackson and Fran Walsh, his partner, when they came to London a few months later.'

Faramir was the weaker of two warrior brothers who come to a tragic end. Orlando would have been thrilled to land the part, even though the role was relatively minor: 'I think as a young actor you take what you can get. At the beginning of your career, you can't expect to get certain roles.'

'My back is a constant reminder of how lucky I am . . . Now if I start to take on too much, my back goes, "Twang! Listen, man, remember who you are."'

He ultimately failed to get the part (it went to Australian actor David Wenham), which may have seemed like a setback, but there was hardly time to draw breath. 'I was given a call, or my agent rather, that the role of Faramir wouldn't become available to me, but would I read for Legolas?' Legolas Greenleaf, Prince of the Elves, was a secondary but much more prominent and more intensely physical role that would feature in each of the intended films of Tolkien's three novels. 'I was over the moon to do that obviously, so I read for Legolas and I was offered the role a few weeks after that. It was a six-month process but a mind-blowing time for me, really.

'I went back and read the books and tried to find out who Legolas really was. I was thrilled when they asked me to play him. I went on tape again and, after they'd checked out how tall I was and everything, I got the call to say I was in . . . I said "absolutely". I got an offer and I was freaking out and screaming and yelling . . . it was too much.'

'The first time we saw Orlando, we rewound the tape, looked at him again, and then looked at each other,' explains Jackson. 'He was straight out of drama school, but we knew we'd struck gold.' Orlando recalls: 'I remember meeting Peter Jackson when he came to see me at school and thinking this would be really amazing. I could feel the mad energy, and I was so excited.'

Orlando's method for getting into his character was imaginative. 'A friend of mine in England has a house in the countryside, and we'd go for walks,' he later explained. 'When I found out I got the role, I practiced walking through the forest and running and sort of imagining what it would be like to be really quiet in the trees,' he laughed at his own grown-up playing. 'It sounds ridiculous, but what can you do? I mean, you are playing a character that's immortal, ageless, never been seen before.'

Orlando would later appreciate how he was at Guildhall 'with some very talented actors, incredible people . . . and I was the one who left only days before graduation. You just have to be in the right place at the right time, I think, for things to happen. I just got there, really early doors. So, thanks for that . . . I guess I've had a lot of really "pinch me" moments in the last few years.'

But the good news didn't stop there. Orlando had won his part in *The Lord of the Rings* only two days before he would graduate from the Guildhall, with a Bachelor of the Arts degree in drama

Orlando Bloom, a new-style hero for the New Age. Taking pride of place among the natural minerals hanging around his neck is his namesake, the Orlando stone.

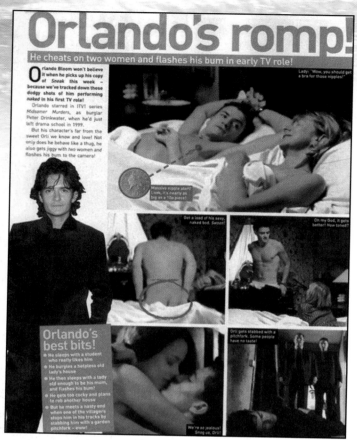

The magazine clipping reads:

Orlando's romp!

He cheats on two women and flashes his bum in early TV role!

Orlando Bloom won't believe it when he picks up his copy of *Sneak* this week – because we've tracked down these dodgy shots of him performing naked in his first TV role!

Orlando starred in ITV1 series *Midsomer Murders*, as burglar Peter Drinkwater, when he'd just left drama school in 1999.

But his character's far from the sweet Orli we know and love! Not only does he behave like a thug, he also gets jiggy with two women and flashes his bum to the camera!

Lady: 'Wow, you should get a bra for those nipples!'

Massive nipple alert! Look, it's nearly as big as a 10p piece!

Get a load of his sexy, naked bod. Swoon!

Oh my God, it gets better! How toned!

Orli gets stabbed with a pitchfork. Some people have no taste!

We're so jealous! Snog us, Orli!

Orlando's best bits!
- He sleeps with a student who really likes him
- He burgles a helpless old lady's house
- He then sleeps with a lady old enough to be his mum, and flashes his bum!
- He gets too cocky and plans to rob another house
- But he meets a nasty end when one of the villagers stops him in his tracks by stabbing him with a garden pitchfork – eww!

Orlando's bare behind was first glimpsed in the 'Judgement Day' episode of TV's Midsomer Murders. Sneak *magazine later ran this feature on his appearance in the TV drama.*

with honours. At virtually the same time, he also won a supporting role in the popular Brit TV crime series, *Midsomer Murders* – an almost-pastiche version of the traditionally genteel rural English murder mystery. 'My agent called and she said, "I've got some news,"' he'd later acknowledge. '"You've been offered *The Lord of the Rings*." I was over the moon. And the very next day I got another call saying, "Do you want to do *Midsomer Murders*?" I was 22, I hadn't left drama school and it was, like, "Here, have a career." Boom. There you go. It was like winning the lottery.'

Orlando may have been grateful for his good fortune, but it was hard for him to gauge just how rapidly his life was going to change at that point. His part in *Midsomer Murders* would obviously have to be shot before he took off for an extensive stay in New Zealand, where Jackson would be shooting on location. Apart from being a more sizeable screen role than his part in *Wilde*, this particular episode of the series, entitled 'Judgement Day', would later gain a reputation for being the first screen appearance to centre on Orlando Bloom's sex appeal. It even managed to give a rare glimpse of his lithe, bare ass as he climbed out of bed with a middle-aged lover.

Orlando played a rural ne'er-do-well named Peter Drinkwater, who, as well as being a burglar, is also a local gigolo. He has simultaneous affairs with two women, one close to his own age (early twenties) named Caroline, and the other named Laura, married and in her forties, who pays for the privilege. But these plot points are red herrings that disguise the reason for his gruesome murder – by pitchfork, no less. As Orlando later put it on camp chat show host Graham Norton's show, 'I got this pitchfork in the stomach,' hamming it up with a death rattle. 'I did this awful death thing. It was terrible.'

Up until 1999, Orlando had been living the life of a young actor just easing his way into the profession. 'I feel really privileged to be an actor, to be paid to do something I love,' he said soon after – a sentiment that would have applied as much to his one-off role in *Midsomer Murders* as his forthcoming part in *The Lord of the Rings*. As is traditional with most actors, throughout their careers, his pleasures were simple and his possessions were few. His car, his first, was 'a deep-green VW Golf. I bought it for 160 quid at an auction in London. I still wish I had it,' he muses wistfully. 'I loved that car.' Also a part of his funky, unpretentious urban lifestyle was his beloved pet dog, Maude – now to be entrusted to the good care of his sister and mother.

Things were about to change irrevocably, taking Orlando's lifestyle about as far from that of a jobbing London actor as possible. As he had the good grace to recognise, 'I had been theatre training for three years at the Guildhall School of Music and Drama, and then suddenly I was given this incredible opportunity to have fifteen months of training in *front* of the camera, working with some of the best people in the business.

'This was three years in front of the camera with a cast and crew that taught me everything there is about making films.'

THE FELLOWSHIP

'I was 22, I hadn't left drama school and it was, like, "Here, have a career." Boom. There you go. It was like winning the lottery.' – *Orlando Bloom*

J. R. R. Tolkien's *The Lord of the Rings* trilogy, to 22-year-old Orlando Bloom, was something for which he held a half-remembered affection. As for Peter Jackson's planned film adaptations, he'd later observe, understatedly, '*Rings* was my first experience out of school, and I was sort of dropped in the deep end.'

Orlando was acquainted with the gentle Oxford University professor's 1954 mythic pseudo-history. 'At fourteen, I read it [the *Lord of the Rings* trilogy] all the way through,' Orlando initially claimed – before correcting himself, 'No, I read *The Hobbit* [Tolkien's precursor to the *Rings* trilogy, a children's novel about Bilbo Baggins, uncle to the *Rings* character Frodo] all the way through. I read half [of *The Lord of the Rings*] and got interested in sport and girls.

'But then I picked up the books again as soon as the casting process began on *Lord of the Rings*, and I read them a couple of times before the movies started shooting. I wouldn't say I'm an authority on Tolkien, but I felt pretty confident about what I was getting into. I had a different experience the second time around I read the books, and when I go back to read them again, which I will do, I know I'll see other things.'

Peter Jackson's $270 million production of the trilogy of novels – respectively, *The Fellowship of the Ring*, *The Two Towers*, and *The Return of the King* – was still a daunting prospect. Its basic story concerns a journey across the mythical terrain of Middle Earth by Frodo Baggins: a young Hobbit, or 'halfling', part of a race descended from Men (a species still in its infancy) and from Dwarves. Guided by the benevolent old wizard Gandalf, his quest is to return the most potent of the Rings of Power back to the fires of Mount Doom, in the dread land of Mordor, from whence it originated – before it can be stolen by nine Black Riders or 'Ringwraiths', zombie-like horsemen whose life is dedicated to retrieving the One True Ring.

What makes its destruction so imperative is that the monstrous hordes of the kingdom of Mordor, the Orcs and the Uruk-Hai, are assembling under the leadership of the Dark Lord Sauron to invade the other regions of Middle Earth. Should the One True Ring fall into his hands, then all Men, all Hobbits, and all the benign races that make up the vast region will be doomed to extinction. In order to save their world, Frodo is joined on his quest by a cross-section of eight allies: one wise old wizard, three fellow Hobbits, two Men, one Elf and one Dwarf. The latter four are all warriors. Collectively, they are the Fellowship of the Ring.

'The story has adventure and beasts and goblins,' born-again Tolkien fan Orlando enthused. 'It has heart. It has magic and love and spirit – a whole range of emotions you can experience. It's so detailed. Tolkien was a professor of history, and he just layered this story with so much. You open up the books, take a look at the pages and get lost in this world.'

'A lot of the charm of the reading of *Lord of the Rings* are the detailed descriptions, and we can't really get any of that in the film,' Jackson would concede. 'To be frank, we have made many changes. The film is extremely different to the book, taken moment by moment and line by line. But we felt we wanted to be as accurate as possible to Tolkien's descriptions of Middle Earth. We wanted to give people the sense that we went on location to Middle Earth. In that sense we took the books as our Bible.'

'A day on set could be spent shooting everything and anything,' confirmed Orlando. 'You never got a sense of each movie because we didn't shoot them chronologically. It was a big haze. A big blur. The books became bibles to me. They helped me to place myself visually when we were jumping between films.'

'One of the first things I did was go to the special effects studio, and there was a warehouse full of armour, thousands of rows of armour and weapons, and that was the first point when I realised, "Oh my God, this is huge!"'

'I literally went through the books and highlighted all the information I felt I needed to know about my character, about the journey of the Fellowship. I really went through them with a fine-tooth comb to try and absorb everything I could about what it meant for Legolas to be a part of the Fellowship.'

Jackson was both fortunate and prescient in his stated desire not to leave his native New Zealand. With its wide-open vistas of space, snowy peaks and volcanic rock formations, it was as if he had the world of Tolkien's mythic pre-history right there at his fingertips. 'I think New Zealand was a great choice for making the film,' said Scottish actor Billy Boyd, who would play one of the story's modest Hobbit heroes, 'because so much of the scenery had not been seen before. Also, you'll never get Peter Jackson to leave it.' As Orlando would put it, 'Peter created a character that wasn't really there, and that was the landscape.'

'When I first got out to New Zealand, to work on *Lord of the Rings*,' Orlando said of his October 1999 arrival in capital city Wellington, the director's hometown and base of production, 'I got off the plane and it took me four weeks of filming before I realised what I was involved with.'

Describing the production of the trilogy as 'a labour of love, a very special project,' he later recalled, 'One of the first things I did was go to the special effects studio, and there was a warehouse full of armour, thousands of rows of armour and weapons, and that was the first point when I realised, "Oh my God, this is huge!" I couldn't quite believe I was in the project until about a month into filming. Then when we finally saw some very rough snippets of a few scenes, which Peter showed us to help keep morale up, I finally, really understood what I was a part of and still couldn't believe it!'

'I mean, imagine being flown to this amazing country and being taught how to shoot a bow and arrow, learn to ride horses and study swordplay,' he testifies, 'It was sick! I was pinching myself.'

But, at first, the prospect was more than a little intimidating. 'I was like, "I've got to do everything I can because he's the character people have created in their imaginations over years." But at one point, I said to myself – because I was so aware of it that it was actually blocking me – I said, "I've gotta let go. I've been cast to play Legolas because I have some quality I can use to try to bring this character to life." So I just did my best to do that. I ended up doing a lot of movement training trying to find the physicality of the character.

The equestrian Elf: for the many battle scenes in The Lord of the Rings *trilogy, Orlando's early life spent 'hacking around' Kent on horseback came in very useful.*

'By the time shooting was underway, I could fire an arrow whilst riding horseback.'

'Legolas is an Elf who represents the Elves in the Fellowship. I'm in quite good company. I have fellow Elves in the movie – I have Cate Blanchett as Galadriel, Liv Tyler as Arwen, Hugo Weaving as Elrond and Marton Csokas as Celeborn. I'm in there literally to offer my bow to Frodo. I offer myself as a warrior really and I act as the eyes and ears for the Fellowship, as it were. Legolas is the first to be aware of danger or the threat of danger. He is very quick with his draw, I use my skills as a warrior and the Elves have these superhuman qualities, as J. R. R. Tolkien has written about them, like superhuman strength and reflex speed and sensory awareness. So, all my senses are heightened and that's what really comes into play for Legolas in the Fellowship.'

Contrary to the stagebound discipline of the last several years, the part of Legolas was the most physical acting role imaginable. Beginning two months before the start of production, Orlando's training and coaching were as impeccable as they had to be: 'I was the first of the cast to arrive and the first thing they did was put a bow in my hand! I started using the bow and getting to grips with the archery, so by the end of the week I was taking paper plates out of the sky, trying to get some real dynamic movement into the way I used the bow. It's an extension of his [Legolas'] body, so I had to be proficient in that . . . .

'I spent a lot of time learning archery, which is basically my weapon of choice in [that] what you'll see me doing for most of the movie is firing arrows. Working on horse training for the second and third movie, swordplay with Bob Anderson who taught Errol Flynn who's amazing.'

Anderson's expertise, and lengthy career, had extended from the days of matinee idol Flynn's swash-bucklers to his coaching of the actor who played Darth Vader in the original *Star Wars* movies.

As Orlando proudly boasted, 'By the time shooting was underway, I could fire an arrow whilst riding horseback.' Though, as he suggested, it wasn't entirely a newly acquired skill: 'I've always loved riding and I used to hack around Canterbury as a kid. It wasn't really a pony club – we'd just go out on horses. So I picked it up again in New Zealand and added a bit more of the style and the posture and the correct riding position. I learned to ride on around 30 different horses, and what you get from that is an understanding that each individual animal has to be treated with sensitivity so you have a mutual respect thing going.'

So richly detailed was Tolkien's Middle Earth that he had devised a basic language for the Elves, taken to its furthest linguistic conclusions by his more eccentric fans. Jackson employed three Tolkien 'linguists' to make sure that Elvish, and the semi-Celtic name pronunciations that permeate the film (the letters 'r' in 'Mordor' rolled mellifluously around the tongue), were accurate.

'It's very hard to grasp hold of,' confirmed Orlando. 'It's like, I dunno, it has this Celtic-ie, Welsh kind of feel to it.

'My first scene on my first day was delivering a line of Elvish to a group of Elves, which wasn't the easiest thing to open with. We were in the studio in New Zealand and it was very hot, and I just remember thinking, God, man, the Elves look really strange.'

The power of Tolkien's archetypal concept resonated with Orlando: 'It's just such a great story. It's a mixture of races – Elves, Dwarves, humans, and wizards all getting together to take on one nasty little Ring of Power. It's great in terms of the universal idea that everybody must come together to achieve something.'

'We decided Elves should be slender and elegant and have high cheekbones. We tried to cast the most perfect human beings we could find, like Cate Blanchett and Liv Tyler and Orlando Bloom.'
— *Peter Jackson, Director,* **The Lord of the Rings**

Despite the focus that the young female audience would later place on Legolas, the main action hero of the *Rings* saga was Aragorn, a displaced heir to the Men's kingdom of Isildur, raised by Elves, played by Viggo Mortensen.

Viggo became something of a mentor to Orlando: as a painter, photographer, jazz musician and poet, he showed how to maintain a level of personal creativity within Hollywood boundaries. 'It was a coming of age time for me working with this incredible group of people,' Orly confirmed, 'particularly Viggo Mortensen whom I worked with more closely than anyone else . . . .

'He's got a lot of grace and humility and integrity and I admire his work ethic. I think he's had a great influence on my life.'

Trapped in their characters for so long, it also led to a jokey offscreen rivalry. 'Vig used to call me "Elf boy", and I'd call him "filthy human",' explains Orlando, whose character's pristine cleanliness reflects the Elves' spiritual purity. 'As an Elf, I never got a scratch on me, never got dirty. And Vig would come out with blood and sweat all over him. And he'd say to me, "Oh, go manicure your nails." . . . . Viggo will go on about Elves and how they're always doing their nails and brushing their long, blond hair, and being all prissy.' Proof, if it were needed, that the length of time spent on the *Lord of the Rings* trilogy, and the total immersion in the characters, was creating its own psychological and physical environment. 'And I just say: Well, at least I'm going to live forever! Got that? LIVE FOREVER!'

'It was a really demanding two months of preparation,' Orlando recalled, 'Fortunately, we were a team, sort of a clan, all the actors. The Fellowship was together very often on location. I ended up spending a lot of time with Viggo and John [Rhys-Davies, who played Dwarf warrior Gimli].' But, equally, Orlando would form a personal alliance with the young actors who played the Hobbits: 'Everyone sat together at table reads, trained together and, as time rolled by, friendships were formed.'

Ostensibly, the head of the cast, wide-eyed, diminutive Elijah Wood essayed the role of Frodo Baggins – the humble Hobbit who inherits the task of carrying the One Ring to the fires of Mount Doom, thus destroying its dark power forever. Already recognisable from his juvenile supporting role in Ang Lee's *The Ice Storm* (1997) and teen fare such as Robert Rodriguez's *The Faculty* (1998), Elijah came to represent the inoffensive little people (average height roughly three foot six) who love the simple pleasures in life and live stress-free existences in their little Hobbit holes.

'My first scene on my first day was delivering a line of Elvish to a group of Elves, which wasn't the easiest thing to open with. . . I just remember thinking, God, man, the Elves look really strange.'

Of the supporting Hobbits, Sean Astin would pick up gradual acclaim as Samwise Gamgee, Frodo's stolid, solid and loyal friend. Comic relief, in Hobbit form, came from the two mischievous friends who come along for the ride and end up risking their lives in the name of fellowship. Young British actor Dominic Monaghan was cast as Meriadoc Brandybuck – or 'Merry', as he's appropriately known, with his love of eating, drinking and smoking the Hobbits' pipeweed.

Billy as Peregrin Took, better known as Pippin, a cousin to both Frodo and Merry, was a deceptively youthful actor already in his early thirties. Accepting Orlando, the Elf, as an honorary member of the Hobbit brotherhood, when asked about his favourite *Rings* character, Billy noted, 'After Pippin, I have to say Legolas. I love his understanding of nature and the world.'

Peter Jackson would feature occasional perspective shots to make the Hobbits and Dwarves seem diminutive against the imposing nobility of the warrior characters. 'We cast for physical features – heights, bone structures, all that stuff. We were using various devices so that Hobbits would appear to be about four feet tall, but even when we were casting Hobbits, we had a rule they couldn't be below five foot four or above five foot eight.' And, of course, Dominic and Billy Boyd still seemed short in stature against Orlando's commanding six foot one.

The most prominent and self-contained member of the Fellowship of the Ring (or 'the Nine Walkers', as they're sometimes referred to) would be the wizard Gandalf the Grey. As played by Ian McKellen, the tall-hatted, pipeweed-smoking sorceror was imbued with power, dignity and good humour.

McKellen, a renowned Shakespearean stage performer and gay rights activist, had been knighted by the Queen back home in London. He is also the vice-president of London's National Youth Theatre – whose alumni include one Orlando Bloom. 'It was like a drama school of its own, being on the set,' enthused Orlando. 'Peter is a genius. Ian McKellen is the greatest theatre actor in Britain. He's somebody I look at and say, "That's what I would like to do." I had studied videos of his performances, so it was bizarre to be thrown into an environment with him.'

McKellen's equal in terms of presence and charisma, though some years his senior, was veteran British character actor Christopher Lee, then in his late seventies. Tall and imposing, he was the perfect choice for Gandalf's counterpart gone bad, Saruman the White. Gimli, the noble Khazad (or Dwarf) warrior of Erebor who commits himself to the quest, was played by Welsh character actor John Rhys-Davies. Boromir, brother of Faramir (who Orlando had originally auditioned to play), was played by fellow British actor Sean Bean. In his late thirties, Bean had acquired heroic status and a loyal following on British TV for the title role of *Sharpe*, a series based on popular novels about a

'It was a coming of age time for me working with this incredible group of people, particularly Viggo Mortensen whom I worked with more closely than anyone else.'

maverick British army officer during the Napoleonic Wars.

Besides one mishap with a horse, Sean Bean would be present on the only other occasion that Orlando inadvertently put himself in danger. As Sean explains, a change in the location schedule meant the cast had to relocate from New Zealand's North Island to South Island. Due to his nervousness as an aircraft passenger, however, he couldn't face travelling in an old Dakota airforce plane. So, in December of 1999, Orlando offered to make the journey with him by car and ferry instead. That was their first mistake.

'He had to stop at every shop to get Christmas presents,' recalled Sean of Orly, the faithful friend and family man. 'It was pouring with rain, so I was saying: "Look, we've got to get going or there's going to be a landslide." And sure enough, there was. We turned back to find another one so we were stuck in the middle of nowhere.'

'Everyone sat together at table reads, trained together and, as time rolled by, friendships were formed.'

'We have suffered some setbacks,' wrote Peter Jackson in his production diary, 'the weather has stuffed the schedule. Two of the actors, Sean Bean and Orlando Bloom, have been caught between two landslides and are now trapped in a tiny town in the middle of the South Island. They have been taken in by a kindly woman who has offered them food and a bed. They were last reported to be cooking spaghetti and cracking into a bottle of red wine.

'We had no choice but to reschedule their scenes . . . . At the height of this insanity we had seven units shooting multiple elements simultaneously for three different movies . . . '

Orlando and Sean managed to rent a house for another couple of days, until the producers came to their rescue. 'They sent a chopper to airlift us out – even worse than a Dakota!' Bean recalls with a shudder. 'It was still raining and we were flying through moutain passes and the windscreen wipers were going like mad. I said: "Can't you just drop us there in that field?", but they wouldn't. I was gripping Orlando's kneecap so hard I must have nearly broken it. He was saying: "It's OK," but he still takes the piss out of me for that.'

Sean also testified to the amount of physical and martial training that the Fellowship's warrior elite went through. Citing the 100 handmade weapons, 2,000 safety weapons and 200 suits of armour produced for the film by specialist blacksmiths, leather workers and armourers, he acknowledged, 'Everyone became quite skilful at fighting.

'We did a lot of research in rehearsals and choreographing sword fights. We developed our own styles as swordsmen. Elves have a very lethal but delicate movement.'

The character of Legolas, serving mainly as an action hero and stripped of much of the Tolkien character's joyfulness, was also imbued with a mysterious charisma. Tolkien had expended a great deal of imaginative energy describing the habitat and customs of the Elvish race – these were not diminutive little helpers from Santa's grotto, but a tall, noble people with highly developed senses and supherhuman reflexes. 'Elves have angelic spirits, deepest sorrow, greatest joy,' explained Orlando.

'Obviously, the books are incredibly detailed, and there is plenty of information about the Elves in them. The Elves are a very interesting culture, and many people are intrigued by them because they're rather magical and mystical. Tolkien created them as the firstborn race – they're angelic spirits placed on Middle Earth by the gods – so they have this otherworldly quality to them. I translated that into them always being centred, poised and focused.'

But they still had the traditional pointed ears. As Orlando later revealed, 'I had to wear a hooded jacket in the car on the way to the set and home every day too if I still had the ears on as security was really tight. We weren't even allowed to take our own photographs. There were a lot of restrictions that were frustrating, but if you think there were eighteen months of filming, if they didn't keep security tight so much material could have slipped out. These movies are going to be released a year apart so they have to be careful.

'They [the Elf ears] weren't uncomfortable other than the two hours it took to put them on. I went home one day without the wig, but with the ears on, because I had a four-hour break and it was in the middle of the night. I crawled into bed with my girlfriend at the time and woke up with one of the ears stuck to the pillow and the other there in perfect form, with my ex-girlfriend taking photos and laughing.'

Surprisingly, Orlando only had one complaint about his costume: 'The only thing that got to be a bit of a drag, because it weighed so much, was my quiver and my bow strapped to my back.' Maybe it's because, as truly elfin as he is in physique, Orlando just doesn't possess a Tolkien Elf's superhuman strength.

'The most difficult race to visualise were the Elves . . . They're this odd combination of preciousness and strength,' testified Jackson. 'And that was frustrating. I think we did OK in the end. We decided Elves should be slender and elegant and have high cheekbones. We tried to cast the most perfect human beings we could find, like Cate Blanchett and Liv Tyler and Orlando Bloom.'

Tolkien could sometimes be vague on individual characterisation, most notably details such as the Elf Prince of Mirkwood's specific appearance or his age. It was Jackson and his fellow screenwriters who decided that, as Legolas, like all Elves, was effectively immortal, they would peg his age at a precise 2,931 years. In order to distinguish Orlando, with his olive skin and distinctive dark brown eyes, from Australian actor Hugo Weaving (who also appears in the *Matrix* trilogy) as dark-haired Elf King Elrond, the peaceful founder of Rivendell, they also came up with the innovation of a long blond wig and deep blue contact lenses to define Legolas's appearance.

Orlando was effectively transformed. His naturally dark hair was cut into the shaven strips of a Mohawk Indian style, like Daniel Day-Lewis's enemies in *The Last of the Mohicans*, so as not to show any traces of his own hairline.

This was at the suggestion of Liv Tyler, daughter of rock superstar Steven Tyler of Aerosmith and Bebe Buell, the ultimate Californian rock chick. 'I was having my make-up done when she arrived and my hairline [was being] raised to give me an Elven featured face. She said, "Why don't you shave it off at the sides? You'd really look cute in a Mohawk."

'I get to transform completely in makeup and costume and become Legolas,' he enthused. 'Then at night, I get to go home with my Mohawk. It's great!'

'It was a demanding two months of preparation. Fortunately, we were a team, sort of a clan, all the actors.'

Tyler brought both beauty and dignity to the role of the Elf maiden who falls in love with Aragorn. 'My character is about 3,000 years old. And I'm thinking, "How am I going to play a 3,000-year-old?" What does that mean? I realised that what makes the Elves so powerful is this inner calm. It's like being the most perfect person you can be, like someone who meditates all the time. A Buddha.'

Orlando took a similarly spiritual view of his Elvish character: 'If you've lived that long, you know, when you have maybe a week of time on your hands where you have nothing to do – maybe you're on holiday, and at some point in time you got really relaxed, you find this moment of tranquility, this moment like you're in another space, another time, another world. And I think that that's the world that Legolas lives in . . .' His view of his character's inner life had much in common with those of Orlando's generation: driven by the need for a new (or New Age) spirituality, loosely in tune with the inner psychological focus of Buddhism.

Liv Tyler spoke with affection of the ensemble cast, and particularly her fellow Elf Orlando: 'I love them all, my co-stars. We would hang out mostly in the hair and makeup trailer, and after work at dinner. We would eat all the time and drink wine and laugh. I was always like, "Let's go get dinner!" We all lived in houses, some of us in apartments. Orlando and I lived right around the corner from where Peter lives on this beautiful bay, up on these cliffs, and we had just the sea in front of us. You wake up to rainbows and dolphins. So, we had each other and work and some of the most beautiful scenery I've ever seen.' Her affection for Orlando, though on a purely platonic level, was obvious.

'I hung out with Liv Tyler a lot,' he good-naturedly confirmed. 'I didn't kiss her, either. But I was always lobbying for love scenes between Legolas and Arwen.'

In fact, one of the major strains of the extended shoot, as it developed into a lifestyle all of its own, was the gradual fracturing of the relationship with his current girlfriend.

'I'm probably a good boyfriend,' he insisted, 'but I'm pretty intense. When you're with me it's exciting, fun and very intense. At the same time I'm easy going. But all that depends on what girl I'm with.'

'I hung out with Liv Tyler a lot, I didn't kiss her, either. But I was always lobbying for love scenes between Legolas and Arwen.'

All the same, his tendency not to kiss-and-tell ensured that very few boy-girl anecdotes survive from the *Rings* period. The present-day Bloom fan grapevine suggests he was engaged to be married at this point, but Orlando remains cagey about the girl he was with at the time. As he says, 'Some things have to be [private] for me, at some point you draw a line.'

Their relationship had ignited briefly before he came to Wellington to begin shooting. 'Out of the blue, I did send a plane ticket to a girl asking her to visit. I guess that's quite romantic,' he later admitted. But the sheer distance strangled the relationship.

'She was a really big love,' a clearly choked Orlando later confessed. 'It's sad. I don't know what happened . . . she spent seven months with me in New Zealand and then two more. We tried, but we didn't know how to handle it.

'We found it very difficult, so we split up,' he reflects on the mystery girl in his life. 'I think that it's something that you have to learn to manage. The sad thing is sometimes relationships will suffer. It isn't easy to be uprooted from your friends and family constantly, but I love what I'm doing. You have to go wholeheartedly into it. A big reason why it didn't work out with my girlfriend was that it was new territory, and we didn't know how to deal with it. In hindsight, there were certain things that I should've done, but you learn as you go.'

In his first metaphorical bloom of stardom, Internet rumours that he had been engaged to Jemma Kidd, long-legged blonde make-up artist and sister of supermodel Jodie, were denied by both parties, who insisted they were just friends.

Similarly, Italian actress Maya Sansa, who graduated from the Guildhall School of Music and Drama at the same time as Orlando, was known to have spent a month with him during location shooting in New Zealand, including a weekend spent skydiving together in October 2000. This was apparently paid for out of the production's budget, which allowed for some of the stars' closest friends to visit them in their beautifully remote corner of the world. According to Ms. Sansa, 'Orlando and I are very close, we have shared very special moments.' But, with a tinge of wistful regret, Orlando insisted, 'My career is about the most special thing in my life . . . and my friends and family. But there's no romance.'

Still, life in New Zealand obviously had its consolations. When he and his Hobbit friends were asked their opinion of Kiwi women, Orly cracked, 'Billy could answer that one. Just go and get the girl.' Billy Boyd was clearly not averse to making hay while the sun shone. But, well-founded rumour has it, that applied just as accurately to other young bucks in the Hobbit-Elf axis.

'Mine and Orly's favourite subject was the girls we were watching in the bars,' laughs Dominic Monaghan. 'He's never had a problem with the girls.'

Orlando with one of his best friends from the Rings *cycle – the lovely Liv Tyler (Arwen).*

Emotional sadness aside, location shooting for *The Lord of the Rings* had more than enough consolations for an adventurous young man.

'I'm a bit of an adrenalin junkie,' admitted Orlando. 'I used the spare time on location to learn surfing, sky-diving and white-water rafting, and I did my first bungee jump there' – and this, remember, was a young man who had broken his back less than two years previously, and was still suffering in silence from the pain.

'I'm probably a good boyfriend, but I'm pretty intense. When you're with me it's exciting, fun and very intense. At the same time I'm easy going.'

'I'm not constantly throwing myself out of aeroplanes . . . but I like to snowboard and I've always been into motorbikes . . . and New Zealand is the place where they invented the bungee – I love that shit.'

Mindful not so much of Orlando's recent injury as the costs to production if any of the main cast injured themselves, producer Barrie Osborne sent out letters forbidding his actors from indulging in New Zealand's extreme sports scene. Almost inevitably, it had the opposite effect. As Orlando recalled, 'There was a memo that was sent around during the filming saying, "We're going down to Queenstown, it's the adventure capital of New Zealand, so please don't do anything stupid" and I sort of ignored it.

'I'd been in Queenstown for like an hour and I walked up this mountain and bungee jumped.

'I went off at the highest bungee-jump in New Zealand, 134 metres, like six times. To throw yourself in the air with only something attached to your feet is a different head space altogether.

'I knew the producers wouldn't be too pleased about it so I only told them afterwards.'

While it might seem like Orlando was tempting fate, or at least provoking the wrath of the film's insurers, he later admitted to having more fundamental issues at heart: 'It's not for the adrenalin. It's because I want to challenge myself and face my fears.' Playing a superbeing in his first major film role, Orlando wanted first to overcome himself, his human weaknesses and fears. As he'd later admit, 'I love anything dangerous. Anything dangerous, you can count me in! And yeah, you'd have thought my accident would have put me off. I did look into whether it [bungee jumping] would be a safe thing for me to do, and it's OK.'

'I don't think there's anyone more unpredictable to spend time with,' Elijah Wood said of his new co-star. Peter Jackson – who, with his squat frame, hirsute appearance and chubby legs in shorts, resembles a Hobbit himself – had a more concise take on Orlando's physical risk-taking: 'He's an absolute nutter!'

'I'm a bit of an adrenalin junkie, I used my spare time on location to learn surfing, sky-diving and white-water rafting, and I did my first bungee jump there.'

'It [New Zealand] really became my home,' Orlando later reflected. 'It was amazing, like the most beautiful parts of England, Ireland, Scotland and Wales all put together on one tiny island; mountains, plains, rolling fields and shit-loads of sheep. And when you're thrown together on such a project, you have no choice but to make friends for life.'

Much of the bonding within the younger members of the Fellowship was based upon who shared Orlando's taste for extreme sports – mostly the four actors who played the Hobbits. As nominal male lead Elijah put it, 'The Hobbits tended to spend their free time together, so the closest friends that I had on the movie were Billy and Dom and Sean. And Orlando, the Elf, who happened to join us as well, much to our dismay. No, he's a good guy. The Hobbits went to Australia . . . we went to Sydney and checked out the *Star Wars* [*Episode Two: Attack of the Clones*] set. The Elf joined us. We went on surfing trips a lot. It was a close union of boys.'

'When I arrived in Wellington I wanted to find some sort of extracurricular activity we could do outside *Lord of the Rings*,' confirmed Orlando, 'just to keep us sane.

'So I was like, "Let's get motorbikes!" and the guys weren't into that at all. They were like, "There's no need to kill ourselves while we're working on this." So one day I just said to Billy Boyd, "Let's buy surfboards." We walked onto the beach with these brand new, sparkling boards, freshly waxed and in our new little wetsuits – the other surfers were looking at us like we were idiots! And the water was freezing. But we ended up being quite good and then the others bought boards – Elijah, Sean, Dom. Even Viggo had a board.' During a break in shooting, the naughty Elf and his Hobbit friends would also check out the waves on Manly Beach, Sydney, in neighbouring Australia.

Much to Barrie Osborne's chagrin. For even the less frenetic sport of catching waves can have its casualties. Peter Jackson described how surf virgin Viggo showed up for shooting one of the famously intense scenes in the mines of Moria with 'a huge swollen face, his right eye closed like a boxer,' after his surfboard had smacked him in the head. 'For the scene we always had to shoot from the left-hand side. We had no choice.'

Also, during a session with the 'surfing Hobbits', as Orlando recounts, 'Me and Billy Boyd . . . were out surfing late one night during the New Zealand shootings. Billy saw a fin and started paddling toward me in panic. It turned out to be a seal, but we were all jittery and got out of the water right away.'

In July Orly and the Hobbits also took a little r&r time out to attend the Queenstown Winter

He's got you in his sights: Orlando Bloom, as Legolas, demonstrates his character's prodigious skills as an archer.

Festival. This being Down Under, July was exactly the right time to ski down some of those snowy slopes that made their way into the sweeping aerial shots of the *Rings* films.

The Fellowship's closeness and friendly rivalries also extended to playing practical jokes on each other. Human warriors Aragorn and Boromir declared a friendly on-set war against the Hobbits and their Elf ally. Viggo had his young son cover Orlando's trailer in duct tape while he was out on a shoot one day. 'They trashed my trailer,' Dominic Monaghan said. 'So, we trashed Viggo's trailer.' As retribution, Mortensen would return to his own trailer to find rotten fish 'and a pile of fake shit' had been dumped inside. Orlando, it was decided, was to blame, so retribution was duly exacted – with the help of the traitorous Hobbits.

'I thought of Legolas as a gun and his arrows as his bullets'

'They broke into his hotel room in the middle of the night,' laughed Dominic. 'They carried him downstairs. Billy and I sat on Orlando's knees and Sean Bean pulled his arms back. Viggo pulled up Orlando's shirt and slapped the hell out of his belly. He was nearly crying, the poor baby.'

'It's all very affectionate,' broke in Orlando, rescuing his credibility. Clearly, his own prowess as a fighter couldn't match that of Legolas. 'We were all in it together. If we got bored, tired or grumpy somebody would slap you around the head and say, "get a grip."'

The *Lord of the Rings* trilogy was suffused with the imagination of Tolkien and the visual power of the maverick Peter Jackson. 'When I was filming I imagined that Legolas was a meditative character who was very thoughtful and had a certain amount of depth to him,' explained Orlando of his crucial supporting role. 'I started working on trying to find this focus that Legolas has, which wasn't really like me.

The odd couple: by the time they ride into battle in The Return of the King, *Legolas and Gimli (John Rhys-Davies) are confirmed allies.*

'So when I was playing Legolas, if the other Hobbit actors were joking around on set, I would usually be more quiet and still, trying to remain as focused and concentrated as I possibly could. I wanted that intensity in the character. It's all in the eyes, I think. It's not in what he says, it's in what he does – even if he's not running or fighting or shooting a bow. And if he does speak, it's because there's danger or something important needs to be expressed. He'll say, "The Orcs are about," or, "There's something unnerving about this situation. We need to move on." That's his mission, his job.'

'I like the fact that Legolas is a man of a few words, because what he doesn't say kind of gives him weight in a way.'

The dialogue spoken by Legolas throughout the film trilogy is, indeed, minimal – 'There is a fell voice on the air;' 'The stars are veiled. Something stirs in the east,' are two of the dryly Tolkienesque warnings he gives the Fellowship.

Interestingly, the young man instilled with a lifelong self-assuredness, and the most thorough theatrical training, was relieved at not having to act too much: 'It wasn't like going into a huge, heavy-dialogue role where I could have potentially made a mess of it – you know, by being overly theatrical.

'I like the fact that Legolas is a man of few words, really, because what he doesn't say kind of gives him more weight in a way.'

He was even stoical enough to credit his near-fatal back injury, which necessitated learning how to move all over again, with helping develop his character's style of movement: 'Legolas' moves are smooth and elegant, like a cat. You know how cats can jump and land steadily on their paws? That's what I'm trying to do. There's a strength in that, but it's very balletic. It's also bloody hard to do without falling over!' And it lent a physical grace to the character that allows him, in one scene, to walk over snow without the slightest hint of slipping or stumbling.

The Elves' mode of combat, however, was the brainchild of Jackson and his team of trainers and choreographers, rather than based on the original novels. 'The Elvin style of fighting is based on an ancient European and Asian style of fighting,' testified Orlando, 'so I learned those kinds of styles with twin blades. Essentially, at the end of the day, I had to learn to slow down the movements for the camera and still make them look flashy.'

Legolas's strange and deadly grace was based in part on the poetic battle scenes that both Orlando and Jackson (who described his performance as 'passionate') studied in the films of director Akira Kurosawa. 'There are these massive battle scenes with tons of CG effects, but all the sword fighting I do is real. It was all modelled on Japanese samurai moves,' Orlando confirmed, 'so I did a lot of training for that. The idea was to keep it all looking very controlled and precise, just like samurai warriors. They don't even get angry when they fight, they just use their swords very efficiently. So I had to master all that.'

> 'Legolas' moves are smooth and elegant, like a cat. You know how cats can jump and land steadily on their paws? There's a strength in that, but it's very balletic. It's also bloody hard to do without falling over!'

Legolas may be by far the prettiest male in a film series that sometimes excels in fantastic images of ugliness, but he's also the most efficient, cold-blooded killer. 'We got to know our characters well over time, and that made for a great working relationship with Pete. We were all on the same page. We all knew what he wanted. It was cool. He would just say one word and it would sum up precisely what I needed to do. He would tell me, "Just remember, you're an assassin," and I would think, "OK, I'm a cool, steely assassin." I thought of Legolas as a gun and his arrows as his bullets.'

Firing off one lethal shaft after another with perfect rapid accuracy, it seemed almost as if Legolas' archery skills were a CGI creation – in fact, in the sequence where he fires off a number of arrows in quick succession, computer graphics did play their part. 'That was really me,' explains Orlando, 'I was doing it all but they put the arrows in afterwards. I pulled out the first one and, I think that day I shot off like 50 or so arrows. The arrows were dangerous and they go off in all sorts of directions. So they put in the arrows CG afterwards.'

In the age of DVD, of course, footage that would once have wound up on the cutting room floor is often resurrected for 'special' or extended editions. 'I have a very cool moment in the first movie when I take out about three Orcs with arrows one after another,' explained Orlando. 'In the restored [DVD] version, I take out about ten with ten arrows. I've had fans come up and say, "Wow, did you really kill those three Orcs like that?" Now they'll see it was really ten!'

As with a standard film shoot, most scenes were shot chronologically out of sync to adhere to the production schedule. But this was compounded by the sheer scale of the project, and the fact that Jackson was essentially not shooting one film, but three. 'He had up to ten units going at one time,' testified Orlando. 'It was ridiculous. You could have done a shot for the third movie in the morning and a shot for the first movie in the afternoon. Keeping on top of everything was like juggling balls. It was like a nightmare in terms of keeping it all in your head. To keep a through line for your character was virtually impossible. And multiply that by a hundred for Peter.'

For all the warnings about the dangers of extreme sports, and the necessity of having a chiropractor present throughout to ensure no further damage occurred to his back, Orlando's only injury during the entire fifteen months of shooting occurred during an action scene where he had to ride horseback with John Rhys-Davies' stunt double. 'I did some pretty wicked stuff on horseback,' he reflected with pride. But still, 'Letting go of the reins and shooting my bow and arrow was tricky stuff.

'We'd done this shot five times and you have to imagine that the Orcs and Uruk-Hai are around you and you are battering them down with your arrows. I had my hand on the rein and [stunt man] Brett Beattie was behind me and had a horse that decided not to stop. I bailed and landed on a rock and Brett landed on top of me.' After cracking one of his ribs and being prescribed painkillers, Legolas was up and riding again within the next two days of shooting.

The constant physical demands also demanded a suitable health regimen. 'When you work on a character for eighteen months you take it away with you a bit,' Orlando later explained. 'I know that while I was filming I didn't smoke or drink and I even tried different dietary things.'

'It isn't easy to be uprooted from your friends and family constantly, but I love what I'm doing. You have to go wholeheartedly into it.'

While not dogmatic about what he eats – he likes starchy or potentially fattening foods like pasta, pizza, rice or baked potatoes – his dietary adjustment for the *Rings* cycle created the image of Orlando the strict vegetarian. But it wasn't quite that way, as he explains: 'When you're working on a film, food is like a fuel. It can help you out or, if you indulge, it can get in the way. While making *Lord of the Rings*, I would get tired after lunch. I ate so much, it knocked me out. So I didn't eat meat. I stopped drinking milk. I wasn't strict, I was just trying to find out what was right. I went to see a guy for my back. He said he had been a vegetarian for 25 years, but he went back to eating one piece of meat every couple of weeks. Because of his blood type, he needed it. I was getting sick with the flu and feeling rundown. So I tried having a steak and I wasn't ill anymore.'

As for the time spent on the project and in character, Orlando expressed surprise that anyone should see that as any kind of imposition: 'I mean, I have a great job. I get to dress up and become somebody else, especially when it's someone like Legolas, who's this super-cool kind of other-worldly Elf. It's, like, I'm lucky, man, so why would I not appreciate that?'

In the final days of shooting, it became inevitable that what had become a way of life would have to go the way of all film shoots, with the participants returning to their civilian lives. 'We all had such a great time together, and we wanted something to remember the experience [by],' recalled Dominic Monaghan. Both Dominic and Orlando agreed that all the nine original members of the Fellowship – Gandalf, Frodo, Sam, Merry, Pippin, Aragorn, Legolas, Gimli and Boromir – should permanently commemorate the time together.

'At first, we talked about a ring, and then we got on to the tattoo.' With tattoos playing such a prominent part in the iconography of Maori (native New Zealand Aboriginal) culture, they seemed both more appropriate and more permanent. 'It was a guy called Roger at Roger's Tattoo Parlour in Wellington,' explains Dominic. 'He didn't open on Sunday, but we only had a day off on a Sunday . . . . We all turned up there, I think at eleven o'clock, and it was a real party atmosphere. We were all taking photos and writing in diaries.'

'It was designed by Alan Lee, who illustrated all of the *Lord of the Rings* books,' explained Orlando. 'It's in Elvish script, and it's the word for nine. We all chose to put them in different places. I got mine on my forearm, because I'm an archer.'

It was initially intended to be a private bond between the nine actors, concealed from the public. When he appeared as an interviewee on the US chat show *Live with Regis and Kelly*, in 2002, co-host Regis Philbin almost got Orly to show his Elvish tattoo to the camera – before he hastily withdrew his arm. 'Yeah, I wish I could,' he explained. 'The thing is, I can't. I'm not supposed to show anyone. It's kinda like the nine of the Fellowship had a tattoo done, and it was like the movie is for everyone else and the tattoos were for us.'

But, as Ian McKellen said, 'There are a lot of naughty Hobbits running around. When we first had this done, it was agreed we would tell no one except those who are in a position to discover it for themselves.' It wasn't long until the Elvish symbol tattoo surfaced in the press.

Later, in December 2001, as Orly explained to Regis Philbin, 'We were in New Zealand just now for the release of *The Lord of the Rings*. And I got Peter Jackson, the director, Barrie Osborne, he's one of the producers, Mark Ordesky, who was one of the executives at New Line, and Richard Taylor, who is head of Weta, this special effects company that Peter owns in New Zealand: I got them all a tattoo that said "ten". They got ten tattooed on them, so they're like the [collective] tenth member of the Fellowship.'

In addition, Orlando was given a further souvenir by one of the makeup artists: a replica of the One Ring itself, bearing the inscription, 'To wherever it may lead.' It seems as apt a motto for the adventurous young actor's life as any.

'Not a ritual that I'll be repeating for future projects,' Orlando stressed. 'I feel really blessed to have been part of this project, really blessed and honoured. The whole experience has been amazing, living in New Zealand, working with the calibre of cast and crew and working with your best mates around you. It was a labour of love. And with the tattoo, it's like the reality of it will be forever left on my skin.' But then, how many film projects could possibly change a life in the way that *The Lord of the Rings* was about to transform his?

Shooting ended in December 2000, when the cast (and, indeed, the Fellowship) disassembled after public appearances at a children's charity showing of *The Grinch*. Over the course of the multi-episode film's release schedule, some of the cast would be called back for reshoots or to shoot extra scenes. 'I'm quite looking forward to going back for those pick-ups,' said Orlando to a London reporter. 'Really hard work – surfing, snowboarding, skydiving, alongside filming *Lord of the Rings*.'

Less flippantly, in the autumn of 2002, he'd observe, 'The thing is, although the three films were all made at the same time, they're not all finished yet. Just a few weeks ago they were filming new stuff for the second one and there's still a lot of work to go on the third.'

'My career is about the most special thing in my life . . . and my friends and family.'

Should any of the actors' physical presences prove unavailable, however, then Peter Jackson had a technical trick up his sleeve: 'All the main cast had their faces scanned and body movements captured by Weta Digital, our New Zealand-based special effects company . . .'

In the first instance, this was so that the characters' virtual selves were seen to perform life-endangering acts not even their stunt doubles could undertake. In *The Fellowship of the Ring*, the great monster battle scene where Legolas jumps on the back of the giant troll in the mines of Moria, to fire arrows into him point blank, had already made use of the technique. Obviously, the fearsome monster himself was a CGI creation. But then, as he had nothing substantial to do battle with, so was Legolas – with Orlando's features and bodily movements morphed into an amazingly lifelike simulation of himself.

In the long term, it also meant that members of the Fellowship would be able to perform heroic deeds without necessarily even being in the country. It would get Jackson out of a tight spot in the celebrated Battle of Pelennor Fields in *The Return of the King*: 'We had planned on that day to do a shot of Orlando jumping up onto the saddle, but he fell off the horse and cracked his rib and we couldn't shoot any more. He went home, and I forgot all about it. Then earlier this year [2003], when I was cutting that scene together, I realised, "We don't have any shots of him getting on the horse. How the hell are we going do this?"'

What he did have was a shot of Legolas looking at the front line of the Uruk-Hai as a horse gal-

The 2,931-year-old warrior prepares for battle. Legolas prior to the climactic war scene, the Battle of Pelennor Fields, in The Return of the King.

lops along behind him. Utilising a CGI composite of Orlando, Jackson would compose a shot where Legolas vaults through the air onto the horse – an action scene that drew spontaneous applause from preview audiences.

The wrap party took place in December 2000, at the Shed 21 club on Wellington harbour, with most of the cast present bar Liv Tyler, who had already returned to the USA. 'The stunt guys did a hucker, which is a Maori kind of pole dance,' Orlando recalled. 'Peter said some amazing things. It was really sad and hugely emotional.

'I have a great job. I get to dress up and become somebody else, especially when it's someone like Legolas, who's this super-cool kind of otherworldly elf.'

'I don't know what I'm going to do,' he said at the time, feeling obviously deflated. 'It's going to be a shock to the system, arriving in the UK in cold winter weather.'

But the Fellowship decided they were not yet fully ready to dissolve. 'After we finished,' Orly later revealed, 'I went surfing in Florida with two of the Hobbits, Billy Boyd and Dominic Monaghan.' Unlike the ephemeral nature of most film sets or location shoots, the *Lord of the Rings* experience really did bond some cast members for life.

'I've grown up here,' Orlando said of New Zealand. 'And it's been a great place to grow up.'

Indeed, so enamoured had he, Elijah, Dominic and Billy become of the Antipodean islands, that, after filming wrapped, they applied for New Zealand residency, with a view toward buying a house together as a timeshare. Orlando was so in love with the country he claimed it was 'the sort of place I would want to raise my kids one day.'

As if to maintain a connection with the nature mysticism that permeates the *Rings* trilogy, Orlando, Elijah, Dominic and Billy also made donations to an organisation called Future Forests, to plant new trees on the Scottish Isle of Skye. J. R. R. Tolkien, romantic chronicler of a disappearing rural Britain, would surely have approved.

Wind forward one full year later, and Orlando Bloom was no longer a newcomer in front of the cameras. But still, he had yet to be seen on the big screen in anything but the bit part he'd played in *Wilde*.

Things were about to change. Prior to its worldwide pre-Christmas 2001 release, Orlando took part in promotional duties for *The Lord of the Rings: The Fellowship of the Ring*, attending the

'We did lots of research in choreographing sword fights. We developed our own styles as swordsmen. Elves have a very lethal but delicate movement.'

world premiere in Wellington, closely followed by premieres in Sydney, London and New York. 'After all the hype, I went to hang out for Christmas and New Year,' he recalls. 'We'd been going on the press tour for ages and it was exhausting. It ended in Australia, so I just decided to get some friends together. In fact, a couple of the Hobbits came with us, and we relaxed. We just had a laugh.

'I was on a beach in India, winding down from the whole process of putting out the movie. In hindsight, I think I would have enjoyed it, but they hadn't released it in India, and there was no access to newspapers or magazines.'

As willfully cut off as he now was from all the hype, Orlando still expressed a nervousness about the audience response, and post-production work on the second and third films. 'At the moment, I am *terrified* about going back. It's just too much. We've done so much *Lord of the Rings*, I'm scared that there's something I *missed*. The pressure of playing one of these characters was very demanding.'

The wave of excitement would build at a much faster rate than he could possibly have anticipated. In *The New York Times*, Elvis Mitchell applauded 'Peter Jackson's altogether heroic job in tackling perhaps the most intimidating nerd/academic fantasy ever.'

'Not since *Gone with the Wind* more than 60 years ago has a movie held up as well to the original book,' ran the cnn.com review. Their reviewer also saw fit to praise the cast: 'The

For many young – and not so young – female fans, Legolas was the whole point of The Fellowship of the Ring.

Rings trilogy is also a monument to ensemble acting of the highest order. McKellen is sheer perfection as Gandalf, and Wood is remarkable as Frodo, the heart and soul of the story. Others, including Orlando Bloom as the warrior Elf Legolas . . . are excellent in their roles and vital to the story.' It was praise of the highest order, but still regarded Orlando's character part as strictly second-string.

Clearly, for many critics the figure of Legolas was almost incidental to the film. One critic managed to miscredit the actor behind the Elvish archer as 'Armando' Bloom.

'I feel really blessed to have been part of this project. The whole experience has been amazing, living in New Zealand, working with the calibre of cast and crew and working with your best mates around you.'

Some viewers – members of the public, rather than critics – would come to see the *Rings* trilogy as a parable for the modern world, and the US-led 'war on terrorism', in the battle of the Fellowship against the forces of the Dark Lords Sauron and Saruman. By the time of the December 2002 release of *The Two Towers*, the title's unfortunate evocation of 'the twin towers' (of the World Trade Centre) would lend further post-9/11 resonance. Orlando respected their concerns, but calmly explained, 'The book has been around for a really long time and the name is part of the culture of these stories. I happened to be in New York at the time [of 9/11] so I know it's very painful, but this film is not about it. It has no relevance to those events.'

Orlando did concede that people could find whatever they wanted to in such an epic work full of fantastic metaphor. 'It has all the best elements of a fantastic story and I think that what Peter's done is he's taken those moments from the book and crystallised them and put them into the movie. And it makes for a very exciting film. I had a phone call from [executive producer] Mark Ordesky, saying that the movie has done like $18 million in its first day in America and it's broken all the records across the board in Denmark, Sweden, Germany. I mean, it's taken more money anywhere than anything . . . which is great.'

It was only on his return from holiday that Orlando began to understand what a phenomenon the movie had become. *The Fellowship of the Ring* had quickly risen to the ranks of the five highest grossing films of all time. 'The enormity of it is only just hitting me,' he admitted. 'I've spent the last few weeks in India so, to be honest, I'm only now realising the craziness.' So many different aspects of the film had connected in different degrees to

Left: Orlando demonstrates his love of New Zealand at the Wellington world premiere of The Return of the King. *Right: Clowning around with the hobbits at the New Zealand world premiere. Billy Boyd is the Hobbit with his finger in the Elf.*

different sectors of the audience: the faithful truncation of the original text to the Tolkienites; the CGI effects to the sci-fi geeks – and, not least, the appeal of Legolas to teenage girls.

The marketing director for 20th Century Fox in Singapore, one Janice Kay, had already predicted that 'older women will go for Bloom. Bloom as Legolas has a quiet confidence, skill and grace in battle. He's an eye-mind kind of hero.' As astute as her assessment was, it seemed she'd misguidedly limited the age range. To a vast number of young girls, it seemed that scenes featuring the ostensible leads Elijah Wood, as the doe-eyed Frodo, or Viggo Mortensen, as the darkly masculine Aragorn, were an irrelevance. Orlando may have appeared some way down the Fellowship of nine on the cast list, but, to the suddenly enthused young female audience, the core of *The Fellowship of the Ring* was Legolas.

Up until the present day, Orlando remains modest about the role that his personal charisma and visual appeal played in the *Rings* trilogy: 'Well, I don't think I can compete with Viggo . . . certainly, I'm [popular] with the six-year-olds and below. He's got the rest covered.' Billy Boyd concurred: 'I imagine that eight-year-olds in playgrounds all over the world want to be Legolas.'

But there was clearly so much more going on. In January 2002, on the Xenite.org fantasy fan website (named after the *Xena: Warrior Princess* TV series, to give some sense of its fanbase), commentator Michael Martinez noted that something extraordinary was afoot: 'Last month I wrote about the movie starring Orlando Bloom. I forget who else appeared in the flick, but in case you missed it, he played an elf named Legolas . . . . Orlando had a supporting cast and all, but it was his movie. I know this because, starting somewhere around December 20, 2001, my email began to explode with anxious queries from young ladies about that gorgeous elf in the movie.' It seems, to paraphrase Jim Morrison of the Doors, that the men didn't know but the little girls understood. The bemused/amused sword-and-sorcery buff noted, 'It seems the young ladies had hijacked our *Lord of the Rings* movie forum and were squeezing out all the other discussion. And that's a pretty active forum even without Orly threads.'

'Orlando Bloom's elf archer, Legolas, looks, with his flaxen locks and impeccable choreography, like an entire boy band in one person.'
– *Daily Telegraph*

Predicting that 'Orlando Bloom will probably be the Tom Cruise of the early 21st century', Martinez also noted, 'No one, and I mean no one, had any idea of how popular this character would become.'

But some of the grown-up papers had got the message. 'Orlando Bloom's elf archer, Legolas, looks, with his flaxen locks and impeccable choreography, like an entire boy band in one person,' commented London's *Telegraph*. The explosion was worldwide. 'Everywhere on the Net, it was, "Yeah, we love Frodo, but who's that Elf?"' said 36-year-old Jasparina Mahyat – a Singaporean housewife who set up her own website, orlandomultimedia.net. 'He had very little screen time in *The Fellowship of the Ring*, but he has that presence and star written all over him.'

Much later, when he'd learned to accept his character's sex appeal to his young fan base, Orlando would perceptively comment, 'There's absolutely nothing sexually threatening about an Elf. Legolas is a good, safe guy for girls to pin their dreams on.'

But the rapid blooming of the Orlando fan cult was almost entirely unforeseen. As Orlando himself observed, 'Legolas doesn't really arrive in *Fellowship* until Rivendell anyway, although there was other stuff shot for *Fellowship* that didn't make it into the film. But there was more of every character that didn't make it into the movie. That was because the film had to introduce the characters and get on with the story. Rather than let *Fellowship* run on too long [and its running time on release was close to three hours], Pete refined every character right down to their essence.'

Given how it developed out of grassroots fandom on the Internet, Orlando/Legolas fandom may be almost unprecedented. When he appeared as a guest on UK chat show *So Graham Norton* in early 2002, the house band struck up 1980s pop band ABC's lyric 'shoot that poison arrow through my heart,' in appreciation of the effect Legolas was having on fans worldwide.

'Orlando Bloom will probably be the Tom Cruise of the early 21st century.' — *Michael Martinez, Xenite.org*

Citing himself as 'a technophobe, I don't have an email, a computer,' Orlando was almost horrified to be told by the camp host, 'We put out an email search, an internet search on your name, and . . . 29,000 results! Apparently,' Norton continued, 'up to 50 fans an hour are joining the clubs for you.' By this time, an original Orlando Bloom autograph had already sold for US$250 on eBay. The young actor was pleasantly bemused. It all seemed to be happening to someone other than

himself. 'I have long blond hair in the movie,' he reminded the audience, 'and I don't think people really recognise me as [of] yet.' Back in London, out of costume, and with his Mohawk newly scalped, he now looked the image of young urban sophistication with his trendy 'Hoxton fin' hairstyle and his eyes, *sans* blue contact lenses, back to their natural dark shade. None the more for that, it seemed the character he affectionately referred to as a 'pointy-eared bow-twanger' had made him into an overnight star.

Norton had great fun showing Orlando the latest action-figure doll based on Legolas. 'You know, he's only trying to get it [the doll's box] open as he's gonna ask me to play with myself!' Orlando joked to the audience. But fellow guest Cybil Shepherd confirmed the appeal of Orly to the older woman, by pushing the doll down her cleavage.

'The girls have got a bit excited,' Orlando would admit, in what may be the understatement of the millennium. 'I spoke to my agent and she says she's wading through the fan mail. We've got bags of it. I'm like, "OK, well, what do we do with that then?" And she explains that we're sending them pictures and stuff, which is great.'

But Orlando also claimed that the initial explosion of popularity was overwhelming, and a little surreal: 'That really freaks me out. That many people taking an interest is scary. The Internet is a scary thing . . . My mum wants me to start an official web page . . . She telephones me and gives me updates

The Elf who made Orlando a movie star. At the right time, in the right place, Legolas scored a bullseye.

Spot the difference: it was Legolas who got him noticed, but the teenage girl's mags were soon interested in the man beneath the wig and the pointed ears.

on stuff about me that's happening on the Internet. It seems to be quite busy, which is flattering. And it's useful that my mum is able to use the internet and tell me about it, because I haven't got myself sorted out on that front yet – I'm just not into computers at all.' Perhaps, given his successful early battle with dyslexia, computer literacy, as opposed to general literacy, was something that just didn't seem worth the effort.

Orlando was inclined to look at it in terms of a career kickstart, rather than being blinded by the reflection of his own sexual charisma: 'I have no idea yet what the impact of my being in the *Rings* films will be. So far, just having done it has enabled me to get representation in America. It has opened up a whole new area of work, which is very exciting to me.'

He also kept things in perspective by seeing them through the eyes of his old friends and schoolmates: 'I spoke to one of them yesterday and he was like, "Oh, man, I'm so chuffed for you! I've seen your doll in Burger King. I've seen your face all over." All my friends and family are really happy for me. My mum is freaked out. She's making a scrapbook.'

'The girls have got a bit excited, I spoke to my agent and she says she's wading through the fan mail. We've got bags of it.'

Sonia Bloom was probably right to suggest her son set up his own website, to control the constant flow of Internet chatter. After all, Orlando would claim that one oft-repeated magazine quote was both glib and inaccurate: 'I don't care much about the money at all. Frankly, if I get the chance to kiss somebody in a movie, they wouldn't need to pay me at all.'

'Women are great,' he protested. 'But I didn't take up acting so I could kiss a girl.' If ever a refutation had a ring of truth about it, that was it. But still, Orlando held out from setting up his own site, claiming that 'the work can do the talking'.

In the place of an official website, any number of unauthorised Orlando Bloom fan sites sprang up. Referring to the most popular one, Ian McKellen observed of his young colleague's popularity, 'Twelve million people logged on to it in January! It is extraordinary.' By late February, the Internet Movie Database confirmed that Orlando had been the most sought-after actor on their site for the previous eight weeks – ever since the release of *The Fellowship of the Ring*. In 2002, more than two dozen unofficial Orlando Bloom websites would also go online. 'That's kind of a lot, isn't it?' understated the man himself. 'That's just mad.'

But much of the attention given to Orlando, the human being, was infused with the same kind of innocent hero-worship afforded to Legolas, the Elf. 'It's weird,' admitted Orly, 'it helps me meet women, but I don't use it to help me pull.'

As *Sunday Telegraph Magazine* interviewer Emily Bearn later observed, 'he is ridiculously good-looking, in a sort of pretty, unreal way that somehow makes one feel it might be more appropriate to admire him than actually to speak to him.' And he was still street-level enough to maintain a healthy distance between the screen image and the guy that young women might run into in London or LA bars.

'This whole heart throb status thing is only recently becoming apparent to me, it's all very flattering. I just hope it won't have an impact on the films I get to make.'

But, as Billy Boyd observed of the Bloom phenomenon, 'Orlando has become a big star quicker than anyone I've ever seen. But because he is so extraordinary looking, people have always noticed him and he's dealt with that. He is just doing it on a world level.'

'This whole heart throb status thing is only recently becoming more apparent to me,' Orly was finally forced to admit. 'It's all very flattering. I just hope it won't have an impact on the films I get to make.'

As to whether his new status was going to distort his personality, Orlando swore that he had too many personal ego-checks in place: 'I have a sister who would never let that happen . . . I've surrounded myself with friends who would beat me, physically beat me, if for a moment I tried to get above myself. And also I think I'm incredibly lucky to be doing what I do.'

But, in the build-up to *The Fellowship of the Ring*'s opening, Orlando had clearly been groomed as a star-in-waiting. In late October 2001, the *LA Times Magazine* was able to report that his favourite fashion designers were Marc Jacobs, Paul Smith (for whose London store he once worked) and Gucci, that he liked 'to break the forms a bit by mixing them with vintage pieces', and that his favourite haunts in LA were The Latin Lounge and Les Deux Café.

Orlando himself would try to play the designer clothes-horse image down. In an interview with *People Magazine* several months later, he'd claim his most treasured item of clothing was 'a pair of old Levi's, and I wear them all the time. I wore them to a premiere with a Fendi suit jacket. They're falling apart, but I keep getting them sewn back together.'

In March 2002, the UK's *Daily Mail* would report Orlando had been seen at a party at the 'palatial mountaintop home' in the Hollywood Hills of Bob Shaye, chief executive of New Line Cinema. Apparently, 'he was surrounded by a bevy of young women vying for his favours.' A reluctant sex symbol, perhaps, but Orlando could still play the role to the hilt.

In the US, *Moveline* selected Orlando's debut as one of their Ten Standout Performances by young actors in 2001. Legolas, they observed, 'moved with crystalline resolve and athletic grace. Even when a million things are happening at once, Bloom grabs your attention and makes you feel that everything depends on the great battle of good and evil.' MTV recognised Orlando with an award for 'Breakthrough Male' at their 2002 Movie Awards that April.

Back home in London, the cinema magazine *Empire* honoured him with an award for 'Best Debut' at their 2002 awards ceremony. It was a democratic vote by the mag's readers, demonstrating how Bloom mania was infecting the public. Orlando also made the hallowed ranks of *Teen People*'s '25 Hottest Stars Under 25' listings – all on the basis of that one film role.

As for the experience itself, he still spoke in glowingly positive terms: 'I graduated from drama school three years ago and I just walked into this job and it's just been probably one of the most life-changing, exciting and memorable experiences of my life, ever. My cousin said to me the other day, "Whatever happens in the next three years, you've got a movie out for the next year." I could do anything and not have to worry because I've got all the *Rings*.' But, as he had already demonstrated, it was not in Orlando Bloom's nature to sit on his hands.

'I just walked into this job and it's just been probably one of the most life-changing, exciting and memorable experiences of my life, ever.'

In the gap between the release of *The Fellowship of the Ring* and *The Two Towers*, in December of 2001 and 2002 respectively, Orlando had made three further films – though only one of them had reached the screen so far. In the interim, he'd done his best to stay in touch with the rest of the Fellowship: 'I went back for a weekend just to visit some of the lads who were doing some reshoots. I was in Melbourne in Australia doing a film about Ned Kelly. So I couldn't be there because I had grown a beard and stuff for this other movie and Legolas was clean-shaven so they couldn't do anything about it. But it was OK because my story with Aragorn and Gimli was in pretty good shape Peter told me. I went over anyway, like for a weekend, just to say, "Hi." Because I was like, "This is bollocks, I feel out of it." I met up with Viggo. And let me tell you, we had one mad night in New Zealand!' Meanwhile, with fan interest in Orlando reaching a hysterical all-time high, conjecture surrounded just who his current paramour might be. Speculation claimed it was most likely to be Hollywood actress Christina Ricci, who Orlando had befriended in LA. After all, one celebrity magazine journalist had spotted them dancing together at a party. But no, according to Orly. 'There's no one in my life at the moment. You know, I'm too busy for a relationship. I know I've been linked to Christina Ricci – and she is great – but all I did was get a lift in her limo to a Hollywood party. Nothing happened, believe me. I was there.' The rumours were apparently fuelled by eyewitness accounts of Christina having a little too much to drink, and having to go outside to throw up. When Orlando swept her hair back off her face, gave her a hug and whispered comforting words to her, it's little wonder that the rumour mill turned them unofficially into an item. 'Don't get me wrong, I love women. I would like to meet someone, but I'm working really hard. I'm tired a lot of the time and also I haven't been in any place long enough to make a real connection.'

All that awaited him back home in England was, it seems, his faithful old dog. 'The most important thing in my life is def-

The eyes and ears of the Fellowship: by the time of the climactic battles in The Return of the King, *Orlando has nicknamed his character 'Action Elf'.*

Liv Tyler and Orlando are greeted by The Return of the King *premiere audience in Wellington. Liv describes his new superstar status as akin to that of her rock star dad.*

initely my family,' Orlando would later testify. 'I'm on the phone with my mum Sonia and my sister Samantha at least once a week. The first thing I always want to know is how our dog Maude is faring.'

While being a very direct continuation of *The Fellowship of the Ring*, *The Two Towers* was a much darker, more action-filled movie than the first segment. As Orlando observed, 'By the end of *The Fellowship of the Ring*, the Fellowship has dispersed. We've lost Boromir, and now we'll go on.' Boromir is dead; Merry and Pippin have been carried off by the Uruk-Hai; Frodo and Sam continue their quest to Mordor alone, as Aragorn, Legolas and Gimli give chase to save their Hobbit friends; the immortal wizard Gandalf is apparently dead, pulled to his doom by the demon Balrog.

'Everytime we landed at an airport, there were thousands of girls screaming for Orlando.' – *Liv Tyler*

In the Battle of Helm's Deep, one of the most celebrated battle scenes in the history of cinema, the besieged castle of King Theoden (Bernard Hill) attempts to provide shelter for terrified villagers, including many women and children, as a CGI-multiplied army of 10,000 Uruk-Hai do battle with only 300 Men led by Aragorn, Legolas and Gimli.

This was where Legolas really came into his own. As Orlando explained it, his laconic hero would have less to say but much more to do, with much more physical movement: 'I became Action Elf in this movie. The bow was my signature weapon, but there's also some close combat stuff where I've got those two white knives and I get them wet . . . . I had a great stunt double called Morgan. He taught me most of my routines – showed me some really flashy moves. Most of those stunt people were amazing: black belts in everything . . . .

'There's a sequence where I slide down these stairs on a shield. They wired me up and I'm firing arrows as I slide down. I had a shield strapped to my feet and I had to kick it off at the bottom and leap into action.'

By now, with three further features under his belt, Orlando could also see the extent of his director's achievement: ' Now that I've seen the pressure of time and money and everything else that goes into making a film, the more amazed and baffled I am at what Peter achieved. It was the way he held it together, his commitment to each and every character and his way of communicating to everyone. The fact that he didn't lose his mind is unbelievable. And he's still working on it. I've been off the film for nearly two years and Peter is still in the cutting room.'

'I have no idea yet what the impact of my being in the Rings films will be. So far, just having done it has opened up a whole new area of work, which is very exciting to me.'

In the British press, much of which seemed to hold a sense of proprietorship about Tolkien's stories, *The Guardian*'s Xan Brooks praised the film: '*The Two Towers* is nasty, brutish and long (it clocks in at over three hours). It bows out to a vista of belching lava and swooping Nazgul [Tolkein's Ringwraiths, or Dark Riders], with barely a crumb of comfort to be found.

'But don't let that scare you off. Because *The Two Towers* is also mightily entertaining; a confident, sure-footed epic that works a kind of alchemy on its cod-grandiose material.'

Typically, however, the Brit crit had a list of criticisms, including a dismissal of one of the cast's finest assets: 'Its three-hour running time flags mildly during the tree-hugging interludes, the thunderous final battle scene perhaps beats you over the head for a few minutes longer than is strictly necessary, and Legolas – frankly – is a self-satisfied bore.' It was part of an undercurrent of incomprehension and derision among the British critics, that Orlando's character should have become one of the trilogy's major crowd-pleasers.

In the USA, the *Dallas Observer* enthused, 'Jackson has forged the middle of his cinematic trilogy with the immediacy of broadsword steel . . . [his] limited but enthusiastic adaptation has made literature literal without killing its soul – a feat any thinking person is bound to appreciate.' Their reviewer, Gregory Weinkauf, was also perceptive enough to describe 'hunky human Aragorn (Viggo Mortensen) [and] elegant Elf Legolas (Orlando Bloom)' as 'two-thirds of every schoolgirl's dream'.

On the Web, flipsidemovies.com offered the following praise: 'Bloom . . . really comes into his own as Legolas, and his growing bond with Rhys[-Davies]' Gimli brings a subtle charm to the proceedings.' Orlando also received the praise he deserved on a more democratic basis, by winning the public's vote for the AOL Moviegoers Award for Best Supporting Actor.

The December 2003 release of *The Return of the King* would be, as Peter Jackson trumpeted, 'the triumphant payoff'. As Orlando had commented the previous year, 'I don't think anyone will get what we were trying to achieve until the third movie comes out.

'I always think the third part of a movie is the best part because you've got closure,' he explained, acknowledging that the three segments of the *Rings* trilogy were, in effect, one big long film. 'I just hope that Pete gets all the recognition and appreciation he deserves for it.'

It was certainly a vivid climax – with Aragorn reclaiming his birthright as king by leading a ghostly army of the dead against the dark forces of Sauron, plus a whole plethora of monsters. Naturally enough, both the director and the co-star continued to up the ante on Legolas' action scenes. 'Leggy is up to his old tricks, slaying Orcs and getting business taken care of,' states Orlando, having adopted the affectionate nickname 'Leggy' for the long-legged Elf who changed his life. In one of the best CGI sequences of the trilogy, Legolas brings down one of the mumakai (huge, mammoth-like war elephants). 'Pete loved the way audiences had responded to Legolas running over the top of the cave and taking down the cave troll in the first movie,' explained Orlando, 'and sliding down the stairs on the shield and hopping onto the horse in the second movie, so for the third he wanted to come up with something that would combine both, so I went back and did the scene where I take down an elephant, which necessitated a very serious conversation with my digital double.'

Orlando also had to return for reshoots on the final film. But now it was for the very last time. 'It was really emotional to sort of say goodbye,' he confirmed. 'We've done the wig for the last time. We've done the pointy ears. I'm done. I did three days and they cut together a little clip for me of all the Legolas moments with music. And it was really kind of sweet and fun and sad. They let me keep my bow and arrow and the clapperboard from my last shot. And an ear or two.'

His friendships with his fellow co-stars continue to this day. 'Whenever I'm in New York I call Liv and if I'm in LA I call Viggo and Elijah and Sean. Then when I'm in England I see the other two lads [Dominic and Billy]. We hang out. It's more than something which you would ever say just passes.' (In fact, during a break in 2003's heavy work schedule, Orly would head to LA's Ventura Beach to catch some waves with Billy Boyd.)

Peter Jackson, like the rest of the cast and crew, marvelled at the way Orlando's star had risen ever since the release of *The Fellowship*, and how he'd adjusted to the fame: 'He was the same guy, fun-loving, enthusiastic and supportive. He doesn't buy into the nonsense.'

Orlando claims there's no professional envy between himself and the other Fellowship members, despite being the only actor whose career has truly taken off as a result of the trilogy. 'These are really talented, special people. Everyone's aware that each actor has his own path, not just in acting but in life. In my case, I feel really lucky to have been in the right place at the right time and right for the role . . . . And I can tell you I've auditioned for everything I've played. It's not like I'm given the pick of the bunch. You still audition.'

But, at the same time, he admitted he often had to take a reality check. 'It is incredible. I mean, I'm stumped by it . . . . I never expected this. I remember seeing myself in *Lord of the Rings* and thinking, I can't fucking believe I'm in this movie.'

'He is ridiculously good-looking, in a sort of pretty, unreal way that somehow makes one feel it might be more appropriate to admire him than actually to speak to him.' – *Emily Bearn*, Sunday Telegraph *Magazine*

As Liv Tyler had noted during the press tours and the *Rings* premieres, Orlando had now attained something closer to rock-star status. 'Everytime we landed at an airport there were thousands of girls screaming for Orlando. It's probably the closest thing to knowing how my dad [Steve Tyler of Aerosmith] feels.'

As for *The Return of the King* itself, Lou Lumenick of the *New York Post* insisted that *The Lord of the Rings* cycle 'takes its rightful place among such classics as *The Wizard of Oz*, *Gone with the Wind* and *Lawrence of Arabia*.' He also felt that it 'towers above its predecessors with cleaner storytelling and a more satisfying balance between terrific acting and eye-popping special effects . . . . unlike last time, Jackson never lets the spectacle overwhelm the human dramas . . .' Extra praise was reserved for Jackson's ingenious CG-improvised scene, where 'the Elf Legolas (Orlando Bloom) . . . performs a horseback stunt that will have audiences whooping.'

In *The New York Times*, Elvis Mitchell emphasised the resonance that he too found in the trilogy: '*King* is a meticulous and prodigious vision . . . It's been a long time since such a commercially oriented film with the scale of *King* ended with such an enduring and heartbreaking coda: "You can't go back. Some wounds don't heal." Mitchell also found space to praise 'the pitilessly sure Elf warrior Legolas (Orlando Bloom, whose physical élan fills out the role)'. It was a measure of how far

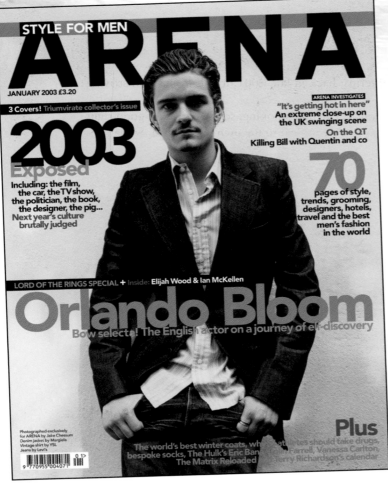

From mythic icon to style icon: Orlando fronts men's mag Arena.

Orly's public profile had risen that the *NY Times* reviewer got his name right this time around.

The Return of the King was the culmination of the *Lord of the Rings* cycle. Defying the logic that said only diehard fans of the first two movies would go to see the film, it performed best of all at the box office – becoming only the second film after *Titanic (*1997) to take more than US$1 billion worldwide. In January 2004, at the Golden Globe awards, *The Return of the King* won Best Dramatic Film, Peter Jackson won Best Director, Howard Shore won Best Original Score, and vocalist Annie Lennox, together with Jackson's partner Fran Walsh, won Best Original Song with their co-composition 'Into the West'. The next month, at the BAFTAs in London, it won Best Film, Best Adapted Screen-play, Best Cinematography and Best Spescial Effects – plus the special award for Film of the Year, as voted by the British public.

But it was at Hollywood's Academy Awards, on Sunday, 29 February, 2004, that this leap year's chickens came determinedly home to roost. *The Return of the King* was nominated for eleven Oscars: Best Picture; Best Director; Best Adapted Screenplay; Best Art Direction; Best Makeup; Best Costume Design; Best Visual Effects; Best Musical Score; Best Original Song; Best Editing; Best Sound Mixing. It won every single one of them, breaking the record for the highest number of Oscar nominations translated into actual awards. Everyone who applauded the accolades realised that this was Hollywood's seal of approval on the trilogy as a whole, not just one film.

'I will take Legolas, and [the] experience in New Zealand, wherever I go.'

And Orlando Bloom? His life, he could see with benefit of hindsight, had been changed almost beyond recognition by the three films. He didn't credit his time on *The Lord of the Rings* so much as a passage to adulthood (he had, after all, been an independent young man since the age of sixteen), but spoke of it as if it wasn't just the start of a shining career, but the apex of total creative fulfillment: 'I think that I've had an interesting life and I feel very grateful. If I died tomorrow, I'd feel like I've lived a very full life. I've loved every moment and, through that, I've learned a lot about people and relationships. I try to apply a set of rules to life to make it easier and that normally means being open and honest so you can enjoy it.'

Ultimately, the role of the Elf Prince of Mirkwood had been a career-defining moment: 'I will take Legolas, and [the] experience in New Zealand, wherever I go. The beautiful thing about being an actor is every character you embrace, when you move on, you take part of the character with you.'

As much as this sounds like a thespian cliché, Orlando seemed to mean it literally. 'Elves live in harmony with the world and I try to do that,' he explained earnestly, claiming that he was aspiring toward living in a 'more elfin style'. In practical terms, back in late 2001, it had meant him striving even further toward physical perfection by giving up smoking and cutting down on his alcohol intake. Only one tiny vice remained: 'I bite my nails. Seriously, I've quit smoking, so it feels pretty good right now. On the other hand I have a tendency to drift off, disappear into my own little world. Some people might take that as if I'm being rude.'

Despite the differences in his on and offscreen appearance, it was almost as if Orlando's public persona was merging with the more spiritual, intuitive side of Legolas. Always spiritually inclined since he and Samantha were encouraged to read from the Bible as children, he had developed that typically modern composite of beliefs that takes in New Age symbolism, Buddhist philosophy and basic Christian morality.

'I think that I've had an interesting life and I feel very grateful. If I died tomorrow, I'd feel like I've lived a very full life.'

Shortly after the release of *The Fellowship*, he showed a reporter from *Newsday* a selection of natural mineral souvenirs hanging around his neck on a necklace: 'here's an Orlando stone. It was given to me by a girlfriend. And here's a power shell from New Zealand. I travel to all these different countries. I like to take a little bit with me.'

More recently, Orlando described keeping a small pyramid of the blue mineral stone lapis lazuli by his bed, 'for wisdom'. According to the New Age earthbow.com website, 'Lapis is said to help your ability to communicate. Its subtle energies amplify your natural talents for speaking and to allow them to develop . . .

'Lapis lazuli can also help you achieve spiritual enlightenment. By calming the mind and soothing the body, it allows you to be more open to the subtle messages of the spirit world.'

'I have a lot of good luck charms and trinkets and things that keep growing as I need more,' says Orly, admitting to a big superstitious streak. 'I need all the luck I can get.'

But he was still counting his blessings, and looking toward the next stage: 'I've had this incredible start to my career, and I'm being a little bit selective at the moment. I've had some very nice offers for some stuff that's coming up, both British and American, and I'm travelling between the two trying to work out which one is going to work at the right time. It's looking really good. I keep pinching myself because I just can't believe it.'

'And,' said friend and mentor Ian McKellen, present at the same interview, 'I'm going to encourage him to do some theatre before he gets swept up in movies and doesn't know the joys of a live audience.' That, after all, had been Orlando's ambition back at the Guildhall School of Music and Drama.

'I never went into acting because I wanted to be an action man,' Orlando insists, 'although I think Legolas is a bit of a superhero.' As we shall see, though, Legolas to a large extent determined the path that Orlando's career would follow, far away from a life treading the boards. 'Theatre is something that I feel is very important for an actor to keep doing,' he would later assess. 'I think it keeps you sharp. But at the moment I'm intrigued with movies and filmmaking. It hasn't lured me away from theatre, but I'm just going to try and ride this wave and then jump into another world and see how far it takes me.' By now, Orlando was realistic enough to recognise that he was a bone fide Movie Star.

'It's great to be able to have that variety [of options], that's the opportunity I've had from working on the bigger films and I think I'll always be grateful to Peter Jackson and Fran Walsh because they gave me the opportunity for *Lord of the Rings*. They put me into a new arena. I was suddenly thrown into the public eye and thanks to that I'm able to make these choices.'

GUNS & POSES

'Orlando proved himself to be an excellent actor in a strong ensemble. He's got that quality that he can do whatever he wants to do.' – *Ridley Scott*

Once filming had wrapped on *The Lord of the Rings*, Orlando's agents – who now included the prestigious International Creative Management (ICM) in the USA – were able to take the crucial next step. 'It's a very hard act to follow,' he acknowledged, turning down the pile of offers for teen heartthrob pap that followed in its wake. However, in early 2001, he was invited to Hollywood to audition for British director Ridley Scott and action movie mega-producer Jerry Bruckheimer on their upcoming film.

He quickly landed a small but highly significant role in a war film based on recent history. When asked, at a *Lord of the Rings* press conference, whether he got the role in *Black Hawk Down* (2002) via becoming noticed in Peter Jackson's masterpiece, Liv Tyler butted in on behalf of her reticent friend: 'He got that because he's talented! People don't understand that.'

'I didn't want to do teen crap,' Orlando later explained, 'and that was what I was getting offered. I did a small part in *Black Hawk Down* because it was Ridley Scott and I had the chance to use an American accent.'

'I just look for good actors,' Scott confirmed, 'wherever they happen to be from. It was tricky to cast this ensemble, because there are some 40 speaking roles. All of them are important . . .'

Certainly, *Black Hawk Down* was one film where Orlando's looks were pretty much an irrelevance. The conflict the film was based on was the 3 October, 1993 massacre in Mogadishu, Somalia, in which eighteen US soldiers died and more than 70 were wounded, alongside more than 100 dead Somalis. It was adapted from journalist Mark Bowden's book about the crisis that occurred after the American military tried to 'extract' two lieutenants of Somalian warlord Mohammed Farrah Aidid.

After two Black Hawk helicopters were shot down in the Bekara Market area, compared in the film to the Wild West, the taskforce found themselves embroiled in a sixteen-hour street battle.

In *Black Hawk Down*, Orlando found himself playing alongside such contemporaries and peers as American teen heartthrob Josh Hartnett, Scottish star and fellow alumni from the Guildhall School of Music and Drama Ewan MacGregor, and Ewan's *Trainspotting* co-star Ewen Bremner. 'The first scene I shot was with Ewan,' recalled Orlando. 'He was the big name that had come out of school. So we chatted about some of the teachers we had at college.' Ewan, like the rest of the unusually large British contingent on the film, was cast as an American military man.

Naturally, a voice coach was required to make all the Brits sound as if they were authentic members of America's bravest. 'I decided to speak in my American voice all day long so that I felt the voice was my own,' explained Orlando. 'Americans are also very strong and focused in the way they communicate, whereas the Brits kind of offer something and then stop a bit. There's also a difference in the body language between the two nationalities. I had to learn to just kind of relax, whereas we're somewhat more formal in Great Britain.

'My character, Private First Class Todd Blackburn, was the youngest and greenest of the Rangers brought over to fight in Mogadishu,' described Orlando. 'He fell 60 feet from a helicopter at the start of the mission, and that was really the beginning of the end, if you like. But he's alive today. The Ranger's code of conduct is that you never leave a man fallen or down. So this one man fell and needed to be removed from that location. This meant that the other Rangers had to land in an area with the worst open live fire since Vietnam and try to take him out. And it became hellish.

'Theirs not to reason why, theirs but to do and die,' he quoted Tennyson's 'The Charge of the Light Brigade' – not ironically, but in admiration. 'They went into Mogadishu, did what they were trained to do and put their lives on the line. The fact that their government soon after pulled out of Somalia was out of Task Force Rangers' hands. These men were the foot soldiers. And anyone who puts themselves in that position succeeds on every level in my book.'

'I used to run around with toy machine guns, wearing all that combat gear, and suddenly I'm being paid for it.'

The parallels with Orlando's own youthful experience are obvious. 'My character breaks his back, and I had mentioned that I had done that when I was up for the part,' he admitted, equivocating, 'Who knows why one actor gets a job and another doesn't? I think it was just good timing that I happened to be there and I had had that experience. – I mean, I was lucky.' In a further piece of synchronicity, 'After I had my fall, I was in hospital lying right next to a young soldier with a paralysing injury. It's surreal how life has these patterns.'

As Orlando acknowledged, overseas filming on 'Black Hawk was a totally different experience. It was a huge machine. It was five months, but it was Morocco which was a very difficult environment to work in, much more so than New Zealand. It was hot and it was dusty and dry.'

Before location shooting the cast had to attend a military 'boot camp' in the southern state of Georgia, with an emphasis on fighting strategy, the handling of firearms, and explosives. Though the cast were given admonitions like, 'I'm going to put you in a world of shit!', Orlando insisted, 'I went to boot camp for *Black Hawk Down*, and I was fine there,' accustomed to pushing himself to physical extremes.

Later though, he admitted, 'I was kind of a joke. Everyone was like, "You don't need a gun, forget about it, you're falling from the helicopter." It was a bit frustrating to say the least.' To add jokey insult to injury, fellow Brit co-star Jason Isaacs insisted, when both appeared on *The Johnny Vaughan Show*, that Orlando only had to attend camp 'because he's a very pretty boy, and you know, it's all men there.'

But when he attended the 17 January, 2002 British premiere at the Empire Leicester Square in London, alongside Hartnett, McGregor and Bremner, Orlando had to fess up to the demands of the role: 'It was pretty gruelling and I didn't do as much of the running around as a lot of the boys 'cause I'm the first man down. The film was more reacting than acting, you didn't even have to act like you were getting shot because you were often getting paintballs fired all around you. But it was fantastic. I used to run around with toy machine guns, wearing all that combat gear, and suddenly I'm being paid for it.'

Almost inevitably, his own action scene brought out the reckless action man in Orly. 'I remember taking helicopter rides in the Black Hawk,' he'd recall, 'those machines are so powerful, and

It's hard to tell, but that's Orlando lying down as critically injured Pte. Todd Blackburn, with Josh Hartnett as Sgt. Eversmann in Black Hawk Down.

we did this zero-gravity thing where they drop the helicopter in mid-flight. You freefall, and for a few seconds you're floating. There are no doors on these things, your feet are dangling out of the side and you're weightless. It's the most freaky thing ever – close to walking on the moon, probably. Talk about exhilarating.'

'Black Hawk Down was pretty gruelling and I didn't do as much of the running around as a lot of the boys 'cause I'm the first man down.'

Black Hawk Down was not only the most harrowingly realistic, but also the most successful war film in years. 'I thought it was rather cheeky of you when *Lord of the Rings* finally slipped from being Number One in the world after about a month,' Ian McKellen teased Orlando in an interview on London's Capital Radio. 'It was kicked out marginally by a new movie called *Black Hawk Down*, and guess who was in it?'

Despite his limited screentime in *Black Hawk Down*, the entertainment media couldn't fail to notice Orlando's appearance in two of the most powerful and successful films of recent times. Orlando Bloom, it was predicted by the London *Times*, was set to become 'an international household name' within a year.

Its youngest British co-star had also made a significant impression on the film's makers. 'Orlando proved himself to be an excellent actor in a strong ensemble,' praised director Scott. 'He's got that quality that he can do whatever he wants to do,' acclaimed producer Bruckheimer. In fact, Ridley Scott was impressed enough to bear him in mind for future major roles.

As for his current situation, Orlando himself felt blessed. 'I don't really know what I'm going to be doing next. But I like the idea of doing something smaller. Which, when you think about it [the scale of his previous films], still leaves quite a few options.'

On the set of 'Denim Invasion', the Gap clothing commercial that depicted the public pressures of stardom. With director Cameron Crowe (left) and Kate Beckinsale.

In fact, though neither of his next two film roles would advance his career in the way that his epic debuts had, he had a big enough store of goodwill and kudos to get by. 'I remember reading something Ewan McGregor once said,' Orlando reflected, 'something like, "You put yourself up on this huge screen just to be taken down." I'm lucky because I am taking those steps up, but I am sure I'll piss somebody off at some point and then they'll want to bring me down.' Fortunately, those days still seemed a long way off.

'Style icon for British men . . . gorgeous, undeniably well-dressed, and one of the future's biggest stars.' – The Times *Magazine on Orlando*

As to his growing status as a sex symbol, and the opportunities for taking advantage of it, Orlando remained coyly reticent. During his *Johnny Vaughan* interview, he claimed, 'I would love to say that I am getting it loads. I really would but . . . in fact, if anyone's interested,' he implored to the audience, to good-natured laughter.

But, over in Hollywood, he'd joined the ranks of the glamorous. In early January 2002, he was one of the guests of honour at E!Online's 'Sizzlin' Sixteen' party, the sixteen being the hottest stars of the year, at the ultra-hip Club AD. In London, the 16 February 2002 edition of *The Times Magazine* cited him as a future 'style icon for British men . . . gorgeous, undeniably well dressed, and one of the future's biggest stars.'

Consolidating his reputation as a casual designer clothes horse, Orlando also filmed an ad to be broadcast in spring 2002 for the Gap summer range. Directed by Cameron Crowe, who made the light-hearted rock-critic biopic *Almost Famous* (2000), he featured alongside fellow Brit and beautiful brunette Kate Beckinsale in a black-and-white vignette with the working title 'Denim Invasion'. In a comment on the kind of intrusive star status that kept threatening to overtake him, Orlando and Kate were seen running down a street from a crowd of fans after setting out on a leisurely romantic stroll together, to the strains of the Troggs' 1960s hit 'Love is All Around'.

That Orlando was becoming the ultimate modern sex symbol, there was no doubt. But his words still betrayed a lack of someone special in his life: 'Maybe our generation is more about sex, but it feels like romance is dying out. In England, when you meet someone, you're normally quite drunk and end up having some messy little snog in a cab on the way home.'

But still, in the spring of 2002, basking in the reflected glory of his previous two films, the world was Orlando's oyster. Screenplays were also being forwarded by both ICM in the States and his new London agent, Fiona McLoughlin, with regularity. Despite the literacy problems of his schooldays, his mother Sonia confirmed, 'He reads scripts all the time. [His dyslexia] hardly affects him now.'

> 'Orlando is a movie star waiting to happen. He's going to be huge because he's a good actor and he has incredible presence. There's a reason why girls go crazy for him. He's in the long tradition of guys like James Dean and Russell Crowe.' – *Gregor Jordan, Director,* Ned Kelly

His most favoured script of the time would entail a return Down Under. 'There's actually a great project coming out of Australia at the moment,' Orlando acknowledged during press interviews for *The Lord of the Rings: The Fellowship of the Ring*, 'and I'm trying to see if I can get in there.' His enthusiasm paid off. His next scene-stealing support role would be in a piece of Australian pop-history that had, over the years, become inseparable from legend.

'I wasn't very well informed about the history of Ned Kelly before I signed up to do the film,' admitted Orlando. 'But in preparation for my role, I read all the books to get my head into the character [of bushranger bandit Kelly's accomplice, Joe Byrne]. So I really enjoyed learning about the history of the Kelly Gang. There are so many different ideas about who the gang were and whether they were heroes or villains, so I took what I thought I needed in order to create the character. It was an amazing project to work on, which I think has to do with the fact that it's such a huge part of . . . Australia's culture. There was something eerie about filming it, because we were filming in locations they'd been in.'

Ned Kelly (2003) was directed by native Australian Gregor Jordan and produced by Working Title Australia, the Antipodean arm of the successful British independent production company, and based on the 1991 novel *Our Sunshine* by Robert Drewe – which drew as much on legend and reputation as verifiable fact in its account of the Kelly Gang.

'He made it sound really great,' said Orly of the director. 'He described it as a bunch of young guys riding on horses, shooting guns, sort of tearing up the town and generally causing havoc.

'But it's all for a purpose. They feel they are hard done by and persecuted unjustly, so it sounded like something to be involved in. Camaraderie, loyalty, friendship, and standing up for what you believe in are all themes I can relate to.'

Jordan's AU$33 million production of *Ned Kelly* began in remote regions of rural Victoria, and Melbourne in April 2002. Orlando was pleased to be back in the Antipodes; 'I love this part of the world,' he confirmed. 'I love the pace of life and lifestyle. And I've made a lot of friends.'

The role of the legendary outlaw went to Heath Ledger, the young Australian actor once tipped to be a 'Hollywood hottie' himself. As Orlando described, 'I play his best mate, Joe Byrne, the most educated of the gang and Ned's right-hand man. He tries to keep a lid on Ned who is fiery and

Orlando in Ned Kelly. *As Joe Byrne, Kelly's loyal, thoughtful but deadly sidekick, he stole every scene he appeared in.*

impulsive. Again, I was riding horses and shooting' – though this time it would be guns, not a bow and arrow.

As Orlando recounts, he was initially offered a choice between Joe Byrne or Steve Hart, the fourth member of the gang and best friend of Dan Kelly. 'I was immediately drawn to Joe,' he confirms, 'he'd live and die for the loyalty of his friends and particularly for Ned. He'd follow him to hell and back and I just felt that was something that I could work with, embellish, and make a strong character.'

'Fear is my staple diet, my demon . . . and I'm pretty sure it was the Kelly Gang's, too.'

Luckily, his accident-prone nature didn't take advantage of the opportunities on offer. 'I didn't break anything, but I got kicked by a horse, just above the knee. I was very lucky!' laughed Orlando, claiming to have 'almost lost a kneecap.'

Since the days of *The Lord of the Rings*, when his main sources of enjoyment were 'flying, travel and excitement', Orly claimed to have calmed down. 'When I'm not working, I prefer to sit and do nothing. Go to a beach. Go for a walk. The simple things have suddenly become more enjoyable.'

With a greater sense of self-knowledge, he explained, 'I think one of the reasons I've had so many accidents is because fear is something I'm utterly afraid of, more so than anything else. That's why I put myself in uncomfortable situations so I can push the boundaries.

'Fear is my staple diet, my demon . . . and I'm pretty sure it was the Kelly Gang's, too.'

Orlando's character, who he describes as a 'very charismatic figure . . . a poet, and quite a thinker . . . a bit of a ladies' man, Irish accent kind of thing,' won him a brief love scene with Rachel Griffith. It was also the kind of role that could justify his publicist playing down the heart-throb status, claiming, 'Orlando's a very serious actor.'

By the time MTV presented him with his Movie Award for Best Breakthrough Performance in spring 2002, for *The Fellowship of the Ring*, Orlando had to link up with the ceremony via satellite from Australia: 'Hey, I'm sorry I can't be there with you in L.A. . . . I'm here in Melbourne, Australia making a movie about a bunch of Irish outlaws, which is quite mad.'

But not quite as mad as the Kelly Gang themselves. 'These crazy bastards put themselves in the firing line,' described Orlando. 'I have to admire their balls.

'If Ned represented the passion and heart of the gang, Joe was the brains of the operation. He was very intelligent, to the point of speaking fluent Cantonese, and apparently quite self-contained.' Joe spoke several languages, was the well-educated son of successful farmers and, as an opium smoker, his calm demeanour and connections to the criminal elements of the Chinese community become all too understandable.

But the drug-addled Joe was also (semi-)literate enough to compose the famous 1879 'Jerilderie letter', so named because of the town where the gang were holed up at the time. 'Joe was very deliberate in his thought and action,' considers Orlando.

'I think we all felt the ghosts of those boys close by,' Orlando insisted of the characters who all died in their early-to-mid twenties. 'I wanted a photograph of Joe but the only one I could buy was a final portrait of him in death, twisted and bloody and hung on a door. I had the programme from Christie's sent over but on the day of the auction, I pulled out of the bidding. The night before I'd had this weird night's sleep, tossing and turning and dreaming uncomfortably. I couldn't figure it out at the time, but now I think it was the fact that I was immersed in Joe Byrne the man, not that poor bastard hanging dead on the wall. I believe in connections and something told me that the photo was wrong energy.'

'. . . stealing all of his scenes is Orlando Bloom, whose rakish swagger and commanding screen presence suggest a formidable star in the making.' – The Hollywood Reporter

Orlando also believes, 'Joe's opium use adds a real twistedness to his soul. That and the fact that he has to pull the trigger on his boyhood friend to protect the gang. That's the moment where Joe loses his innocence, because it's one thing to shoot a stranger, another matter entirely to do it to a mate.'

For authenticity's sake, once the Kelly Gang were firmly ensconced in Australia's outback, Heath, Orlando and the rest of the crew grew big, bushy beards in line with how the gang would have appeared at the time. Visiting studio executives were reported to have baulked at the sight of their heartthrobs looking like they should be playing the Irish folk music that Orlando enjoys. The relevant scenes had mostly been shot, and they feared resistance among the teen audience. 'That's not really true,' insisted Orly, of the idea that they alienated their core audience. 'And it's more about the way you wear it, isn't it?

'It was great to work with my own hair,' laughed Orlando, who'd grown an abundance of it for the role.

Towards the end of production of this violent film, in late May 2002, Orlando demonstrated his sympathy with the serene philosophy of Buddhism, by attending a 20,000-strong audience with the Dalai Lama at Melbourne's Rod Laver Arena. The gun-toting Iron Man himself, aka Heath Ledger, also attended.

Three months later, back in Hollywood, Orlando and Heath were seen hanging out together with model Rachel Hunter, Rod Stewart's ex, at the opening of a major Express designer clothing store. Who said spirituality and glamour can't co-exist side by side?

Ned Kelly premiered in Australia on 27 March, 2003. As might be expected, the story's familiarity

One reviewer claimed Orlando's performance in Ned Kelly 'demonstrates why he has become a bigger star' than Heath Ledger, who took the title role.

and iconic status translated into good box-office numbers in Australia. Press response was uneven, but Australia's *Daily Telegraph* opined, 'If any doubt remains that this English-born lad from Kent is headed for major movie stardom, his role as "the most handsome one of the [Kelly] bunch" (so-called in the movie) should put it well and truly to bed.'

Joblo.com's Australian reviewer, Craig Dixon, praised the cast as 'uniformally excellent all round', singling out Orlando: 'Bloom shows why he's going to be a very big star with an immensely charismatic and believeable performance.' The efilmcritic.com site also found time to credit Orlando for being 'all charm as the womanising Joe Byrne'.

'I really enjoyed learning about the history of the Kelly Gang. It was an amazing project to work on.'

For his part, director Gregor Jordan was forced to agree: 'Orlando is a movie star waiting to happen. He's going to be huge because he's a good actor and he has incredible presence. There's a reason why girls go crazy for him. He's in the long tradition of guys like James Dean and Russell Crowe.'

Ned Kelly didn't fare so well overseas. Opening in the UK in late September 2003, it was the subject of a critical article by historian Andrew Mueller in *The Guardian*, which at least found time to praise 'Orlando Bloom as a twinkling Joe Byrne'. The BBC's *Film Reviews* website also praised the second name on the cast list: 'Bloom, in particular, is brilliant, proving much more than a pretty face as Ned's right-hand man.'

Expected to open in the USA around the same time, the distributors' lack of faith would push the film back for another year. When it finally saw a theatrical release in March 2004, Jack Mathews in the *New York Daily News* was critical of the film's 'credibility gap wider than the screen' and 'smouldering blarney'. Mythic embellishment aside, Mathews followed the general tone by acclaiming, 'Bloom – Legolas in *The Lord of the Rings* – is a dashingly mischievous Joe Byrne.'

More positively, *Los Angeles Daily News* film critic Glenn Whipp commented, 'the charismatic

As Joe Byrne, Orlando's normally boyish good looks are disguised by the authentic look of an unshaven bushranger.

Bloom, playing Kelly's right-hand man, demonstrates why he has become a bigger star than head-liner Ledger.' Best of all was Erin Free's review in *The Hollywood Reporter*: '*Ned Kelly* is a striking, stately and ultimately deeply moving experience.' Once again, she compared the prospects of the two male leads: 'Australian actor Heath Ledger is still chasing a hit. A fixture on magazine covers and drawing all kinds of heat, he's yet to go over the top at the boxoffice . . . stealing all of his scenes is Orlando Bloom, whose rakish swagger and commanding screen presence suggest a formidable star in the making.'

Despite such critical approval, the Orlando Bloom fan community could not rescue *Ned Kelly* – either in the US or the UK, where it fared equally badly at the box office.

Ultimately, *Ned Kelly*, while sporadically violent, especially in the climactic twenty-minute shootout scene at the Glenrowan Inn, remains a criminally underrated film outside Australia. Orlando, who, with his dark, curly hair could easily pass for an Irishman himself, still saw it as an overwhelmingly positive experience. 'I loved that Irish accent,' he said at the time of its Australian release, by which time he was ensconced in a fistful of film projects. 'Sometimes I'll even use it here in L.A. when I go out with friends.'

His next project, beginning immediately in summer 2002, took him all the way back home. 'London is my home and will always be my home,' Orlando insisted, 'I may travel away from it for stretches of time, but I'll always come back to it.'

'I love doing big epics like *The Lord of the Rings*, but it's great to play a character who's less cool. This milkman is just an everyday geezer, a bit naïve, who's suddenly thrown into the public eye. I can relate to it.'

The Calcium Kid was a further move toward the smaller, more intimate type of movie he wanted to make. 'I also wanted to work in England. I'd been out of drama school for about four years and I hadn't done anything in my own hometown, so being in South London was great. It was good to be home and have my mates around me.' It was also Orlando's first ever starring role. As he said, 'I wanted my first lead to be in a film that wouldn't require me to be hugely responsible for a budget of a hundred million dollars.

'I like films that have integrity and a great story. But I also see myself doing comedy because I think people find me amusing. I can be a bit geeky, which is what people don't expect.'

According to producer Natascha Wharton, he won the role of milkman and amateur boxer Jimmy Connelly simply because, 'Orlando just had this sweet innocence about him.' Or, as he put it, 'A mate asked me to do it, and I couldn't say "no".' That mate was music video director Alex De Rakoff. Orlando laughed about how 'the budget of *The Calcium Kid* was the same as the after-party for *Lord of the Rings*.

'It's a real working man's hero piece,' explained the respectably middle-class Orlando, claiming, a little unfeasibly, 'Jimmy is an everyday geezer. He's not trying to be anything. In fact, he's just like me.

'I play a milkman who's a boxer. By a freak accident he gets a shot at the world title and he's got six days to prepare, but his harebrained manager gives him all the wrong advice.'

Ironically, given how the arduous demands of *The Lord of the Rings* led him to become a near-vegan, Orlando confirmed of his character, 'I drink a lot of milk.' It's this old-fashioned three-pints-a-day regime that strengthens Jimmy's bones so much that the British middleweight world contender breaks his hand on his amateur sparring partner's jaw – leaving Jimmy to face US and world champion Jose Mendez (Michael Pena). Unlike Orlando himself, Jimmy's bones are far from easily broken.

Orlando as amateur boxer Jimmy, in The Calcium Kid. *Jimmy's endurance in the ring is due to his intake of milk – a product Orlando himself avoids in his non-dairy diet.*

'I have a lucky punch, lay him to the ground. He gets up, furious, does a flurry of punches and then lays a huge right on me and breaks his fist on my head.' There was a small irony at work here, in that dairy products were the source of his character's rock-hard bones. 'It's funny isn't it?' Orlando recognised. 'I've been avoiding them as they don't make me feel too hot.'

A horseman, an archer and a swordsman he may be, but Orlando is, at heart, reputedly no fighter. 'If only it were true in real life,' he self-deprecatingly told an interviewer. This doesn't matter so much in the role itself, as the unassuming Jimmy is a mediocre boxer at best, drawn into the ring by a sheer fluke. But, as Orlando says of his training for the film, 'You watch two huge guys slugging it out and you're like, "Well, okay." But when you actually stand in the ring and try to punch for three minutes, it's exhausting.'

According to one uncredited friend, however, Orly was taking his training as a boxer seriously: 'He'd always been known as a sprightly actor and had never been asked to build himself up before.

'But he knew that, if he was going to pull off playing a boxer, he was going to have to gain a few pounds.

'He's been jogging to get his fitness levels up and also hit the gym. I'm not joking when I say he's as hard as nails now. It's amazing to see the transformation.'

'I wanted my first lead to be a film that wouldn't require me to be hugely responsible for a budget of a hundred million dollars.'

'I wanted to get super fit so I did a lot of preparation,' confirmed Orlando. 'I really enjoyed it. Then I came over to Australia to film *Ned Kelly* and kept it up. I was trying to put on weight and develop shape because I'm a bit skinny. This is the one time that I thought, "I've got to give it a go. I've got to get the boxing thing going and get the physique right."'

Alex De Rakoff described shooting the scene where Jimmy goes head to head with Brit middleweight contender Pete Wright (Tamer Hassan), on the *Sky Movies Premiere* TV show. 'We were doing a scene where Orlando has to punch him,' said De Rakoff. 'And I actually let Orlando hit me!' said Hassan, who was also on the show. 'And Tamer's a bit of a nut and he was an ex-boxer,' elaborated the director, laughing. 'Orlando's not a nut and he's not an ex-boxer!' 'I hated it!' admitted Orlando. 'He didn't want to do it!' laughed Alex. 'I kept saying to him, "Orlando, hit me!"' confirmed Tamer. 'He was like, "Lay it on me, son, come on, lay it on me!"' recalled Orly.

Just like his character, who begs his trainer to knock him out before the start of his title bout, he was not a natural born pugilist. Eventually, things were resolved in classic style: 'Tamer said a few interesting things to Orlando,' said Alex, 'and Orlando chinned him!' 'I did,' he perked up with pride, 'a couple of times!'

Much of the film's comedy content comes care of Anglo-Iranian comic Omid Djalili as Jimmy's manager, Herbie Bush – the man promoting Mendez and Jimmy's clash as the 'Melee on the Telly'. As Orlando describes, '[Jimmy] puts his trust in all these people around him like his promoter, who turns everything he touches to shite . . . . Herbie Bush puts him in some ridiculous situations which are just funny, you know?'

Other character roles included TV impressionist Ronni Ancona as Jimmy's tarty mum – a 'massage therapist' who embarrasses him with a constant stream of male visitors to her flat. Billie Piper, the former teenypop singer, was shoehorned into a short cameo as one of 'Jimmy's birds', named 'Angel'. The film also features brief cameos by two of Britain's best-loved boxers, Chris Eubank and Frank Bruno – acting up their respective eccentric/buffoon roles so familiar to British TV audiences.

Back on home turf, it seemed strange that the international heartthrob was not pursued with hysterical fervour through the streets. Where were all the groups of girls who, it was already customary, would pursue him at any events he attended with cries of 'Marry me Orly!'? Maybe it was

Opposite above: Orlando as Jimmy, with Anglo-Iranian comedian Omid Djalili as his manager, Herbie Bush, in The Calcium Kid *and below: Orlando locks lips with Billie Piper, as one of 'Jimmy's birds' in* The Calcium Kid.

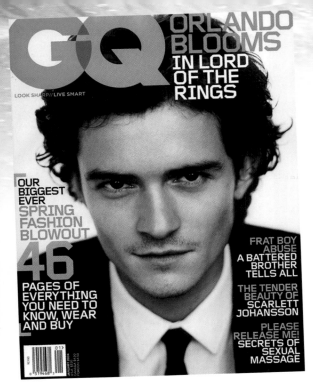

For The Return of the King, *GQ featured Orlando on their cover. They broke their sales record, selling 290,000 copies.*

simply that it was *him*, and not Legolas, moving around the streets. 'I was lucky because of the wig,' admitted Orlando. 'I can still ride my bicycle around London. It's not like I can't walk down the street.

But still, the most fervent young fans had him under surveillance. When the film began shooting in September 2002, one young fan named Katie put a posting on the Orlando Bloom Central website. The subject was the fanatical interest in who Orly may or may not be dating – in this case, the focus was his friend Joanne Morley, who had recently appeared with Julie Walters and Joanne Whalley in *Before You Go* (2002).

'I know Orlando,' boasted Katie, 'and I was down at *The Calcium Kid* set today. Anyway, the thing is, I have a little sister, and her friend is besotted by Orlando and she regularly checks out the websites and told me there was a rumour about Orlando and Jo (who, may I add, is really nice). Joanne was on the set today as she has a cameo in the movie. Her and Orlando are friends, but I can safely tell you that there is nothing going on between Orlando and Joanne . . .'

As Orly laughingly commented, 'It all comes back to the fact that I just wanted to be an actor. The idea of all this other stuff wasn't something I ever really contemplated . . . . The fame, or the celebrity aspect, is just a by-product. You just have to find ways of dealing with it where it doesn't drive you crazy.'

Inevitably, perhaps, there would be one eventual tear in the fabric of Orlando's privacy. More than a year later, on 7 December, 2003, the UK's oldest Sunday scandalsheet, *News of the World*, would run a kiss-and-tell interview with Maddy Ford – a blonde model who frequently appears in popular UK 'lads' mags', and had a bit part in *The Calcium Kid*. She also alleged that Orly had had a part of himself in her.

'When your friends read about you more than they get to see you, then you have to keep reassuring people that you aren't changing.'

'I was just a bit of eye candy in the movie,' she admitted to the reporter. 'My character didn't even have a name.' Claiming that Orlando made the first move, she recounted how he 'waited until the "wrap" party [at London's Q Bar] before working his magic . . . . it was clear what was on offer. I don't normally sleep with guys so quickly but I was single and I really liked him.' And, of course, assuming that her story's genuine, it may have been a once-in-a-lifetime chance to bed Orlando Bloom.

Although Ms. Ford described how a friend of Orly's drove them both to the flat that he was renting at the time, she explained, 'that night I didn't stay because I knew he had to be up early to go to L.A. But a few days later I got a sweet card from him. It said, "To Maddy, thanks for being one of Jimmy's birds, X."'

For mostly any young man in his position, the company of women would be a perk of the job. The merest hint of scandal in the *News of the World* piece arose from the fact that Orlando was, by then, in a steady relationship – but this wasn't the case back when he was filming *The Calcium Kid*.

Around the same time as the tabloid piece ran, an interviewer from *GQ* would jokingly ask Orlando if the downside of stardom might be that he started sleeping with strippers. 'There's nothing wrong with sleeping with strippers,' he retorted. 'Thankfully, I've got a lot of that stuff out my system.' He may refuse to talk about it, but the boy has clearly sown his share of wild oats.

It would be a full eighteen months from the end of production to *The Calcium Kid*'s simultaneous release on both sides of the Atlantic, in April 2004. Reviews on both sides were mixed but, on the whole, negative.

'The release date of the British mockumentary *The Calcium Kid* has been moved several times,' noted London *Times* reviewer Wendy Ide, 'presumably to maximise the impact of its newly bankable star, Orlando Bloom . . . . Bloom, however, gives a performance that's as bland as a pint of semi-skimmed.'

'Orlando Bloom, pulchritudinous star of *Lord of the Rings* . . . puts a lot of youthful buttocks on seats,' dismissed Peter Bradshaw in *The Guardian*, 'and that demographic calculation can be the only reason for releasing this shamingly bad British comedy . . . . There are no funny lines, no funny scenes, no funny characters, no funny anything.'

'It's as wholesome as a pint of the white stuff, but *The Calcium Kid* is in desperate need of a backbone,' damned Stella Papamichael in her BBC Films website review. 'Orlando Bloom is distinctly wishy-washy as the eponymous underdog boxer made good in this mild-mannered mockumentary . . . Over-egged, half-baked, and too darn sweet, *The Calcium Kid* is little more than cinematic creampuff.' Fanbase or no fanbase, sometimes it just didn't pay for Orlando to be too nice.

'It all comes back to the fact that I just wanted to be an actor. The idea of all this other stuff wasn't something I ever really contemplated. The fame, or the celebrity aspect, is just a by-product.'

In the US, there was little mercy shown. 'Orlando Bloom . . . is the marquee draw in Brit mockumentary *The Calcium Kid*,' noted *Variety*'s concise review, 'but few outside his young femme fan base look likely to support the low-fat pic . . .'

'*The Calcium Kid* was creatively the most rewarding experience I've had,' Orlando had earnestly insisted, 'loads of dialogue, exercising muscles that had been lying dormant. I can only hope the people who write me thousands of letters will go see this. I feel proud of what it meant for me.'

'It remains to be seen, however,' observed Matthew Turner in his review for the viewlondon website, 'whether "the Bloomers" (as they may or may not be called) will be sufficient in number to turn *The Calcium Kid* into a box office hit -–after all, where were they for *Ned Kelly*, eh?'

Sadly, not many of them showed up for *The Calcium Kid* either. In London, where it was filmed and where a good proportion of its potential audience resided, the film was pulled from every single cinema within two weeks of its opening. *The Calcium Kid* turned out, in the end, not to have very much bottle.

But, by the time it opened, Orlando Bloom had returned to a much bigger universe. Released from the gritty intensity of London, he was free to travel the world again – for work, or simply his own wanderlust, as in a recent visit to the ancient Mayan city of Tikal, in Guatemala. ('The temples there were awe-inspiring. I remember climbing these steps and looking over this huge forest. It's a pretty amazing place.')

As at the start of his career, Orlando's concerns didn't begin and end with the movie industry. He also remained remarkably unpretentious: 'It sounds slightly self-indulgent to hear some actor wanking on how you get into your role,' remains a characteristic comment.

But, at the end of the day, Orlando had become a Movie Star. That autumn, he would tell *Rolling Stone* of his first big 'Hollywood moment'. At a hungover meeting with Nick Cassavetes, actor/director/screenwriter of *Blow* (2001), Cassavetes had to stop to take a call from another actor: 'Halfway through the call, he looked over and mouthed to me, "Mar-lon Bran-do!" Can you fuckin' believe it? That was surreal!'

Starstruck, but with his own star in the ascendant, Orlando Bloom was about to return to the exotic, epic movie universe where he first came to prominence – via adventure on the high seas.

SALTY
SEA DOGS

'As soon as I found out Johnny was attached to the project I was like "Where do I sign".' – *Orlando Bloom*

Orlando Bloom had, it seemed, made the huge jump to the Hollywood A-list without so much as a successful leading role. But also without any struggle, or resistance. With producers vying for his presence, he was the first actor that came to the mind of *Black Hawk Down* producer Jerry Bruckheimer for an old-fashioned role in a perversely old-fashioned movie.

Bruckheimer's confidence in the young star's suitability for the role came from impromptu interviews with his teenage daughter's friends. 'He's on the radar of all these young girls. He's one of the most sought-after actors on the Internet right now. I didn't know that was going to happen [at the time of *Black Hawk Down*]. I had no idea.'

'It's a good choice,' the opinionated Bruckheimer later insisted of his project. 'The movie has a broad spectrum. This will help Orlando down the path of becoming a true movie star.' It was also a calculatedly commercial franchise flick, based on one of the oldest and most popular attractions in the world's various Disneyland complexes. 'Pirates of the Caribbean', with its overhead cannonballs, rum-drunk buccaneers and ghostly skeleton sailors had been a mainstay of the original Disneyland in Anaheim, California since 1967. The director was scheduled to be Gore Verbinski, who made a hit horror movie of *The Ring* (2003) by adapting it from its original Japanese source.

Initially, however, Orlando was reluctant to commit out of loyalty to Alex De Rakoff, as it looked as if the production schedule might clash with that of *The Calcium Kid*. 'When I got the script for *Pirates* [*of the Caribbean: The Curse of the Black Pearl*, to give it its full title] I didn't want to tempt myself with the idea of getting involved with something I didn't think I was going to be able to do,' he explained. 'Then I was in Australia working on *Ned Kelly* and Geoffrey Rush [who played the Kelly Gang's police adversary] was really excited about coming on to do *Pirates*. He said: "There's a great role in this. You have to read it if nothing else."

'I only made the film because Geoffrey Rush said I'd be an idiot if I didn't. I'd seen the script and I knew about the ride, but it just didn't feel like my cup of tea. Then I was hanging around with Geoffrey on the *Ned Kelly* set and he said that he thought it would be a really fantastic experience.'

The movie would also be shot in the idyllic tropical environment of the Bahamas. At first, however, Orlando took a little convincing. It was, after all, a return to action fantasy on a fairly epic scale, rather than the smallscale character portraits he'd dreamt of downsizing to.

Ultimately, Orlando would admit his signing up for the $125 million production was a 'no-brainer'. 'It's a big action adventure with a lot of swordplay, scars and long hair. And I've teamed up with Bob Anderson again, who was the sword master on *Lord of the Rings*.

'In the physicality of doing a sword routine, you can lose a sense of the character, but [Bob] was good at making sure you stay on top of that.'

As Orlando confirmed, although his injured back 'still gives gyp,' he was in exactly the right shape and state of mind to take on the action sequences. It would also entail the chance to work with leading man Johnny Depp, an actor Orlando had admired since his teenage years. As he observed, 'As soon as I found out he was attached to the project I was like, "Where do I sign?"'

It was partly the coaching by Bob Anderson, now approaching his eightieth year, that would earn Orlando the rather throwaway title of 'the new Errol Flynn', once he'd completed his latest action-adventure film. Despite the fact that Depp played the devil-may-care pirate character who once would have been played by Flynn, there was no denying that the dark-haired Orly, with his pencil moustache and hair in natural dark brown curls, had a definite likeness to the young Errol. And, by his own account, 'I looked at a lot of Errol Flynn films like *Captain Blood* [1935] and *The Master of Ballantrae* [1953].'

'When the camera is on Orlando, he is so natural. He's got that look, as if he could have come from another time.' – *Jerry Bruckheimer, Producer,* Pirates of the Caribbean

'The thing I remember most was always running to the house on Sunday afternoons,' reminisced Orly, 'whenever there was a really old classic black and white film on the telly, and watching someone like Errol Flynn go through his stuff. What a hero he was!' But, at least in the sense of his alcoholic, destructive lifestyle, Flynn couldn't be further away from the health-conscious, body-conscious young stars of today like Orlando Bloom.

But even they have their moments – as Orlando revealed, from the making of *Pirates of the Caribbean*: 'There was one time Johnny Depp, Jerry Bruckheimer and I got flown to St Vincent [the Caribbean island where filming would be based] in a private plane to meet the Prime Minister. So Jerry was up at the front of the plane with his wife, and me and Johnny and Johnny's friend Sam were at the back of the plane and we sat there and drank red wine, and – I don't know, maybe the altitude had something to do with it – but when we got to the island we just, like, crawled off the plane, staggering.'

According to an account in the UK's *The Face*, Johnny came out singing in a transatlantic or trans-Caribbean patois. The assembled dignitaries were greeted with, 'Ya mon, 'tis so good to be 'ere in the Carabic wid you, mon!' In his wake, tears of laughter streaming from his eyes, Bailey's liqueur staining his lips brown, was a prostrate Orlando, crawling down the tarmac.

Orlando acclaimed Depp's character, Captain Jack Sparrow, as 'a real deal pirate who's completely cool and roguish,' and both Depp and Rush's pirate character, Barbossa, 'have the full-on [pirate] paraphernalia, which I'm a bit envious of to be honest.' He also admitted to envy of Depp's courage 'in how he develops a character and puts himself out there. He's not afraid to fall on his face.'

But Orlando was not initially impressed by the screenplay – although writers Ted Elliott and Terry Rossio's love for popular folklore and pop culture could already be seen in their popular animated hit *Shrek* (2001). Even his eventual praise of the film and its basic concept seemed a little faint. 'It doesn't feel like a typical Jerry [Bruckheimer] movie,' he insisted, given the producer's reputation for big-budget action and even bigger explosions. (Though he had, of course, produced *Black Hawk Down*, which realistically, if noisily, described the horrors of war.) 'The supernatural element to this film – the idea that there is a curse on these pirates, that they go skeletal when they

Orlando, as romantic lead Will Turner, teams up with Keira Knightley in Pirates of the Caribbean.

pass through moonlight – combined with the love story, the roguery of Johnny and the bad pirates, makes this a really fun film that everyone can enjoy. Which is good, I guess, for a summer film.'

'Offering a perfect counterbalance to Depp's shenanigans are Orlando Bloom and Keira Knightley – two individuals who prove they are stars in the making.' – *Mark Sells,* Film Threat

The basic storyline is that the Black Pearl, a stolen pirate ship, sails through seventeenth-century British waters in the Caribbean with a traditional rag-tag crew of sea-scum. Traditional, that is, apart from the fact that, in moonlight, they're revealed as ghostly walking corpses. Due to a curse placed upon the stolen pirate ship and those who sail in her, these particular pirates can only return to the land of the living by stealing the last gold medallion that remains from the forbidden treasure that placed the curse on them, and spilling the blood of pirate Bootstrap Bill's offspring.

'My character, Will, is kind of the earnest young man type,' explained Orlando, 'a kind of true blue straight shooter. He's not an obvious pirate. That's part of his arc – discovering that he's from that stock [Jack reveals Will's father was a pirate] and realising that it's something he needs to come to terms with.' Will does this via a number of acts that would have seen him hanged for piracy on the high seas – breaking Sparrow out of jail, recruiting a shipload of pirates, and stealing the fastest British vessel in the fleet, the HMS Interceptor.

'Had Johnny played his as more of the hero character, it might have conflicted. But Johnny left

'My character starts off as a blacksmith and
then teams up with Johnny Depp who's like a
real deal pirate – completely roguish! I'm sort
of a pirate who's not a pirate!'

ORLANDO BLOOM: WHEREVER IT MAY LEAD

it wide open for me just to go the whole hog on the hero number, because the hero element to his is much more character-based. So it kind of left it open for me, which was great. And then I would be like, "Forget the close-up, just give me a two shot," because it was great to do stuff with him.

Playing the straight man between Johnny's camply drunken Captain Jack Sparrow and Geoffrey's spectral, villainous Barbossa, Orlando's latest supporting role at least had the advantage of being a romantic one – for it's his character, Will Turner, who becomes romantically involved with the delectable governor's daughter Elizabeth Swann (Keira Knightley), and teams up with the drunken Jack Sparrow to save her from the undead Barbossa – though the feisty Elizabeth shows that she can throw herself into the action every bit as much as Jack or Will.

Director Verbinski said that he specifically cast Orlando last because, 'We really needed some-body who could hold his own as the love interest-Errol Flynn character, so the audience wouldn't think Keira was going to end up with Johnny Depp.' After Geoffrey Rush, who'd recently worked with Orlando on *Ned Kelly*, suggested him as the romantic secondary lead, Verbinski set up a din-ner with himself, Keira Knightley and Orlando: 'I just kept looking at them across the table and thought, "This could work."'

Keira Knightley was from the younger part of Orlando's generation, still only eighteen. Naturally, this started the latest snowballing conjecture about Orlando and his love life. Particularly as his feminine romantic lead fulfilled so many of his own preferences: 'I respect tough women, but I'm attracted to nice, sweet girls. Keira is beautiful. I had a crush on her when we filmed *Pirates*,' he admitted, before uttering his get-out clause. 'She's got a boyfriend, damn it! She's in love with him, he was around the set the whole time, and I couldn't compete! I was heartbroken!'

But Orlando still managed to give Keira her first onscreen kiss. Keira recalls: 'We were filming our kiss, and someone brought her daughters to the set. I thought I was going to be lynched by a little blond mob.' Keira insists they kept their romantic scene 'very professional, but we always had a giggle. He was kind enough to make sure he had mints and mouthwash beforehand. I have noth-ing but good things to say about the kiss.

'My character, Will, is kind of the earnest young man type, a kind of true blue straight shooter. He's not an obvious pirate.'

'He's fanciable. I think he's got that androgynous sort of boyish look,' she spoke warmly of the man eight years her senior, 'a totally attractive boyish look. He's sort of unthreatening to teenage girls. I suppose, I mean, gorgeous.'

But Orlando is still less relaxed when it comes to screen kissing time: 'It's definitely a sort of nervous thing. You're sort of like – to tongue or not to tongue? Should it be real or shouldn't it?'

There were other issues to playing the role of Will Turner; 'my character starts off as a black-smith and then teams up with Johnny Depp who's like a real deal pirate – completely cool and roguish!' remarked Orlando, 'I'm sort of a pirate who's not a pirate!'

Orlando's solution for getting around this character point was tantamount to hero-worship: 'We were on a flight over to St Vincent and I was like, "I really want to be doing what Johnny is doing!" So I said to him, "Oh, maybe I could do an impression of you . . ." And he said, "Yeah, you should." And Jerry Bruckheimer was there and he said, "Yeah man, we'll write that in!"' So they improvised the scene where stout-hearted Will briefly parodies salty sea dog Jack. It was also noted on set by *Details* magazine that Orlando was wearing his multivarious rings, strips of leather and talisman-like trinkets around his neck in a distinctly wannabe-Johnny style.

'I'd be doing a scene with him and the writer from the very beginning said, "You guys have these great characters to be working with because it's almost as if the whole time you're looking at him,"' confirmed Orlando. 'And in terms of the context of the character, Will is looking at him going, "What the fuck is this guy doing?" But actually, it's me . . . going, I can't believe I'm doing this . . . and I loved that. I always felt so privileged to be sharing the screen with him.'

As Orlando revealed, the jokey swordfights early on in the movie, between his character and Johnny Depp's, and the later, more intense clashes with Geoffrey Rush as the villainous Barbossa, were initially scheduled to be shot close together. 'They wanted to do all that on about the second day of the shoot,' he confirms, 'and I just said, "No," and that I wanted it to be rescheduled, so that we had at least two or three weeks' rehearsal. That's what happened. Inevitably, Johnny and I had a few scrapes, minor cuts and bruises, but that's what happens.

'There's always some little nips and jabs when you're doing stuff like that. In one scene in the blacksmith's shop, where Johnny started throwing hammers at me, I got hit by a couple of them and I have the bruises to prove it.'

For all the swashbuckling and swordfighting, and being an old hand at fencing, Orlando was less prepared to take professional risks. 'Johnny Depp's taught me to respect the stunt men,' he admitted. 'He said, "Let them get injured. They're good at it." And as for the wholesome action hero image I seem to have earned through *The Rings* . . . I'm working on that too.'

Not that the role of wholesome action hero Will would do a great deal to dispel it. During his time spent sword-sparring with Johnny, there was far more footage than the movie could possibly use.

'And that was because Johnny and I worked out so many little moves and one-liners that, if we'd had them all included, the film would have run for four hours, rather than just over two. He wanted, at one point, to slap my butt with the broad of his sword, so we practiced and shot that. That's an out-take, but you get the line when he asks whether I am a eunuch – but not, thank God, the bit when I collapse in tears at his ad-lib question. Some action sequences in these movies are over in a few minutes, but the great thing is that the directors can allow up to two weeks to get them absolutely right, with hundreds upon hundreds of shots.'

As Orlando modestly admits, 'I could never take Johnny. On any level' – either as an actor or a fighter. But their choreographed swordsmanship, along with that of the supporting actors, ensured that *Pirates* would be largely an old-fashioned fantasy-adventure, with very few CGI effects added in post-production. What we see on screen is largely what the actors did.

On its July 2003 release *Pirates of the Caribbean: The Curse of the Black Pearl* became Orlando's fourth film in a row (after the first two instalments of *The Lord of the Rings* and *Black Hawk Down*) to take over $46 million on its opening weekend and $80 million in its first week, leading to a total of $300 million at the US box office – or over US$650 million worldwide. Like his previous showstoppers, it went straight to Number One at the US box office.

The early July US premiere took place at Disneyland itself. The brouhaha and spectacle included Johnny, Orly, Keira, English supporting actor Jack Davenport, Verbinski and Bruckheimer floating into the exclusive screening on a wooden log raft along the 'Rivers of America' waterway, and a bevy of go-go dancing girls dressed as pirates. For the first time in its 48-year history, Disneyland, California was closed to the general public – at an estimated cost of $2 million.

And then there was the screaming: hundreds of young female voices screaming for leading man Johnny Depp, but mostly, one suspects, for relative newcomer Orlando Bloom. *Newsweek*'s Kate Stroup described walking with Orlando down a 1,050-foot red carpet at the Disneyland premiere as pure hysteria threatened to break out. '"Get out of my way!" one [girl] screams at me, eyes glittering with hatred and pink eye shadow. Soon the entire girl-gaggle is chanting Move! Move! Move!'

'I do think it's a phenomenon that they have glommed onto him so completely when he has not done a movie with a major role,' Alyssa Petrano, entertainment director of *YM* magazine, was quoted in the *LA Times*. 'It's really been a groundswell from teenage girls who are hooked into his looks and his charm.'

The London premiere saw several thousand teenage girls and young women surrounding the celebrities' red-carpeted walkway at Leicester Square. For the most part, it wasn't for Johnny Depp. One young girl told a BBC reporter she'd been camped out all night just to catch a glimpse of Orlando.

Orlando stops a while at Disneyland's Main Street, 23 June, 2003, for the world premiere of Pirates of the Caribbean.

'It's just such a circus,' their hero bemoaned. 'In groups the girls get rather intimidating, it makes me nervous. I'm trying to adjust to all the changes that are happening. There's mountains of fan mail and it's really a lot to deal with. It's flattering but it doesn't mean anything to me. I'm not interested in being a celebrity or a movie star. I'm just trying to be an actor.'

'I respect tough women, but I'm attracted to nice, sweet girls.'

The film's reviewers took the girls' point, but saw things their own way. '*Pirates* is a must-see, if only for one reason: Bloom's co-star, Johnny Depp,' wrote journalist Derek O'Connor in an even-handed *Irish Times* piece. 'As a disheveled, down-on-his-luck sea salt named Jack Sparrow, Depp offers a one-man masterclass in show-stealing. He makes the movie. Young Bloom, on the other hand, can't compete – very few young actors possibly could. He contents himself with playing the straight man – a noble young blacksmith with a mysterious past – with a certain understated nobility, and gets to save the day and kiss the girl. Everybody's happy. The critics will love Johnny, but the punters won't forget our Orlando.'

Andrew Sarris in the *New York Observer* also noted, 'amid all the feverish Depp-worship, the indispensable contribution of Orlando Bloom as Will Turner, the romantic blacksmith-swordsman who wins Elizabeth's heart after saving her skin, has been much underrated. Yet is it not the guy who gets the girl, or loves her *a la folie*, who lies at the heart of any popular film franchise?'

'Offering a perfect counterbalance to Depp's shenanigans are Orlando Bloom and Keira Knightley,' wrote *Film Threat* website reviewer Mark Sells, 'two individuals who prove they are stars in the making. Bloom supplants his role as Legolas in *Lord of the Rings* and Knightley elevates beyond her *Bend It Like Beckham* soccer sidekick. These two match Depp's whimsy with wit and humour of their own. It's one of the true pleasures of the film.'

As a consequence of his role as Will Turner, *Entertainment Weekly* christened Orlando one of the '"It" Boys of Summer'. 'That is a huge honour,' deadpanned the man himself. 'Massive. What is "It", though?'

Veering between a desire for smaller, more character-based roles and his alma mater in the world of costume epics, Orlando couldn't conceal his enthusiasm: 'I love making film like *Pirates*. I love dressing up.

'I prefer the simpler things in life. I love just walking the streets, taking my mum and gran out for lunch, going to see a movie, or having dinner with mates.'

'You know, when I look at my career so far, on paper, it's amazing. I've got all these skills – horse riding, archery, sword fighting, and to get the opportunity to play an Elf, a soldier, an outlaw, a boxer and now a pirate – it's every boy's dream. Unbelievable.' Unlike the career in the theatre he might once have envisaged, Orlando had never had to suffer periods of unemployment, insecurity or soul-searching. In fact, he didn't even have to grow up.

Looking again to his mentor, Depp, Orlando was urged not to agonise over his life or his career. 'Johnny said to just enjoy it,' confirmed Orlando. 'It's not open-heart surgery. Enjoy the whole process. You keep certain things private, don't you? There are things in your life where there is a line . . . this I'm prepared to talk about. And anyway, the truth is that I understand people wanting to know about your private life in some way, because they want to feel like they are getting closer to you.'

But it was easier said than done. The press and the paparazzi were prone to snoop on any social encounter, casual or otherwise, that he might have with a woman. 'There's the odd occasion where you were just doing something and somebody will freak out a little bit,' Orlando admitted. 'I mean, after *Pirates* came out it was more intense than anything really.'

There was also, it seemed, someone special in his life by this time. Someone who may not have been a permanent fixture at first. 'Yeah, I'm sort of "dating", I guess, but I'm not in a relationship,' he explained, enigmatically, at the time of *Pirates*' release, 'although I don't want to talk about it too much because my personal life is my personal life. But if you ask me what I find romantic, I'd say it was the little subtle things you can do that mean more rather than the big gestures.'

Naturally, at first he was reluctant to give too much away, citing his partner's feelings rather than his own. 'I'm quite sensitive to women,' he insisted. 'I saw how my sister got treated by boyfriends. I read this thing that said when you are in a relationship with a woman, imagine how you would feel if you were her father. That's been my approach, for the most part.'

The special girl would eventually be revealed as twenty-year-old Kate Bosworth, who played the lead in teen surfer movie *Blue Crush* (2002). Orlando had been seeing her since the end of major production on *Pirates of the Caribbean*, and she also visited him in New Zealand in April 2003, when he was filming pick-up shots for *The Return of the King*. But when reporters initially confronted him with her name, he clammed up. 'She is a great girl but I don't like to talk about that stuff,' he snapped. 'It's not necessary. People want to know everything.

'I will say that it's difficult to keep a relationship going when you're not in the same country as the person you're seeing,' he was courteous enough to explain to a curious female fan. So far, though, the relationship seems to have flowered where others have wilted under the strain.

Rumour soon had it that they were engaged to be married.

Orlando himself admitted to living a romantic dream. 'I'm in love with love,' he mused aloud: 'It's heavenly when you're falling for someone and you can't stop thinking about her. I love the experience of waiting hours, minutes and seconds 'til we can meet again.'

With his feet still grounded in London, Orlando had plans to settle and buy his own home – principally because, he claimed, 'my mum was losing her mind' at his nouveau-gypsy lifestyle. Although, for obvious reasons, he refused to give the exact location away, 'I saw this great place in the estate agent's last time I was over. I really want to buy it, although it's stretching the pounds. It's south of the river, mind, which will make getting a black cab home a fucking nightmare.' Rumour had it that the house was in the more salubrious, less funky part of southeast London – specifically Dulwich.

Characteristically, it wasn't just for Mum that he was buying a permanent home – it was for all the devoted Bloomers too: 'I've been getting loads of fan mail, really intense amounts of it. And I always feel these people have put all this time and effort in so you really want to respond to it in some way, and I'm never in one place long enough to do it.'

As to whether his popularity would continue growing at its prodigious rate, Orlando claimed, maybe a little disingenuously, 'I've only just realised I've got heartthrob status! It's weird and I hope it won't get in the way of me making the right choices over films I appear in. But I think you sometimes have to get used to being popular for your looks, just to get to do the movies you want to do.'

'When I first got the script [for the original *Pirates of the Caribbean*],' insisted Orlando, 'I was like, I'm not really interested. And then it was put to me in a different way, which was that if I opened a door like this, it will ultimately put me in a marketplace where I can get projects made that I want to get made . . . .'

The phenomenal success of *Pirates of the Caribbean* had the Disney machine grinding back into action very quickly. There was a sequel already on the cards. 'And that looks as if it will go on in late 2004,' confirmed Orlando, 'provided that we have everyone in the original cast on board and that Gore Verbinski directs again.

'I'm not interested in being a celebrity or a movie star. I'm just trying to be an actor.'

'I know that Johnny is up for it. He's always said that he'd never do a sequel, but he's also been on record as saying that he wants to do more movies for his kids, so . . . And I know that Jerry Bruckheimer also wants to give it another shot, so, well, hey, why not?'

In October 2003, *Variety* announced that Disney were considering filming two sequels to *Pirates of the Caribbean*, back-to-back – in the legacy of *The Lord of the Rings*' great success. In early December, an anonymous source told the Coming Attractions website, 'I work for . . . Fantasy II F/X in Burbank, CA . . . . I just saw some composite artwork for *Pirates of the Caribbean: Treasures of the Lost Abyss*. I'm not sure if that's just the working title or not.

'"The Lost Abyss" is in reference to the first pirate ship that sailed in the Caribbean . . . . I have no information about the script. Disney had a rep here with the artwork. Very hush hush!'

According to a later posting on various sites, Orlando was purportedly more than ready to spill the beans on the screenplay: 'Brilliant! That was my spontaneous thought when I had read the first draft of the script for the sequel of *Pirates of the Caribbean*. At the beginning, the wedding of Will, thus me, and Keira Knightley alias Elizabeth Swann is in full preparation.

'Everything goes after plan – then Elizabeth is kidnapped in the night before the wedding. A lot points toward Johnny Depp, alias Jack Sparrow. Since the end of the first part he and Will haven't seen each other. Will only knows Jack as a sort of Robin Hood of the seas, who robs the rich in order to give money to the poor.

'With his new friend Jim, Will goes on the search for Jack and Elizabeth. On an island they get held captive by nasty guys. Will has then to fight in an arena like a gladiator against a one-eye monster.

'Only in the last second he is able to behead the monster . . .

'Now it really becomes mean: Jack is also held captive on that island – and now he should fight in the arena against Will! It's clear to Will: Jack doesn't have anything to do with Elizabeth's kidnapping. Eventually its turns out that a woman is behind it all: Bermuda Barbossa, daughter of Captain Barbossa – probably played by Salma Hayek. She wants to take revenge on Jack and Will for the death of her father.

> ## 'When I look at my career so far, on paper, it's amazing. I've got all these skills – horse riding, archery, sword fighting, and to get the opportunity to play an Elf, a soldier, an outlaw, a boxer and now a pirate – it's every boy's dream.'

'At the end of the film it comes to a gigantic showdown: A battle on the high seas with four ships – among them the Black Pearl II.'

It all sounded very contrary to his ultimate acting ambitions: 'It's like Johnny Depp told me. Be brave and courageous with the roles. Don't go for the money. The money will come.'

Indeed, rumour insisted it already had –with the press suggesting that, as of *Pirates of the Caribbean*, ICM's asking price for each Hollywood film Orlando had appeared in had gone up to $2 million. It was something else he refused to either confirm or deny. 'I said to Johnny on *Pirates*,' recollects Orlando, '"Isn't it crazy how much money we get to do a job that we love?" and he [Johnny} said that privacy and trying to live a normal life becomes quite expensive. I mean, there are suddenly a lot of people in my life who weren't there before and they're all on the payroll.'

But Orlando was clearly itching to switch from action to more character-based roles. And, once again, Depp was his role model: 'Johnny had to do [teen TV cop series] *21 Jump Street*. I mean at this stage of my career I'm not getting the opportunity to play really great characters but it's like a rite of passage.'

On the other hand, he was forced to acknowledge his good fortune: 'I could be out of work, struggling to make rent, living in London, not doing much. I've just had a different path. It is mad. It is mad,' he repeated for emphasis. 'It does sort of freak me out a bit.'

But the route to the kind of independent films he wanted to make would still be lined with epic monuments. And the pace certainly wasn't about to let up. 'When you start to realise that there's pressure on you, you have to face up to it whether you like it or not. There's responsibility. There's professionalism. There's integrity towards the work and towards yourself. Sometimes I want to be a kid and go, "Fuck it all!" and run away and bury my head. And then I go, "Look, be realistic. You chose this path. So fucking deal with it. Be a man about it." But I do constantly feel like putting the brakes on.

'It's an interesting time for me and I'm figuring it out right now. I'm trying to keep my head and I look at myself and wonder if I'm coming apart at the seams. I ask my sister, who's a couple of years older, "Am I still normal?" . . . . She says I'm doing good.'

LONDON
– LOS ANGELES –
PARIS

'I feel really lucky to have been in the right place at the right time and right for the role.' – *Orlando Bloom*

The seeds of Orlando Bloom's next epic costume drama were sown back in early 2002, shortly after the release of *The Fellowship of the Ring*. Expatriate German Wolfgang Petersen had long specialised in action films. Now an established Hollywood director, Petersen was shown a screenplay about the legendary Trojan War – which purportedly took place around 1200 years before the birth of Christ, in a walled city situated on what is now the Northwestern coast of Turkey.

At the time that Orlando was still filming reshoots for the *Lord of the Rings* trilogy, his agents, ICM, set up an audition for the vital role of Paris, lover of Helen of Troy. 'I'd seen the first *Lord of the Rings* and was expecting this blond-haired, pointy-eared guy to walk in the room,' said Petersen. 'I didn't even recognise him at our first meeting.

'I knew there was a real buzz happening around him but I was thrilled to see he was a good actor and really grounded. There was no attitude about him at all.'

'What can I say? I'm an actor and I like to get dressed up!' said Orlando of the sixth big-budget costume drama of his career. 'To be honest, it's just worked out that way. I don't sit around consciously thinking, "Ugh – here's a contemporary film, so I don't want to do it." I've just been really lucky to have had the opportunity to work on some great movies that happen to be based on great stories – *The Iliad* [the Greek poet Homer's epic account of the Trojan War], for instance, is one of the best stories in the world.' Just a couple of films down the line, however, the young actor would start to rethink his attitude toward costume dramas.

But for now, he was happy to take the role of the Trojan prince he described as 'just a misguided youth'. For in 1193 BC, according to legends preserved in epic Greek and Roman poetry, Paris seduced and stole away the beautiful Helen, wife of King Menelaus of Sparta, and so began the ten-year Trojan War.

Orlando had already played the other side of the triangle on stage, as Menelaus in a production of Euripides' *The Trojan Women*, at the Guildhall School of Drama and Dance. Now, he

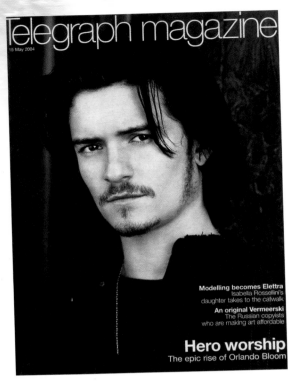

This cover shot of Orlando, for the Telegraph *magazine, was timed to coincide with the release of* Troy.

would be the Trojan prince who stole the fabled Helen, 'the face that lauched a thousand ships'. For Orlando, it was a chance to display the other side of the coin, to get caught up in the chaos and the ambiguity of human emotions.

'Will in *Pirates* and Legolas, they're obvious hero types. Paris is an anti-hero,' he explained. 'Because of him the whole thing turned to shit.

'For me, it was like playing a character whose actions fundamentally are wrong – he goes against all the ideas of manhood and the male energy of the time. He's a lover, not a fighter. He falls in love with a woman and creates a war because of it, because of his lust for this woman. It's like the indiscretion of youth.'

Along this blood-stained path, Paris will realise the consequences of his actions and be forced to face his own cowardice, in contrast with the bravery of his brother Hector. 'So the challenge for me there was to try to find a way to make the character still likeable in some way. To humanise him, you know what I mean? It doesn't happen every fucking day. Imagine if we were at war right now because Bush stole bin Laden's missus. It's a story, it's the story of stories, but it does deal with jealousy, with love, with anger, with greed, with power – it's all those basic instincts that we as humans all have.'

'I've been really lucky to have had the opportunity to work on some great movies that happen to be based on great stories – The Iliad, for instance, is one of the best stories in the world.'

As Paris, Orlando would wear a full mop of his naturally dark, curly hair. And, as is now almost customary, he would appear several names down the cast list – after Brad Pitt as Achilles, Greece's fiercest warrior and the hero of the Trojan War, and the Australian Eric Bana, one of Orlando's many co-stars on *Black Hawk Down*, as Hector, Troy's greatest warrior.

Pitt would be the latest to join the unofficial fellowship of Orlando's acting mentors: 'It's amazing, because they're the guys you think of when you think of great actors, the people in the generation above mine who are really kicking it. As a young actor, I would watch Johnny [Depp]'s films and Brad's films and go, "Wow, that's the stuff to do." I feel lucky because I get to pick their brains about how they go about maintaining their cool and keeping it real and not losing their shit.' They were the standard to which he now aspired.

Against the bloodthirsty warrior that Pitt became for *Troy*, and Bana's more modest but self-sacrificing Hector, 'Paris is like a dysfunctional little prince,' acknowledges Orlando. 'He's romantic and dashing and handsome and sort of swans to the ladies and does the whole thing. He doesn't really think about the consequences of his actions.'

However, 'Putting on those togas and the short armoured skirts,' he emphasises, 'you feel like you're fighting for the fair Helen.'

Helen would be played by elegant German actress Diane Kruger, a ballet-trained former model who had appeared in *Elle* and *Harpers & Queen*, having won the part during an international casting process. 'She has to be believable as the face that launched 1,000 ships and caused the Greeks to go against Troy,' said director Petersen. 'She has to be that beautiful.'

As Paris's/Orlando's lover, the five foot seven Helen/Diane has an ethereal quality and sad, far-away, almost feline eyes. 'I rub it in to all my girlfriends,' boasted Diane of her romantic scenes with Orlando, 'saying, "I got to kiss him again today."'

'Orlando is a great kisser and I know he'll be happy to hear me report it.'

As ever, speculation surrounded how well the most attractive male on set got on with the alpha female. 'Do I feel grateful to be around beautiful girls?' asked Orlando, rhetorically. 'Of course I do! I'm a guy. All guys love gorgeous girls, and I get to work with Diane Kruger in *Troy*, and with Liv Tyler and Cate Blanchett in *Rings*!'

'He's romantic and dashing and handsome and sort of swans to the ladies and does the whole thing. He doesn't really think about the consequences of his actions.' – *Orlando on his role of Paris in* Troy

The love affair between Paris and Helen would remain at the centre of an intense and violent film (an importance it never held in *The Iliad*) and even included a romantic fantasy sequence where they dream about going off to live an idyllic, isolated life together, and a brief lovemaking scene where Helen gives herself totally to Paris.

'I had this costume that had clasps on the shoulders,' recalls Diane. 'When I released them, the costume fell to the floor leaving me naked.

'It was the first scene we filmed together and there I was having to stand naked in front of Orlando with 100 crew members looking on.

'I didn't know whether he was more embarrassed for me or for himself.' Sonia Bloom's little boy may have been taught to follow his personal passions without compromise, but he was, nonetheless, raised to be a gentleman.

Other prominent members of a glittering cast include 1960s superstars Peter O'Toole as King Priam, father of Paris and Hector, and Julie Christie as Thetis, Achilles' mother. Both were veterans of the beautifully-filmed epics of British director David Lean: O'Toole as the enigmatic hero of *Lawrence of Arabia* (1962), and Christie as Lara, whose tragic love story unfolds against the Russian Revolution in *Doctor Zhivago* (1965).

By this stage of the game, the 26-year-old actor was no longer daunted by working with such a stellar cast. 'I am getting much more comfortable,' he acknowledged. 'I was doing a scene [with Peter O'Toole], and to be standing there not feeling as petrified as I would have been a couple of years ago . . . I wasn't as intimidated. I felt more comfortable to

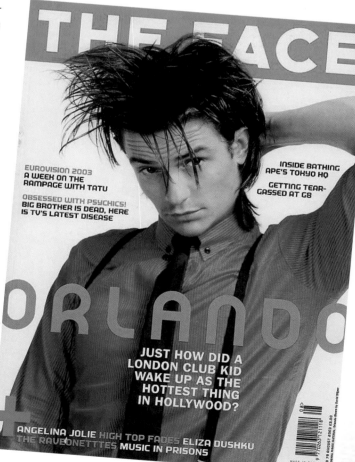

The style-conscious star on the cover of style magazine The Face.

'Paris is a lover, not a fighter. He falls in love with a woman and creates a war because of it'

do what I needed to do, and not let my fear of anything get in the way of the work . . . . It's fantastic to work with these people . . . . They raise the bar. That's a new target to aim for.'

Orlando was apparently relishing the chance to depict human weakness and folly, rather than his usual heroism. 'There's this one scene we're shooting next week in Malta for Troy,' he told an interviewer, 'I'm really anxious about it. I have to confront Menelaus, scared and beaten. I'm standing in front of the woman I love, my father, my brothers, my entire country, and I have to run away like a girl. I mean, how am I going to get away with any dignity?'

In one of many changes to the source material, Paris would be rescued by his brother Hector, who kills Menelaus – thus incurring the wrath of Agamemnon and Achilles. This completely deviates from the ending of *The Iliad*, where Menelaus survives and wins back Helen, who pours out a drugged wine that makes everyone forget there ever was a Trojan War! (And, of course, it differs from *The Trojan Women* – back at the Guildhall, Orlando had played Menelaus *after* the Greeks have taken Troy.)

Filming was scheduled to begin in London, followed by location shooting in Morocco, where Orlando had enjoyed filming *Black Hawk Down*. But world events would soon interfere with production. In February, the imminence of the US invasion of Iraq, and the fear of reprisals by Muslim zealots in Morocco, led the production to pull out.

'Putting on those togas and the short armoured skirts, you feel like you're fighting for the fair Helen.'

Mexico would eventually replace Morocco for location filming. In such hot foreign climes, Orlando's complexion became the opposite to that of the milky-white Legolas. 'I have olive skin,' he had to remind an interviewer from *Elle*, 'I walk under a light bulb, I get a tan.'

Petersen also decided that the set of the city of Troy itself would have to be built twice – one version in Malta for dialogue sequences, and again in Mexico in July for the battle scenes, thus further inflating the budget. 'This feels so much bigger in so many ways,' observed Orlando, making a comparison to *The Lord of the Rings*. 'The money, the vastness of the sets, and I'm playing more of a principal role. That means you assume more responsibility, and it forces you to be more immersed in things.' Unfortunately, while Paris is indeed a pivotal figure in the Trojan War, few critics would agree that his character dominated the screen, when competing with so much other muscular male talent. But the fans, as ever, would know better.

Orly's personal entourage were along for this major stint of location filming. 'My mates came out to Mexico when I was filming *Troy* and we had a great time,' he confirms. 'It's great to be with people who are like, "Oh, shut up, don't be a tosser."'

Before the Bloom posse could converge on Mexico, however, Orlando would receive a further education via the film's male lead – a star who first became famous when the young Orlando was riding horses through the Kent countryside.

Filming in Malta was, on the whole, a relaxed experience for Orlando. It was here that the main spotlight of attention was taken off of him and placed onto the film's main star. 'It was written in a newspaper in England that if you're going on holiday this summer,' Orly laughed, 'why not go to Malta because Brad Pitt's filming there. And you might bump into him.'

One Saturday night, when the cameras stopped rolling on *Troy*, Orlando witnessed movie superstardom on a whole other level. He and Brad went into town together: 'We left the restaurant and walked down the street. I was just chatting to Brad, and before you knew it, there were flashbulbs. It felt like the whole of Malta was in the street, just screaming and yelling from the rooftops. It was incredible. I was so impressed with the way he kind of kept his composure. But it's bizarre to see how one person can have that kind of effect on that many people just immediately. It was really scary.'

Opposite above: The face that launched 1,000 ships, (Diane Kruger as Helen) and the man who risked all-out war to make her his own (Orlando as Paris), and below: Hector (Eric Bana) and Paris lead their troops to defend the walls of Troy.

Of his own, slightly less universal stardom, he admits, 'It's all still a bit odd, all that adulation. I'm genuinely not used to it at all. Brad Pitt gave me some very interesting advice . . . keep smiling and keep moving. Well, I've learned the smiling bit, but I'm not so good at the moving on. I like to give fans what they've been waiting for.'

It was during the Maltese stages of filming that the Bloom fan base began to expand. '*Pirates of the Caribbean* hadn't come out when we started filming in Malta so nobody recognised him,' explained Diane Kruger. 'He could go wherever he wanted.'

Then *Pirates* was released. 'Suddenly hordes of fourteen-year-old girls were lining up just to get a glimpse of Orlando. He couldn't go anywhere. He became a prisoner of his celebrity.'

Orlando's fans would turn out to see him in *Troy*. But, ultimately, the film belongs to Brad Pitt as the mighty Achilles – a merciless, muscular warrior, all buffed-up, despite unfounded rumours that his legs looked thin enough in a skirt to require a double. Few, apart from his most diehard fans, would claim that *Troy* took Orlando up to the next level.

'I'd only done six movies before Troy and Orlando had gone straight from drama school into Lord of the Rings. We felt so young and inexperienced in the company of so many heavyweights, so we really bonded.' – *Diane Kruger*

After a special screening at the Cannes Film Festival, *Troy* was released on both sides of the Atlantic in May 2004. *Empire Online* had already reviewed the trailer, featuring the three male leads, in March. 'Women will queue round the block because Brad Pitt, Orlando Bloom and Eric Bana are oiled up and prancing about in scanty clothing,' the reviewer logically predicted – which proved even truer when the finished film granted a fleeting profile shot of Orly's lithe, bare behind, and even more of Brad's butt when he's first seen in a tent with two nubiles, post-threesome.

The UK's *Daily Telegraph* were not nearly as kind to the third name on the cast list: 'While one can easily imagine his Paris stealing the beautiful Helen away from Menelaus, it is more difficult to believe him as a Trojan warrior waging serious battle.'

In the US, feelings about the bloody epic were mixed. In *The Hollywood Reporter*, Kirk Honeycutt was underwhelmed, dismissing 'a much too pretty Orlando Bloom' as Paris. *Variety* critic Todd McCarthy agreed. Describing the 'affair between Helen, Queen of Sparta (Diane Kruger), and the equally lovely Paris (Orlando Bloom)' as 'no more than a lusty diversion for both even at its peak, hardly the sort of passion that might result in the deaths of thousands and the ruin of a city,'

Other US reviewers were kinder – although David Denby in *The New Yorker* had very mixed feelings about the romantic leads: 'Sometimes the lack of play and fantasy leads to simple banalities, like the earnest love scenes between a dewy young Paris (Orlando Bloom) and a rather anxious Helen (Diane Kruger). These two are the movie stars of the Trojan War; it's hard to believe they weren't wickedly turned on by being at the centre of so much gossip, but, when they get together, they are so placid they might be a young suburban wife and a handsome lawn man smooching in an afternoon soap opera.'

After completing filming on *Troy*, though prior to its release, Orlando suffered a small bout of disenchantment. 'I'd really like to take a role that doesn't involve a sword,' he testified.

'I've had enough of being the cool, clean-shaven Elf; the cool, wholesome pirate slayer,' he spat, almost venomously. 'Do I want to be a pin-up? Do I want to just be a poster boy? No I fucking don't! People turn to me sometimes and ask, "So you only do costume dramas now, do you?" I'm like, "fuck off".'

Diane Kruger and Orlando as star-crossed lovers Helen and Paris in Troy.

'Orlando is a great kisser and I know he'll be happy to hear me report it.' – *Diane Kruger*

For the time being, however, he was 'going to go back to London and take some time. I just feel like I need to take some time. I'm really stretched.

'I haven't read [a screenplay] that's really made me sit up, so I'll keep reading until I do.' It wouldn't be long. Orlando would find the means to fulfil his ambition to balance big Hollywood epics with smaller-scale, more personal independent movies. And still, the manic pace of the last year would continue unabated.

The second of his independent projects, if the spectacularly unsuccessful *The Calcium Kid* is included, was *Haven* (2004). Co-starring Orlando with Bill Paxton and Gabriel Byrne, this low-budget crime drama brought him closer to his ambition of playing grittier character-based roles, an ambition partly realised by his acting as the film's producer.

'It's the first time I've done that,' he acknowledges. 'By getting involved in something you believe in you can help forward a film. In terms of the role that I've been playing as a producer, it's been really just a sounding board; it's very much a collaborative effort and we're all just mucking in and getting on with it.' Given how his star has risen, having Orlando's name attached as both actor and producer can only have made the film more bankable.

Production began on the film in November 2003, in the Cayman Islands where the film is set. *Haven* is the feature-film debut of writer/director Frank E. Flowers, who previously won the HBO

Troy veterans Orlando, Eric Bana and Brad Pitt at the Cannes Film Festival, May 2004.

best short film award at the American Black Film Festival for *Swallow*, his salutary tale of the dangers of acting as a drug mule. The film features Paxton and Byrne as two crooked American businessmen who escape to the Caymans to avoid prosecution for crooked real estate trading. Orlando's crucial role is that of a young British guy sucked into their web of deception, who ends up committing a crime with serious reverberations.

'As a young actor, I would watch Johnny Depp's films and Brad's films and go, "Wow, that's the stuff to do."'

'It's a pretty intense little film, both visually and emotionally,' testifies Orlando, 'and I feel an audience will feel the impact of that. I play a young character called Shy who is a happy-go-lucky young man who's been brought up in the Cayman Islands. He's in love with this young Caymanian girl [Andrea, played by Zoe Saldana, who also appeared in *Pirates of the Caribbean*]; he's kind of from the wrong side of the tracks and she's from the right side of the tracks . . . they get together to the fury and anger of their families.' Reputedly, *Haven* will feature a love scene between Shy and Andrea after she's just passed eighteen, the islands' legal age of consent. Sneaking into her house late at night, he has to run for it, shirtless, the next morning, chased off by her father, and leading to a violent attack by Andrea's brother.

As for the usual speculation about liaisons between Orlando and his leading lady, this was confounded by the arrival of Kate Bosworth in the Caymans during the last week of shooting, in December 2003. According to Orlando, one part of life that never becomes less complicated, however famous or glamorous the person, is emotional and sexual relationships: 'When you're famous, people write you off as out of their league or they think that you're something you're not. Then when they meet you they're either intimidated or let down by the real you.'

In November 2003, British 'high society' magazine *Tatler* had belied the notion that Orly's appeal is limited to teenage girls by featuring him as 'Britain's most eligible bachelor'. As editor Geordie Greig said, 'Bloom is the name, face, body and mind that all young women would seem to feel happy having on their arm.'

But it was already common wisdom that Orlando may have found his perfect girl: 'I want a fun-loving girl who I can also spend quiet hours with,' he described her in the most hypothetical terms. 'I need her to realise what it's like to be an actor – so she accepts that I travel a lot and that we won't get to see each other as often as I'd like to.'

And who more sympathetic or understanding in this sense than another actor?

'It's all a bit odd, all that adulation. I'm genuinely not used to it at all. Brad Pitt gave me some very interesting advice . . . keep smiling and keep moving.'

Kate Bosworth had recently taken a brave career step recently herself, accepting the part of the girlfriend of coke-addicted ex-porn star John Holmes (Val Kilmer) in the controversial true-life story *Wonderland* (2003). It was also around this time that *News of the World* ran their exclusive on Orlando's purported one-night stand with Maddy Ford. But, as great an intrusion as this was, it had also taken place before he first started seeing Kate in April 2003.

Asked by the press how their relationship was enduring, Orlando snapped, 'Kate is a great girl, but I don't like to talk about her. I try to keep my private life separate from my professional life.' It's known, however, that the couple spent a romantic Christmas 2003 together in Kate's native Los Angeles.

Pumped by an interviewer as to the state of his relationship, Orlando refused, as ever, to be specific. But he did exhibit some touchingly human insecurities: 'I'm rubbish. I'm out of touch. I don't know how to love. I randomly start crying for no reason.' As he infers, the pressures of life and love on a superstar-in-the-making are no less trying than on anybody else.

'I like to think I'm romantic. I try to be,' he says, almost apologetically. But anyone who can spend £36,000 repeatedly flying his girlfriend from L.A. to a Mexican film set, as Orlando did with Kate once separation became unbearable, can at least be said to have a romantic streak – as well as much disposable income.

Orlando's New Year's resolution for 2004 would be, 'Hold it together, boy!'

At the beginning of 2004, Orlando Bloom remained in the peculiar position of an international movie star who had never taken a lead role in a major film. It was about to change with the production of Ridley Scott's *Kingdom of Heaven* (2005). Scott had borne Orlando in mind as a potential male lead ever since his small part in *Black Hawk Down*.

The film appears to be both a typical Hollywood epic and an unusual story that may or may not take a few historical liberties. It also reversed Orlando's disenchantment with the historical epic genre. Orlando's role is that of Balian – his second blacksmith, after Will Turner, but this time he was a character whose story plays out against the authentic historical events of the twelfth century. 'It's about a young man who goes off to the Crusades and in the process falls in and out of love,' he explains. 'I swore to myself I wasn't going to do another movie with a horse and a sword, but

Orlando clutches his 2003 Actor of the Year award from GQ won by his performances in the second Lord of the Rings/first Pirates of the Caribbean *films.*

here I am. I'm excited. It's a really big deal.' As his first lead role in a major Hollywood film, it may also be the means whereby he's finally able to balance the costume dramas for which he's become known with the independent movies he wants to be involved in.

Given the greater need for realism than the *Pirates of the Caribbean* romp, director Scott insisted that Orlando bulk up a little for his role. Intending to spend time in the gym, 'building up', he reacted to a *Sunday Telegraph* interviewer's suggestion that he simply eat more by insisting, 'it would be the wrong sort of weight gain. And I imagine that I wouldn't feel that great,' recalling the dietary restrictions he placed on himself to fulfil the physical demands of *The Lord of the Rings*.

It's the interpretation of historical events that makes *Kingdom of Heaven* potentially controversial. Balian becomes a knight and falls in love with the Princess of Jersualem (Eva Green), in the course of defending the city that's been held by the European Crusaders since 1099. According to a studio spokesperson at Fox, the intention is to show the cordial relations between the three great religions of the Middle Ages – Christianity, Judaism and Islam – before they were wrecked by the Second Crusade, and the attack of the Christian Knights Templar upon a Muslim caravan.

'I did a lot of partying when I was younger, got that out of my system, so I don't enjoy it, I don't need it.'

Distinguished members of the mainly British and Irish cast include Eva Green as Sybila, the Arabic princess who Balian falls in love with, Liam Neeson as Balian's father, Jeremy Irons as Tiberias, a Jewish-Spanish philosopher-scholar, Brendan Gleeson (Menelaus in *Troy*), Bloom favourite Edward Norton, and respected Brit character actor David Thewlis as a priest. Shooting began in January 2004, in Morocco – the Islamic country where filming had to be abandoned for *Troy*, pre-Iraqi war. Location shooting in Morocco would be preceded by shoots in various parts of Spain, where some

Kingdom of Heaven reinforces Orlando's reputation as a star of costume dramas. It's also the first epic in which he takes top billing.

of the architecture testified to the ancient Moorish (North African) invasion, and the lasting Arabic/Islamic influence in certain regions.

First, in early January, the cast and crew pitched up at Loarre Castle in Ayerbe, part of the Huesca region of Spain, which would stand in for the Holy Land. The Roman-style castle makes the perfect setting for the film's opening, where the adjoining village is surrounded by fire, Balian's workshop is destroyed, and his family are among the casualties of the attack. It's this tragic incident that leads to him joining up as a Crusader. According to spectators in the town, the opening scenes entailed 'green riding horses and Bloom practising being attacked by different real dogs'. The funeral of his mother also takes place there, filmed under artificial snow, as did some of Orlando's horseriding scenes.

'I swore to myself I wasn't going to do another movie with a horse and a sword, but here I am.'

On 13 January, however, it would be the hotel, not the castle, that found itself under siege. It was the day of Orlando's 27th birthday. As if to demonstrate that Bloom-mania was truly international, hundreds of his Spanish fans, now aware of his presence, turned up at the hotel to deluge him with presents. Semi-disguised in a beanie hat, he was able to spare only about five minutes on arriving back from filming. Reputedly, Orly's bodyguard and his personal assistant ran out of arm-space in which to gather up all the gifts. Fans had come from as far as Barcelona in the north, bringing with them a range of personalised gifts – including six young women from Zaragoza who presented him with a basket of vegetarian and health food.

In Seville, the attention from Orlando's fans was similarly intense, when he stayed at the luxurious $1,000-a-night Hotel Alfonso XIII in San Fernando. 'Orlando has been dealing with all the girls hanging around him very well,' publicist Quinn Donoghue told the tabloid press. 'He's very down to earth and pragmatic, and knows that the fans are only after his persona [i.e. Legolas or Will Turner] and not him.'

But this time, no one could even fantasise that he was up for grabs. Kate Bosworth, who he'd now been seeing for nearly a year, came to spend time with her man. Described by one of the executive producers on *Kingdom of Heaven* as 'practically inseparable and . . . very much in love,' the movie's casting director, one Billy Dowd, observed how, 'They have a lot of fun, despite the girls waiting at every turn.' Booking themselves into restaurants under false names, Orly and Kate celebrated Valentine's Day 2004 by going to dinner at the Taberna del Alabardero, a former nineteenth-century palace that now plays the multiple roles of hotel, culinary school and restaurant. According to on-set spies (and possibly jealous fans), Kate, who had recently been working in Germany, playing 1960s icon of purity Sandra Dee in *Beyond the Sea*, spent almost all of February in Spain with Orlando on the *Kingdom* set.

Kingdom of Heaven is due to open in the movies' 'early summer' season, on 6 May 2005 – a US

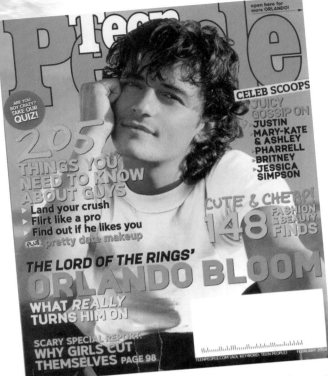

Sex appeal that straddles generations: 'What Really Turns Him On', promised the cover of Teen People . . .

'When you're famous, people write you off as out of their league or they think that you're something you're not. Then when they meet you they're either intimidated or let down by the real you.'

holiday weekend which has provided big openings for blockbusters like Scott's own *Gladiator*. In April 2004, more than a full year before its release, the movie's first promotional poster was released to the press. It featured Orlando's pensive face hovering god-like over the stone pillars of a temple, gazing on a similarly superimposed sword that obviously belongs to Balian. 'Against the tide one man will rise,' promises the promo blurb. While it refers to the film's main character, it could also be seen as marking the point that Orlando Bloom, who has become an international screen presence via largescale epic movies, has moved from being a charismatic support actor to the star attraction.

As to his own religious or spiritual beliefs, Orlando remains resolutely a child of his age: the New Age of alternative spirituality and superstition. The charms and talismans on a chain around his neck continued to grow. 'I have a lot of these things with me all the time,' he displayed to an interviewer from *GQ* – the magazine which, on the basis of *The Two Towers* and *Pirates of the Caribbean*, had made him their Actor of the Year. 'I get given some and find others. One was a key ring that Johnny [Depp] gave me as a wrap gift for *Pirates*. Here's a piece of greenstone Billy Boyd gave me. I found this shell on the beach in Thailand. This is a prayer baton I got in India. I picked up this tiny silver ball in Tokyo. This is a New York City handcuff key, so if I get into any strife, I can get myself out . . . .

'I've always kept all these funny little things, even as a kid. But I'm trying to cut it out, become more streamlined. Otherwise it starts to feel like the things own you. These things fill up my heart. If I were ever to lose them, I'd be really devastated. Isn't that pathetic?'

On the other side of the coin to *Kingdom of Heaven*, another independent project that may fulfil Orlando's need to diversify is *Elizabethtown* (2005). It's to be directed by Cameron Crowe, for whom he previously appeared in his Gap commercial, 'Denim Invasion', with Kate Beckinsale. As a small-to-medium-size independent production, he sees it as another step toward doing 'a major studio film where I'm not wielding a sword or wearing a historical costume.'

As Drew Baylor, a young training shoe designer who loses his job after his line of sneakers are withdrawn at a cost of $1 billion to his corporation, Orlando's latest role seems to be a gentle, bittersweet but life-affirming comedy-drama of a different emotional tone to anything he's done so far.

Contemplating suicide, Drew gives away all his possessions and consumer items before trying to kill himself by rigging his bike with a Ginzu knife. What saves his life is, by a sad irony, a call back to his family's small hometown of Elizabethtown, Kentucky after the death of his father. Entrusted with handling his dad's final affairs, en route back home he meets with a flight attendant named Claire, played by Kirsten Dunst. Forming an attraction, the blossoming love affair between the two incites Drew to get his shredded life back on track, to come to terms with the southern family roots that seem totally alien to him, and deal with the unfinished business that all families and sons have to face at some point. All the indications are that it will be a small, intimate, talky 'anti-epic', set against a parochial background that reflects the human scale of the story.

'You don't really have choices until you get to a point where there's enough people who are behind you and you have enough of an audience who are interested to watch you, to have choices,' explains Orlando, hopeful that at least part of the audience who pay to see him in epics will now turn out for his smaller films. 'If I've got the choice, I would start to downscale a bit and do more human, dramatic, character-driven pieces where you get to see less of a show and more of an actor.'

Friendship and familial ties remain as important as ever: 'I'm a hero to [my mum] but what is really important to me is my family and my friends and the people who are closest to me. I try to maintain some sense of reality through work, friends and family.' But still, this is the young superstar whose asking price has risen to a rumoured £3 million (US $5 million) per film – unless he's lending his presence and his patronage to a smaller independent project.

'It's been such a whirlwind since the release of the first *Rings* film, and it feels as if it's beginning to catch up with me.'

Orlando's roots remain firmly in the southeast of England – specifically, in his adopted hometown of London. 'I hope I won't become a prisoner of fame,' he pondered aloud, 'but if going out becomes more of a hassle, why would I want to deal with it? I have a big place and I want to create a nice environment for my mates so they'll want to stay and never leave.

'It's in London,' he explains, still leaving its whereabouts unknown. 'It's really nice. I feel lucky to have it. Now I've got a place I can put stuff in, so that if I go around the world and I buy something, I can send it there . . . Especially the things I would never have thought of buying before, which I am thinking of buying now.'

As for superstardom, of which he's sampled a small taste of himself and seen at second-hand in the life of Brad Pitt, 'I wouldn't like that to happen,' Orlando swears. 'It's not something I'd choose for myself. I avoid going to parties. I did a lot of partying when I was younger, got that out of my system, so I don't enjoy it, I don't need it.'

In terms of personal ambitions, the desired balance between period epics and smaller independent films may now be taking place. 'I'm holding out for fucking three guys sitting around a table playing cards,' Orlando has said, only half-jokingly. 'Not that I'm not grateful for the opportunities and experiences I've had, but I just think it would be good for me to do something like that just to show that I'm not just an action-reaction, one line man . . . . There's more to me than that, and hopefully I can get an opportunity to show that.

'I'd like to do more character-driven, dark, gritty, human stories. I feel like I'm growing in experience and confidence as an actor and that will lead me to those.'

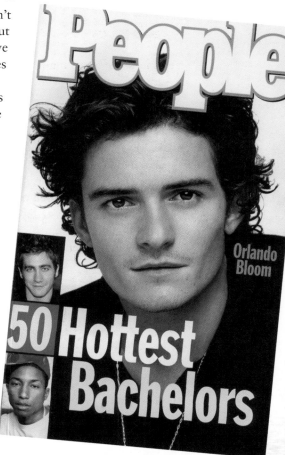

. . . *while* People *magazine, catering to a slightly older market, gave Orlando prominence among their '50 Hottest Bachelors.*

Besides *Haven*, another very important personal project is *The Journey is the Destination*, adapted from the personal journals of 22-year-old Reuters news photographer Dan Eldon. Eldon was stoned to death by an angry crowd in Somalia in 1993 – who held him, and his colleagues, responsible for a United Nations taskforce bombing which missed its target (a local warlord) and killed 72 innocent people.

'My sister had bought the book for my mother years ago even before I went to drama school,' explains Orlando. 'At the time I looked at it and asked, "Why are you giving this to Mum?" It was a fantastic book but it's a young guy's book. So it sort of came into my life then, and then while I was doing *The Lord of the Rings*, one of my friends was talking about it, and when I went to Los Angeles for the first time and acquired a manager and an agent, I asked them to find out more about the rights, and then on her own Cathy Eldon [the photographer's mother] came to me. So it's kind of like I've been on a long journey with it; so we've got to do it.'

As of early 2004, both Orlando and young woman director Bronwen Hughes were attached to the project, which remains in development. As the director explains of Dan Eldon's tragic end, acclaiming him as 'a humanitarian artist', he 'was killed in Somalia before *Black Hawk Down*. In the old days, journalists were off-limits. Now journalists are prime targets.'

Another personal project, and perhaps more problematic, is *Deaf Road* – a film to be shot entirely in sign language, which Orlando has made a verbal commitment to learn. British ad director and photographer Malcolm Venville's screenplay is based on the true story of his profoundly deaf uncle's attempts to lose his virginity in post-war Tangiers. However, despite Orlando's name being attached, the first-time director has so far failed to raise the project £10 million budget. 'I need risk-taking producers,' he complains, 'but no one in Britain wants to know.'

'I suppose I'm getting into that position, which I suppose all actors want to be in, where I have some control over what I'm doing.'

As to his own requirements for a film project these days, 'It's the question of personal challenge,' insists Orlando, 'combined with a sort of "does this excite me?" thing. I also have to totally trust the material . . .'

As to his privileged position in the world of mass media and popular entertainment right now, Orlando Bloom can only admit, 'It's been such a whirlwind since the release of the first *Rings* film, and it feels as if it's beginning to catch up with me. I guess the novelty's wearing off . . . It's funny when you start to sort of live the dreams that you always hoped maybe [for], but never really imagined possible. And when you start to live them – it's kind of overwhelming. There's a lot of other stuff that goes in alongside and it's like, "Ugh."'

His apprehension and neuroses mirror that of many a young actor who will never rise to his sudden heights. 'I'm constantly asking myself, "Am I making the right choices?". . .

'I suppose I'm getting into that position, which I suppose all actors want to be in, where I have some control over what I'm doing, yet what goes with that is a whole new set of pressures.'

For all the doubt and insecurity, for all the agonising over the choices that most young men will never have, Orlando remains realistic about the stardom that fell upon him like an arrow shot from the heavens. 'Fear would say to me, "Do you really want to deal with all that?" My career is really at the point that I either stop now and vanish or I keep moving forward, take the opportunities and make the most of what's coming. On a good day, I realise I'd be crazy not to.

'I don't want to lose sight of the important things in life,' he insisted in late 2003. But then, he conceded, 'I don't have a regular life, but what is a regular life, anyway? Whatever happens in life is just fine. Just trust in that.'

In wherever it may lead.

Bloom-mania becomes truly international as Orlando graces the front covers of magazines from all over the world.

ure

DAY TIMES

Elf an
fitnes

Orlando Bloom blosso
into Hollywood's new h

age
e
est
nd

G SUMMER MOVIE P

REMIERE

BOY
LANDO
OM
UP
C

N
NO
l
vol. 2
G
RS'

ПОСТЕР: «ТАЙНЫ С

Серил

спрала – 2 марта

РОВАННАЯ
ОУН

АРИИ
Е

C
ЛЬШОМ
ОДЕ

ОРЛАНДО
ЛУМ ВЛАСТЕЛИН

He
HIGH QUALITY FOR WOMEN AND MEN

IT'S ON AGAIN!
THE HQ SHORT
STORY CONTEST
WIN $3000

AN ACCIDENTAL
MATRIARCHY
The women
rebuilding Rwanda

MY BODY
FOR A BULLET
Human shields: noble,
naive, next big thing?

MAX MARKSON
You've got a story to tell,
he's got a story to sell

Oh! Orlando
Looks this good

The Heart-Throb
Orlando Bloom
GQ's Actor Of The Year
By Alex Bilmes

Orlando Bloom photographed for GQ by James Dimmock

MAN AT HIS BEST // NOVEMBER 2003

squre

JFK at 86
존 F. 케네디는 86세의
나이로 아직까지 미국인들
마음속에 살아 있다.

활의 제왕

ORLANDO
BLOOM

「木更津キャッツアイ」開幕！ スマ・・かね / 友沢在島 DVD情報も満載

キネマ旬報

8月下

KINEJUN
no.1387

超速報！
2004年話題作
キャサリン・ヘプバー

ジョニー・デップ
オーランド・ブルーム

ノーヒアンン 呪われた海賊たち

アイアルII（鎖暁歌り）

ym

"WHAT'S
IS DEAL?"
W BOYS THINK

k cool for
DER $20

P YOUR MEAN
D NOW!

Z: ARE YOU
SS CASE?

ELLY WAS
HIGH SCHOO

lebrity New Year's
ichelle Branch
ter Facinelli

Lord of the
ORLAND
BLOO
HE'S HOT, H
AN ACCENT
EVEN RECIT
POET

ANUARY 2003

U.S. $3.50/CANADA $4.9

FLAUNT

ORLANDO BLOO

FILMOGRAPHY

Wilde
UK 1997, 118 mins
Directed by Bruce Gilbert
Screenplay by Julian Mitchell, based on the book Oscar Wilde by Richard Ellmann
Production Company: Polygram Filmed Entertainment
Cast: Stephen Fry (Oscar Wilde), Jude Law (Lord Alfred 'Bosie' Douglas), Vanessa Redgrave (Lady Speranza Wilde), Jennifer Ehle (Constance Lloyd Wilde), Orlando Bloom (Rentboy)

Midsomer Murders
Episode: 'Judgement Day'
UK 1999, 100 mins
Directed by Jeremy Silbertson
Teleplay by Anthony Horowitz
Production Company: Chrysalis Television
Cast: John Nettles (DCI Barnaby), Daniel Casey (DS Troy)
Guest appearance: Orlando Bloom (Peter Drinkwater)

The Lord of the Rings: The Fellowship of the Ring
USA/New Zealand 2001, 178 mins
Directed by Peter Jackson
Screenplay by Fran Walsh, Philippa Boyens and Peter Jackson, based on the novel by J. R. R. Tolkien
Production Company: New Line Cinema/WingNut Films
Cast: Elijah Wood (Frodo Baggins), Ian McKellen (Gandalf the Grey), Liv Tyler (Arwen), Viggo Mortensen (Aragorn), Sean Bean (Boromir), Ian Holm (Bilbo Baggins), Sean Astin (Samwise 'Sam' Gamgee), Cate Blanchett (Galadriel), John Rhys-Davies (Gimli), Christopher Lee (Saruman the White), Sala Baker (Sauron), Billy Boyd (Peregrin 'Pippin' Took), Dominic Monaghan (Meriadoc 'Merry' Brandybuck), Orlando Bloom (Legolas Greenleaf), Hugo Weaving (Elrond), Andy Serkis (Gollum)

Black Hawk Down
USA 2001, 144 mins
Directed by Ridley Scott
Screenplay by Ken Nolan, based on the book by Mark Bowden
Production Company: Revolution Studios/Jerry Bruckheimer Films/Columbia Pictures Corporation
Cast: Josh Hartnett (Matt Eversmann), Eric Bana (Norm 'Hoot' Gibson), Tom Sizemore (Danny McKnight), Ewan McGregor (Danny Grimes), Sam Shepard (William Garrison), Orlando Bloom (Todd Blackburn)

Ned Kelly
Australia 2002 (released 2003), 110 mins
Directed by Gregor Jordan
Production Company: Working Title Australia/Working Title Films
Screenplay by John M. McDonagh, based on the novel Our Sunshine by Robert Drewe
Cast: Heath Ledger (Ned Kelly), Orlando Bloom (Joe Byrne), Geoffrey Rush (Francis Hare), Naomi Watts (Julia Cook), Joel Edgerton (Aaron Sherritt), Laurence Kinlan (Dan Kelly), Phil Barantini (Steve Hart), Kerry Condon (Kate Kelly), Kris McQuade (Ellen Kelly), Emily Browning (Grace Kelly)

The Calcium Kid
UK 2002 (released 2004), 89 mins
Directed by Alex De Rakoff
Screenplay by Derek Boyle, Alex De Rakoff and Raymond Friel
Production Company: Working Title Films
Cast: Orlando Bloom (Jimmy), Omid Djalili (Herbie Bush), Michael Pena (Jose Mendez), Rafe Spall (Stan), David Kelly (Paddy), Michael Lerner (Artie Cohen), Ronnie Ancona (Pat), Billie Piper (Angel), Doug Cockle (News Reporter), Tamer Hassan (Pete Wright)

The Lord of the Rings: The Two Towers
USA/New Zealand 2002, 179 mins
Directed by Peter Jackson
Screenplay by Fran Walsh, Philippa Boyens, Stephen Sinclair and Peter Jackson, based on the novel by J. R. R. Tolkien
Production Company: New Line Cinema/WingNut Films
Cast: Elijah Wood (Frodo Baggins), Ian McKellen (Gandalf the White), Liv Tyler (Arwen), Viggo Mortensen (Aragorn), Sean Astin (Samwise 'Sam' Gamgee), Cate Blanchett (Galadriel), John Rhys-Davies (Gimli/Voice of Treebeard), Bernard Hill (Theoden), Christopher Lee (Saruman the White), Billy Boyd (Peregrin 'Pippin' Took), Dominic Monaghan (Meriadoc 'Merry' Brandybuck), Orlando Bloom (Legolas Greenleaf), Hugo Weaving (Elrond), Miranda Otto (Eowyn), David Wenham (Faramir), Brad Dourif (Grima Wormtongue), Andy Serkis (Gollum)

Pirates of the Caribbean: The Curse of the Black Pearl
USA 2003, 143 mins
Directed by Gore Verbinski
Screenplay by Ted Elliott and Terry Rossio, story by Elliott, Rossio, Stuart Beattie and Jay Wolpert
Production Company: Jerry Bruckheimer Films/Walt Disney Company
Cast: Johnny Depp (Jack Sparrow), Geoffrey Rush (Barbossa), Orlando Bloom (Will Turner), Keira Knightley (Elizabeth Swann), Jack Davenport (Norrington), Jonathan Pryce (Governor Weatherby Swann)

The Lord of the Rings: The Return of the King
USA/New Zealand 2003, 201 mins
Directed by Peter Jackson
Screenplay by Fran Walsh, Philippa Boyens and Peter Jackson, based on the novel by J. R. R. Tolkien
Production Company: New Line Cinema/WingNut Films
Cast: Elijah Wood (Frodo Baggins), Ian McKellen (Gandalf the White), Liv Tyler (Arwen), Viggo Mortensen (Aragorn), Sean Astin (Samwise 'Sam' Gamgee), Cate Blanchett (Galadriel), John Rhys-Davies (Gimli), Bernard Hill (Theoden), Billy Boyd (Peregrin 'Pippin' Took), Dominic Monaghan (Meriadoc 'Merry' Brandybuck), Orlando Bloom (Legolas Greenleaf), Hugo Weaving (Elrond), Miranda Otto (Eowyn), David Wenham (Faramir), Andy Serkis (Gollum/Smeagol), Thomas Robins (Deagol), John Noble (Denethor), Paul Norell (King of the Dead)

Troy
USA 2004, 163 mins
Directed by Wolfgang Petersen
Screenplay by David Benioff, based on the poem The Iliad by Homer
Production Company: Warner Bros.
Cast: Brad Pitt (Achilles), Eric Bana (Hector), Orlando Bloom (Paris), Diane Kruger (Helen), Brian Cox (Agamemnon), Brendan Gleeson (Menelaus), Sean Bean (Odysseus), Peter O'Toole (Priam), Julie Christie (Thetis), Saffron Burrows (Andromache), Garrett Hedlund (Patroclus), Rose Byrne (Briseis), Tyler Mane (Ajax), Owain Yeoman (Lysander)

Haven
USA 2004
Written and Directed by Frank E. Flowers
Co-Produced by Orlando Bloom
Production Company: El Camino Pictures
Cast: Bill Paxton (Carl Ridley), Victor Rasuk (Fritz), Orlando Bloom (Shy), Razaaq Adoti (Richie Rich), McKeeva Bush (Leader of Government Business), Zoe Saldana (Andrea), Agnes Bruckner (Pippa Ridley), Stephen Dillane (Mr. Allen), Serena Scott Thomas (Mrs. Allen)

Kingdom of Heaven
USA 2005,
Directed by Ridley Scott
Screenplay by William Monahan
Production Company: Twentieth Century Fox
Cast: Orlando Bloom (Balian of Ibelin), Eva Green (Sybilla), Liam Neeson (Godfrey of Ibelin), Jeremy Irons (Tiberias), Brendan Gleeson (Reynald), Marton Csokas (Guy de Lusignan), Edward Norton (King Baldwin IV), David Thewlis (Hospitaller), Jon Finch (Patriarch of Jerusalem), Ghassan Massoud (Saladin), Ulrich Thomsen (Templar master)

Elizabethtown
USA 2005
Written and Directed by Cameron Crowe
Production Company: Vinyl Films/Paramount Pictures
Cast: Orlando Bloom (Drew Baylor), Kirsten Dunst (Claire Colburn), Susan Sarandon (Hollie Baylor), Judy Greer (Heather Baylor), Jessica Biel (Ellen), Alec Baldwin (Phil)

Pirates of the Caribbean II: Treasures of the Lost Abyss
USA 2006
Directed by Gore Verbinski
Screenplay by Ted Elliott and Terry Rossio
Production Company: Jerry Bruckheimer Films/Walt Disney Company
Cast: Johnny Depp (Jack Sparrow), Orlando Bloom (Will Turner), Keira Knightley (Elizabeth Swann)

BOOKS BY JOHN TOLAND

Hitler: The Pictorial Documentary of His Life
Adolf Hitler
The Rising Sun
The Last 100 Days
The Dillinger Days
But Not in Shame
Battle: The Story of the Bulge
Ships in the Sky

HITLER
The Pictorial Documentary of His Life

JOHN TOLAND

HITLER

The Pictorial Documentary of His Life

BALLANTINE BOOKS · NEW YORK

Portions of this book have previously appeared in *Adolf Hitler* by John Toland.

Portions of this book have previously appeared in *Adolf Hitler*
by John Toland.
Copyright © 1976, 1978 by John Toland

Library of Congress Catalog Card Number: 77-76145

ISBN 0-345-28369-4

This edition published by arrangement with
Doubleday & Company, Inc.

Manufactured in the United States of America

First Ballantine Books Edition: May 1980

1 2 3 4 5 6 7 8 9

To
Carolyn Blakemore
Ken McCormick
John W. Stillman

Contents

Foreword

This book is a supplement to my biography, *Adolf Hitler,* and should help bring it to more vivid life. Since pictures can also give false impressions when taken at face value, I have written a rather lengthy commentary.

Some viewers may be appalled at the pictures depicting the horrors and destruction perpetrated by the Nazi regime. I hope everyone is appalled and I chose the most shocking examples I could locate. For these are an integral part of Hitler and National Socialist Germany. So are the photographs reflecting his achievements, the adulation of crowds, and the intimate scenes of his private life.

Hitler was a builder and a wrecker; a creator and a destroyer. He was to the end a man of the most complex contradictions. That is what I have attempted to portray.

John Toland

December 1977

HITLER
The Pictorial Documentary of His Life

ONE

"Deep Are the Roots"

1889–1918

Adolf Hitler's parents both came from the Waldviertel, a remote rural area of Austria, northwest of Vienna, not far from the present Czechoslovakian border. His father was born on June 7, 1837, in the village of Strones to an unmarried woman, Maria Anna Schicklgruber. Strones was too small to be a parish and so the baby was registered in nearby Döllersheim as Aloys Schicklgruber, "Illegitimate." The space for the father's name was blank, generating a mystery that remains unsolved, but he was probably a man from the neighborhood. However, he might have been a wealthy Jew named Frankenberger or Frankenreither, the son of the family for whom Maria Anna had worked as a domestic. In any case the Jewish family paid her support money for some years, and this later became a family scandal.

When Alois (as his name would be spelled henceforth) was five, Maria married Johann Georg Hiedler, a drifter from nearby Spital. But she died five years later and the stepfather wandered off leaving Alois to be brought up by Hiedler's brother, Johann Nepomuk Hiedler. At thirteen young Alois Schicklgruber ran away. Eventually he became a full inspector of customs, and the man who had brought him up was so proud he convinced Alois to have his name changed legally from Schicklgruber to Hiedler. On June 6, 1876, Johann Nepomuk Hiedler and three other relatives made the short trip to the town of Weitra where they falsely testified before the local notary that Hiedler's brother —they spelled his name "Hitler"—"had several times stated in their presence" that he had fathered an illegitimate son, Alois, and wanted him made his legitimate son and heir. The change of name from Hiedler to Hitler was probably to becloud the issue.

The following day Johann Nepomuk Hiedler traveled with the three relatives to Döllersheim where the original birth record of Alois was registered. The elderly parish priest affirmed from the parish marriage book that a man named Georg Hiedler had indeed married a girl named

1

Schicklgruber in 1842 and agreed to alter the birth register. With some reluctance the parish priest changed the "illegitimate" to "legitimate" and crossed out the "Schicklgruber" in the space for the child's name. In the last space he wrote in an extremely cramped hand: "It is confirmed by the undersigned that Georg Hitler whose name is here entered as Father, being well known to the undersigned, did accept paternity of the child Aloys, according to the statement of the child's mother, and did desire his name to be entered in the register of baptisms of this parish."

Alois Hitler was a strict father. His eldest son, Alois, Jr.—unable to endure his beating and discipline—ran away from home. Adolf, according to his sister Paula, also "got his sound thrashing every day" and one night tried to leave home by escaping from the upstairs window. His father caught him as he was wriggling through the narrow opening, but instead of beating chose a punishment Hitler found even harder to bear—ridicule. It took Hitler, he later confided to a friend, "a long time to get over the episode."

In 1900 Hitler started at the Realschule in Linz and did poorly. Gone for the moment was the cockiness of his village days; in the city school he seemed lost and forlorn. One day early in January 1903, his father went

1. Alois Hitler, Inspector of Customs.

into the Gasthaus Stiefler for his morning drink, remarking that he did not feel well. Moments later Alois Hitler was dead of pleural hemorrhage. The family moved to an apartment in Linz, but without his father's discipline, Adolf did even more poorly academically. He failed to graduate from high school.

In early 1908 Hitler moved to Vienna, with his friend Gustl (August) Kubizek following soon after. Gustl enrolled in the Academy of Music and was an immediate success, but Hitler failed to get into the Academy of Fine Arts and became bitter. The two youths had little money but saw many operas and haunted the museums. Hitler spent his time sketching, and writing stories and plays; he even started an opera with Gustl's help. That fall he again failed to gain admittance to the Academy of Art. Depressed, he went off on his own and when his money ran low began sleeping in bars, cheap flophouses, and the crowded "warming room" on Erdbergstrasse established by a Jewish philanthropist. By December 1909 the twenty-year-old Hitler was forced to seek charity at the Asyl für Obdachlose, a shelter for the destitute.

By the early fall of 1918 the German Army was close to defeat and there were strikes at home. Hitler was among those at the front who believed they were being betrayed by the pacifists and Jewish slackers at home who were "stabbing the Fatherland in the back." He and those like him burned to avenge such treachery: Out of all this would come the politics of the future. On October 14, 1918, Hitler was blinded by gas in Belgium and sent to a hospital in the Pomeranian town of Pasewalk.

2. Document discovered by author in Vienna in 1971 showing that Aloys was illegitimate. It also shows later alternations by the parish priest.

3. Alois Hitler himself had several illegitimate children and was twice wed before marrying Adolf Hitler's mother, Klara Pölzl, in 1885.

4. Angela, Hitler's half sister, and Alois, his half brother, with Granny.

5. The Veit family, relatives of Alois Hitler, who once advised young Josef Veit: "Drunkards, debtors, card players that lead immoral lives can't last."

6. Angela (Hitler) Raubal and son Leo.

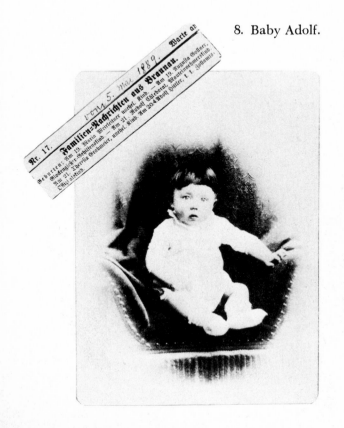

7. The first three children of Alois and Klara Hitler died before the fourth, Adolf, was born on April 20, 1889, in Braunau on the Inn River, just across from Germany. Note his recorded name, Adolfus.

8. Baby Adolf.

9. Adolf and mother.

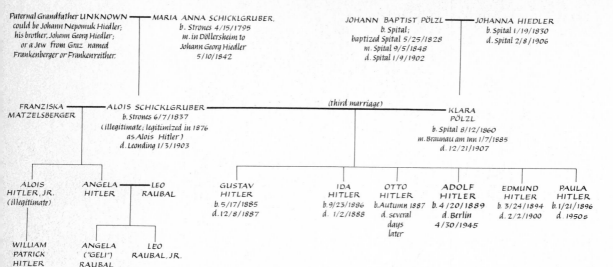

Paternal Grandfather UNKNOWN
could be Johann Nepomuk Hiedler;
his brother, Johann Georg Hiedler;
or a Jew from Graz named
Frankenberger or Frankenreither.

MARIA ANNA SCHICKLGRUBER,
b. Strones 4/15/1795
m. in Döllersheim to
Johann Georg Hiedler
5/10/1842

JOHANN BAPTIST PÖLZL
b. Spital;
baptized Spital 5/25/1828
m. Spital 9/5/1848
d. Spital 1/9/1902

JOHANNA HIEDLER
b. Spital 1/19/1830
d. Spital 2/8/1906

FRANZISKA
MATZELSBERGER

ALOIS SCHICKLGRUBER
b. Strones 6/7/1837
(illegitimate; legitimized in 1876
as Alois Hitler)
d. Leonding 1/3/1903

(third marriage)

KLARA
PÖLZL
b. Spital 8/12/1860
m. Braunau am Inn 1/7/1885
d. 12/21/1907

ALOIS
HITLER, JR.
(illegitimate)

ANGELA
HITLER

LEO
RAUBAL

GUSTAV
HITLER
b. 5/17/1885
d. 12/8/1887

IDA
HITLER
b. 9/23/1886
d. 1/2/1888

OTTO
HITLER
b. Autumn 1887
d. several
days
later

ADOLF
HITLER
b. 4/20/1889
d. Berlin
4/30/1945

EDMUND
HITLER
b. 3/24/1894
d. 2/2/1900

PAULA
HITLER
b. 1/21/1896
d. 1950s

WILLIAM
PATRICK
HITLER

ANGELA
("GELI")
RAUBAL

LEO
RAUBAL, JR.

10. Hitler's family tree.

11. Nazi version
of the family tree.

12. Angela and Adolf went to school here. The schoolmaster recalled that Adolf was "mentally very much alert, obedient but lively."

13. Adolf (top row, second from right) had excellent grades at the elementary school and also attended choir school at the monastery under the tutelage of Padre Bernhard Gröner. Hitler later told a friend that as a small boy it had been his "ardent wish to become a priest." On the way to choir school Hitler would pass by a stone arch in which the monastery's coat of arms had been carved—a swastika its most prominent feature.

14. Padre Gröner.

15. The Hitler family moved in 1898 and then again
in 1899 to this house in Leonding, a suburb of Linz.

16. In the Leonding school Adolf was a success. He got good marks, learned to
draw, and enjoyed himself reading Karl May's cowboy and Indian stories and
then re-enacting them. When the Boer War broke out, Adolf became inspired
with German nationalism and also played war. These games were influential
in his life. Later he claimed that he got the idea for concentration camps from
the British camps in South Africa and from American Indian reservations.

17. After Hitler became Chancellor the Karl May Museum was established near
Dresden.

18. Hitler at sixteen as sketched by F. Sturmberger, a schoolmate who still lives in Linz. Having discontinued his studies, Adolf was enjoying the carefree life of a young Bohemian dandy. He painted, went to the opera, and daydreamed; he read voraciously, filled sketchbooks with drawings, and made plans to redesign the buildings of Linz.

19. In 1905 he finally made a real friend, Gustl Kubizek, who dreamed of being a musician. Hitler would orate for hours of his own plans to be a great architect and artist. It was like a scene from a play, recalled Kubizek. "I could only stand gaping and passive, forgetting to applaud."

20. Hitler's Certificate of Origin, 1906. Every move in Germany and Austria had to be recorded at the local police station.

21. Postwar photograph of the Spital farmhouse bedroom where Hitler and his mother slept during his happy summer vacations there. His mother was born in this house, and his father as a boy lived next door.

22. The family moved across the Danube to an apartment in the suburb of Urfahr. Early in 1907 the idyllic life of young Adolf came to an end when he learned that his beloved mother had cancer.

23. Dr. Edmund Bloch, a Jew, treated Frau Hitler. One breast was removed but the cancer persisted, so Dr. Bloch, with Hitler's permission, began a painful iodoform treatment on the open wound. Adolf nursed his mother during her last agonizing weeks; she died on December 21, 1907. This picture was taken in 1938 by order of Martin Bormann for the Führer's "personal film cassette." The inscription reads: "The Führer often sat on the chair beside the desk."

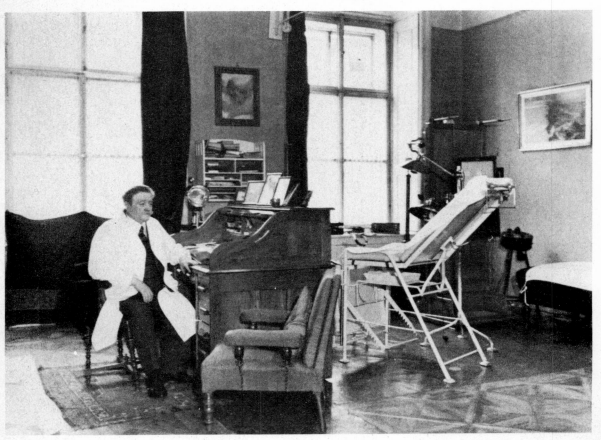

24. Asyl für Obdachlose.

25. Dormitory in the Asyl für Obdachlose.

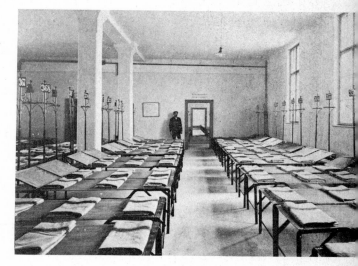

26. Hitler's sketch of Auersberg Palace, Vienna, 1911–12. Architecturally accurate, but the figures are far out of proportion.

27. On August 1, 1914, a large enthusiastic crowd at Munich's Feldherrnhalle learns that war has been declared against Russia. No one wanted war more than Hitler, the supreme German nationalist, and he enlisted in the 1st Bavarian Infantry Regiment. "I am not ashamed to say that, overcome with rapturous enthusiasm, I fell to my knees and thanked Heaven from an overflowing heart for granting me the good fortune of being allowed to live at this time." To him it meant the realization of the Greater Germany he had dreamed of since youth.

28. Military identification.

29. Hitler (seated, far right) kept his dog, Fuchsl, in the front lines for several years and taught him a variety of circus tricks such as climbing up and down a ladder. Hitler was crushed when Fuchsl was stolen in 1917. "The swine who stole my dog doesn't realize what he did to me," he wrote.

30–31. The western front, 1917–18. In December 1914 Hitler had written his landlord, Herr Popp, of his first action against the enemy: ". . . with pride I can say our regiment handled itself heroically from the first day on—we lost almost all our officers and our company has only two sergeants now."

32. Casualty announcement. On October 7, 1917, a shell exploded near Hitler, wounding him. He begged his commanding officer to let him stay with the regiment but he was evacuated to a hospital near Berlin.

33. Hitler decorated with the Iron Cross.

34. The Strasser brothers, all lieutenants. Gregor (center) later became a staunch supporter of Hitler. Otto (right) became a reluctant one, and then a sworn enemy of Nazism. The third brother, Bernhard, is now a priest in Nebraska.

35. A rare display of humor in 1918.

36. The Big Three: Field Marshal von Hindenburg, the Kaiser, and General Erich Ludendorff, the junior but dominant member of the German high command. Both Hindenburg and Ludendorff later played important roles in Hitler's career.

37. Hitler's hospital room.

38. He was treated by a psychiatrist, Professor Edmund Forster, for hysterical blindness. By early November his sight returned, but when he heard on November 9 that the Kaiser was abdicating and that the fatherland had become a republic, he again lost his sight. "That night I resolved that, if I recovered my sight, I would enter politics." As he lay in despair on his cot several nights later, he was suddenly delivered from his misery by a "supernatural vision." Like St. Joan he heard voices summoning him to save Germany. All at once "a miracle came to pass"—he could see again! And he vowed he would "become a politician and devote his energies to carrying out the command he had received."

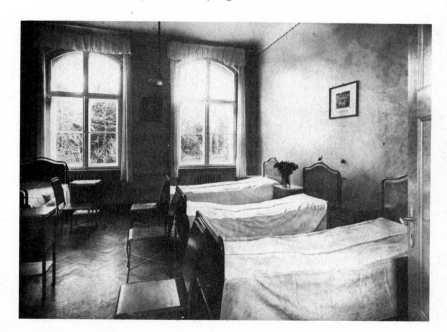

39. Defeated German troops cross the Rhine at Koblenz.

40. The Guards enter Berlin.

TWO

Birth of the Nazi Party
1918–1923

At the end of November 1918, Hitler left Pasewalk hospital and headed for Munich. He must have passed through Berlin, which was in the hands of the left-wing Spartacists. Free Corps troops, veterans of the Great War who shared with Hitler the shame of surrender and rising Communism, marched into Berlin, where most of the governmental buildings were occupied by the Spartacists, and crushed the Red centers of resistance. Berlin—eventually all of Germany—would probably have gone Communist but for the Free Corps, who also murdered the Spartacist leaders, including Rosa "Red Rose" Luxemburg.

In Munich Hitler found himself in the new Bavarian Socialist Republic. Its leader, Kurt Eisner, appeared to be the very model of a revolutionary and the tool of Moscow. He was, in fact, the very antithesis of the ruthless, pragmatic Bolshevik. He was striving for a unique kind of radical democracy. But the January 1919 elections had brought a resounding victory for the middle-class parties and a demand for Eisner's resignation.

The March Communist revolution in Hungary, led by Béla Kun, inspired one in Munich that April. In retaliation for murders of workers by attacking Free Corps troops, the Reds slaughtered some of their hostages. On May Day Free Corps troops marched into Munich to the cheers of the relieved citizenry. In vengeance these troops randomly executed more than a thousand so-called Reds.

The Red regime in Munich and the harsh Treaty of Versailles imposed on Germany a month later changed Hitler's life and turned the course of world history. He blamed Jews for the revolutions, since most of the leaders, including Rosa Luxemburg and Eisner, were Jewish. He decided to form his own political party and that autumn took over a little group calling itself the German Workers' Party. Its program was a bizarre combination of socialism, nationalism, and anti-Semitism. This moribund party, he recalled with amusement, was "nothing more than a debating society." In quick order he transformed it into the German National Socialist Party with a rapidly growing membership.

On February 24, 1920, Hitler spoke to his first mass audience. The great Festsaal of Munich's Hofbräuhaus was jammed with almost two thousand people. Hitler presented the twenty-five-point program of the new Nazi Party. It was accepted enthusiastically and Hitler became a political force in Bavaria.

In the next two years, the Nazi Party grew into a formidable force.

Runaway inflation, the Ruhr crisis, growing resentment over the Versailles Treaty, and Mussolini's recent march on Rome inspired Hitler to stage his own march on Berlin. It began in Munich on November 9, 1923, and started from a beer hall, the Bürgerbräukeller. It ended in the death of sixteen comrades and his own imprisonment.

41. On the morning of February 21, Kurt Eisner wrote out his resignation and was en route to the Landtag to deliver it when he was assassinated by Count Anton Arco-Valley, a cavalry officer who had been refused entrance into an anti-Semitic group since his mother was Jewish.

I. Of Old Vienna. Hitler water color.

II. Ruins of Becelaere, Belgium. Hitler water color.

III. Food market and St. Peter's Church, Munich. Hitler water color.

IV. German postcards of World War I, 1914 . . .

V. . . . and 1915.

VI. "In the Beginning Was the Word," by Hoyer.

VII. During 1923, inflation was so severe that an egg could cost a million marks. Here, a five-hundred-million-mark note is converted into one for twenty billion.

VIII. Hitler Putsch, November 9, 1923, Munich. Painting by Schmitt.

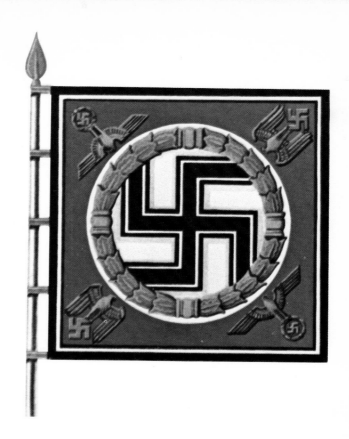

IX. "Führer Standard" for Hitler's
Mercedes, designed by his private
chauffeur, Colonel Kempka.

X. Detail showing the "Führer Standard" as it was mounted on the Führer auto.

XI. "High Nazi Morale amid the Rubble," by Tschech.

42–43. Revolution
in Munich, 1919.

44. Sterneckerbräu in Munich where NSDAP was founded in 1920.

45. Hitler in early party days.

46. Gottfried Feder, founder of the German Fighting League for the Breaking of Interest Slavery, inspired Hitler in the early days.

47. Dietrich Eckart—poet, playwright, drug addict, and coffeehouse intellectual —became Hitler's first mentor. He gave Hitler a trench coat, corrected his grammar, took him to good restaurants, and introduced him to influential citizens.

48. Alfred Rosenberg (wearing broad-brimmed hat) also exerted great influence on Hitler. A fanatic anti-Semite and anti-Marxist, he had brought to Munich from his native Estonia a copy of the *Protocols of the Elders of Zion*. This book purported to prove that the Jews conspired to conquer the world and was supporting evidence for Hitler's own prejudices.

49. Early party meetings at Hofbräuhaus in Munich. Gregor Strasser is at Hitler's right. To his left Franz Xavier Schwarz, party treasurer; Max Amann, the party's publisher and the Führer's former sergeant; and Ulrich Graf, the bodyguard.

50. Pistol permit issued to Hitler by the Bavarian police on November 26, 1921.

51. Leaving party meeting.

52. Hitler and friends at the Café Heck, one of his favorite meeting places.

53. Hitler spoke on the Marsfeld in Munich, January 28, 1923. He denounced the Treaty of Versailles: "Down with the November criminals!"

54. Hitler speaking near Munich on April 15, 1923.

55. Hitler and Julius Streicher, the virulent anti-Semite, on a Munich sidewalk.

56. Hitler and Streicher at the German Day Celebration in Nuremberg that September. The streets were a sea of Nazi and Bavarian flags as the crowd roared "Heil!" waved handkerchiefs, and tossed flowers at General Ludendorff and the marching units.

57. Preparing for the Beer Hall Putsch. Ludendorff; Dr. Friedrich Weber (wearing glasses), veterinary and leader of the Bund Oberland; and Hermann Göring, then leader of the SA.

58. The Bürgerbräukeller.

59. Göring in battle dress.

60. The Beer Hall Putsch, November 9, 1923.

THREE

A Mind in the Making
1924–1930

After the Putsch's failure, Hitler escaped to the country villa of his Harvard-educated aide, Ernst (Putzi) Hanfstaengl, where an SA doctor set his dislocated shoulder. A few days later the police arrested him there and took him to Landsberg Prison.

In Landsberg Prison Hitler, depressed and sullen, went on a hunger strike for several weeks. At first he refused even to give evidence for his coming trial.

At the trial in Munich in 1924, Hitler turned prosecutor and confounded the court. Even so he was convicted of treason and sentenced to five years in prison. On the day of the sentencing, the courtroom was crowded with women bearing flowers for their hero; several requested permission to bathe in Hitler's tub. The request was denied.

Returned to his cell at Landsberg, Hitler proselytized the warden and most of the guards. He also began dictating *Mein Kampf* to his chauffeur, Emil Maurice.

"If at the beginning of the war and during the war," Hitler declared, "twelve or fifteen thousand of these Hebraic corrupters of the nation had been subjected to poison gas . . . the sacrifice of millions at the front would not have been in vain. On the contrary, twelve thousand scoundrels eliminated at the right moment and a million orderly, worthwhile Germans might perhaps have been saved for the future."

In July 1924 when a Bohemian-German National Socialist visiting him in Landsberg Prison asked if he had changed his position concerning the Jews, Hitler replied: "Yes, yes, it is quite right that I have changed my opinion concerning the methods to fight Jewry. I have realized that up to now I have been much too soft! While working out my book I have come to the realization that in the future the most severe methods of fighting will have to be used to let us come through successfully. . . . For Juda is the plague of the world."

It took Hitler two years to rebuild the party because of dissension be-

61. Landsberg Prison.

tween its factions, and a public-speaking ban. But by 1927 he had patched the differences in the party—winning over both Gregor Strasser and Joseph Goebbels, leaders of the more Marxist-oriented northern faction—and was again permitted by the authorities to speak publicly.

Hitler's skill in speaking had improved and he now addressed himself to the basic concerns of the average German. No longer was he the racist fanatic, the frightening revolutionary, of the Beer Hall Putsch, but instead a reasonable man who sought only the welfare of the Fatherland. His "reasonable" words masked one of the most radical programs in history: conquest of Europe by any means and the elimination of the Jews. It was a program that, in one way or another, would affect the lives of most people on earth.

In September 1927, 20,000 Nazis flooded into Nuremberg for the third Party Day. There Hitler called for more living space for the German people.

62. Hitler's sister came to the prison expecting to find him despondent. "Never in my life will I forget this hour," she wrote their brother, Alois Hitler, Jr. "I spoke with him for half an hour. His spirit and soul were again at a high level. . . . That which he has accomplished is as solid as rock. The goal and the victory is only a question of time. God grant it be soon." Once more Hitler had bounced back from adversity. The discovery of this letter ended the myth that his family did not enthusiastically support his political career.

The same year he wrote another book which was not to be published in his own lifetime. Perhaps he did not want to reveal the ultimate mass-murder plan that hid behind its vague wording. Shortly after finishing this work, Hitler voluntarily visited a Munich psychiatrist, Dr. Alfred Schwenninger, to allay a "fear of cancer." This paranoid fear, along with his obsession to eliminate all Jews, persisted to the last days of Hitler's life.

63. Hitler reading in prison.

64. Hitler's cell at Landsberg.

65. Rare picture Hitler autographed while in prison.

66. With (left to right) Emil Maurice, his chauffeur; Colonel Hermann Kriebel, military commander of the Putsch; Rudolf Hess; and Dr. Friedrich Weber of the Bund Oberland. Ilse Pröhl, later Frau Hess, smuggled in the camera that took this and other prison pictures.

67. Paroled and freed in December 1924,
Hitler returned to Munich and politics.

68. One of his first visits after prison was on Christmas Eve to the Hanfstaengl's
new home, Haus Tiefland, in Herzog Park. He entertained the young son, Egon,
by imitating a World War battle, reproducing the noise of howitzers, 75s, and
machine guns. Alone with Frau Hanfstaengl, he dropped to his knees and put his
head in her lap. "If I only had someone to take care of me," he said. She asked
him why he didn't marry. "I can never marry because my life is dedicated to my
country."

69. Hitler at a meeting in party headquaters about 1925. From left to right,
Philipp Bouhler, executive secretary of the party; Arthur Ziegler; Alfred Rosen-
berg; Walter Buch; Franz Xavier Schwartz; Hitler; Gregor Strasser; Heinrich
Himmler.

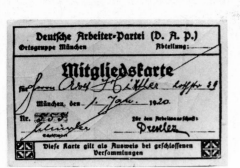

70. Hitler's first party card. He was only the seventh member, but, to make the membership look larger, it was numbered 555.

71. Hitler's party card issued in 1927 made him number one.

72. Hitler at a rally with the Blood Flag, the banner carried in the Putsch.

73. A budding Brownshirt.

74. Göring, early leader of the SA, reviewing newly formed SS troops.

75. Early picture of Hitler in full Sturmabteilung (SA) uniform. By 1930 the Brownshirt storm troopers had grown into a powerful force of 60,000.

76–78. Hitler addressing the SA.

79. Hitler fraternizing with storm troopers.

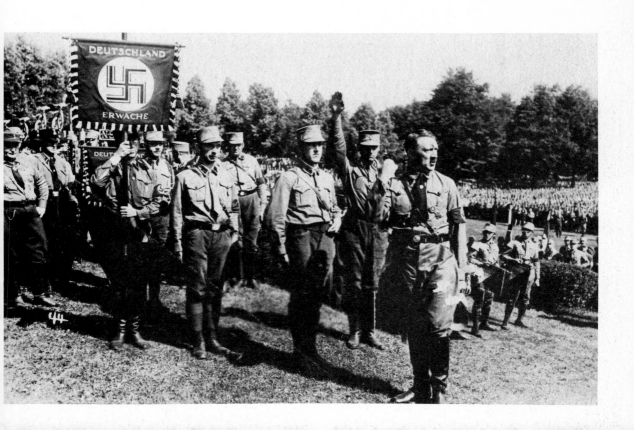

80. Horst Wessel, at left, looking over his own shoulder, the poet and future martyr of the SA.

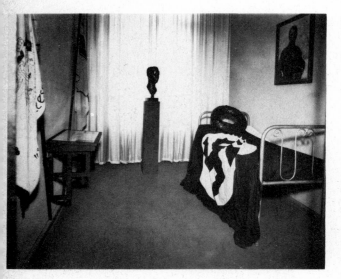

81. The room where Wessel was shot fatally by a Communist in 1930. A marching song he had written became the party anthem.

82. On January 1, 1931, the Brown House, new headquarters of the party, opened.

83. Hitler at work in his office at the Brown House.

Ananas-
Bowle

84. Hitler liked to relax downstairs in the small refreshment room, where he sat at the "Führer" table.

85. In 1931 Hitler picked a strong leader for the SA, Ernst Röhm.

86. The rise of the Brownshirts brought on retaliation. In October 1931 the Berlin police evicted them from their barracks.

FOUR

The Loves of Adolf Hitler

The great love of Adolf Hitler's youth was Stephanie Jansten, who also lived in Urfahr. He composed numerous love poems to her, including one entitled "Hymn to the Beloved," and read them to his faithful friend, Kubizek. Adolf confessed that he had never spoken a word to her. Kubizek urged him to introduce himself, but he refused and never did more than dream about her. Fancy built on fancy. If all else failed, he told Gustl, he would kidnap her. Then in despair he decided to jump off the bridge into the Danube, taking Stephanie with him in a suicide pact. Years later it would come as a complete surprise to Stephanie to learn Germany's Führer had once been her devoted admirer.

Hitler's experience with women seems to have been limited to fantasy until he entered politics. Some early associates felt sure that Jenny Haug, sister of one of his drivers, was his mistress. She was devoted to him and reportedly carried a pistol as voluntary bodyguard. Frau Helene Hanfstaengl could not take this story seriously, and told her husband that Hitler was "a neuter." But one of his closest companions during those days disagreed. Emil Maurice, who also served as Hitler's chauffeur, claimed that they "chased girls together" and would spend time at the art academy and in artists' studios admiring models posing in the nude. Calling himself "Herr Wolf," Hitler would roam the night spots and streets for girls. As Maurice was especially attractive to women, he would act as go-between. Every so often, according to Maurice, Hitler would entertain one of these conquests-by-proxy in his little room on the Thierschstrasse. In Berchtesgaden he flirted with a sixteen-year-old girl, Mitzi Reiter. Years later Mitzi claimed that Hitler went beyond flirtation. On one walk around the lake he suddenly kissed her. "He said, 'I want to crush you.' He was full of wild passion." Before long they were lovers, and while she had visions of marriage, he only talked of renting an apartment in Munich where they could live together. During the summer of 1927, in a fit of jealousy, Mitzi tried to commit suicide by choking herself with a clothesline tied to a door.

87. Geli Raubal with her mother (left) and Paula Hitler.

88–89. Geli as a young woman.

Hitler's true love, however, was Geli Raubal, the daughter of his half sister, Angela. She was nineteen years younger and this time it was Hitler who was the jealous partner. Once he angrily objected to what she wanted to wear at the Fasching carnival. "You might as well go naked," he said, and designed a proper costume. When Hitler moved to a nine-room apartment on Prinzregentenplatz in 1929, Angela let the twenty-one-year-old Geli take a room in Uncle Alf's new lodging while pursuing her medical studies in Munich. Although maintaining the role of uncle, Hitler discreetly began to act more like a suitor. He would take her occasionally to the theater or the Café Heck. "I love Geli," he confided to a friend, "and I could marry her." At the same time he was determined to remain a bachelor. There was no doubt that Geli was impressed by her uncle's growing fame; and his fondness for her went far beyond that of an uncle. But although he deeply loved Geli it is unlikely they had sexual relations. He was too reserved to openly court any woman and too cautious to ruin his political career by taking a mistress into his own apartment—particularly the daughter of a half sister.

By 1931 Geli had become secretly engaged to Maurice, and it was

90. A postcard of Berchtesgaden sent Hitler by Geli in October 1928: "On a stroll to Berchtesgaden we came across this postcard of our house. Wolf [Hitler's dog] feels very well here, we don't have him on a leash: he always runs about free. Only his qualities as a watch dog are very poor. He has forgotten how to bark. . . . Greetings from your little niece. Geli."

known among the inner circle that they were lovers. Finally Maurice confessed to Hitler. He flew into a rage and dismissed him as his chauffeur. That summer Geli became involved with another young man, an artist from Austria, and Hitler again tried to break up the liaison. On September 17, after Hitler heard that Geli had phoned her voice teacher that she was taking no more lessons and leaving for Vienna, they had a violent argument, with Hitler storming out of the apartment to head for an important meeting in the north.

91. Early picture of Emil Maurice with Hitler in Landsberg Prison.

92. Eva Braun as a child.

93. Eva (fourth from right in bottom row) at convent school.

94. "My first Fasching costume."

95. Eva with cat.

96. Eva (left) with Hans, her first love, and her sister Gretl.

Geli locked herself in her room with instructions not to be disturbed. During the night the assistant housekeeper, Frau Reichert, heard a dull sound but thought nothing of it. But the next morning she became alarmed when she found Geli's door still locked. A locksmith opened the door. Geli was lying on the floor next to a couch, a pistol beside her. She was shot in the heart.

Hitler had just left his hotel in Nuremberg to continue his journey to Hamburg when he learned of the tragedy. He was torn with grief. For several days he went into seclusion and refused to eat. It was felt that his political life might be over. Then he came out of his depression and

97. Eva sits on a lap.

98. "Mammy!"

99. Eva meets Hitler for the first time.

100. The Führer's mistress.

101. Eva with puppies.

102. Eva's dressing table, with their photographs side by side.

headed north for the meeting. At breakfast the following morning he refused to eat a piece of ham. "It is like eating a corpse!" he told Göring.
Nothing on earth, he vowed, would make him eat meat again.

Hitler's next love was Eva Braun. He had met her two years previously and occasionally took the seventeen-year-old girl to tea at the
Carlton Café or a movie in Schwabing. On the day Geli had her argument with Hitler, Anny Winter, the housekeeper, had seen her angrily
tear a letter in four parts. The housekeeper pieced them together and
read a note from Eva to Hitler thanking him for his wonderful invitation
to the theater. "I am counting the hours until I have the joy of another
meeting."

In 1932 Eva, who worked at the shop of photographer Heinrich
Hoffmann, became Hitler's mistress. On the first of November she shot
herself with a pistol as Geli had done. While Eva had fallen desperately
in love, Hitler had become so involved with the elections that he spent
little time with her. To add to her misery, a rival for the Führer's affections showed her photographs of the electioneering Hitler posing with
beautiful women. After writing a farewell letter to her lover, she shot herself in the neck, severing an artery. She got to the phone and gasped out
to a surgeon that she had shot herself in the heart. Hitler left the campaign trail to visit the private clinic where Eva was recovering and
learned from the doctor that she had done it for love of him. "Obviously
I must now look after the girl," he told Hoffmann, who objected. Who
could possibly blame him for what happened? "And who do you think
would believe that?" said Hitler, who knew more about human nature.
Also, there was no guarantee that she might not try again.

41

FIVE

The Brown Revolution

1932–1933

In early 1932 Hitler decided to run for President of Germany against Field Marshal Paul von Hindenburg. Still an Austrian, he hastily became a citizen of Germany through the machinations of the Nazi Minister of Interior in Braunschweig, who made him a councilor of that state.

The campaign was tumultuous, for economic depression and political rancor had turned Germany into a quasi-battlefield. Hitler appealed to both the defeated middle-aged and the idealistic youth with a simple slogan: "For Freedom and Bread." But Hindenburg remained the choice of the solid burghers and won by more than 7,000,000 votes. However, since there were many parties, the Field Marshal did not have quite a majority of the votes and a runoff election between the two leaders was necessary.

This time Hindenburg did not make a single speech, spurring rumors that he was dying, and on Sunday, April 10, Hitler got an additional 2,000,000 votes, raising his total to 13,418,051. Hindenburg raised his total by less than 700,000, yet still had a solid majority of 53 per cent. In London the *Daily Telegraph* predicted that this was the end of Adolf Hitler.

Germany was still torn by dissension, and the new government of Chancellor Franz von Papen was forced to invoke emergency powers. Using the argument that the Prussian Government could no longer deal with the Reds, Papen made himself Reich Commissioner of Prussia, which not only meant the end of parliamentary government in that state but would also set an unfortunate precedent for the future. Any political leader willing to use the emergency authority granted by the constitution could make himself dictator.

Hitler entered the Reichstag elections set for the end of July and in the last two weeks of the campaign appeared in some fifty cities, generating rabid enthusiasm wherever he went.

103. Moments earlier Hitler was made a German citizen. To his right, adjutant Schaub; to his left, adjutant Brückner and Hess.

This time the Nazis won almost 14,000,000 votes, half a million more than the combined total of their closest rivals the Social Democrats and Communists. Elated, Hitler now decided, against protests from Goebbels and Strasser, to run for Chancellor.

During the following hectic campaign, he was distracted by the attempted suicide of Eva Braun and embarrassed when Goebbels joined the Reds in a Berlin transport workers' strike. But it was not the first time that the two parties, with many goals in common, had fought together.

The election on November 6 was a disaster for Hitler. He lost more than 2,000,000 votes along with thirty-four seats in the Reichstag. The Hitler flood tide had finally ebbed and the strategy of gaining power through the ballot box had reached a dead end. Hitler is said to have threatened suicide. A month later Gregor Strasser, disgusted with Hitler's chief advisers, resigned from the Nazi Party. "Göring is a brutal egotist who cares nothing for Germany, as long as he becomes something," Strasser complained to Hans Frank. "Goebbels is a limping devil and basically two-faced, Röhm is a pig. This is the Old Guard of the Führer. It is terrible!"

The future of the NSDAP was bleak. Goebbels wrote in his diary on December 24, "The past is difficult and the future is cloudy and dark. The terrible loneliness overwhelms me with hopelessness. All possibilities and hopes have disappeared." Hitler was even more depressed. "I have given up all hope," he wrote to Frau Wagner after thanking her for a

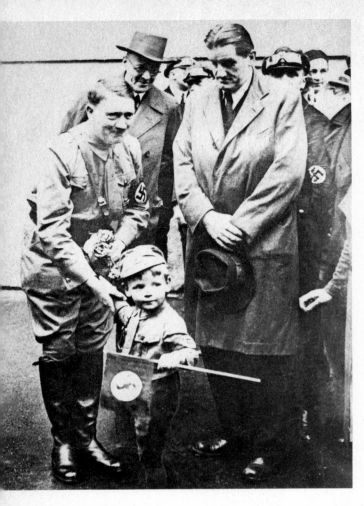

104. Hitler electioneering with Putzi Hanfstaengl, who was now acting as his foreign press secretary.

105. "Workers, Vote for the Frontline Soldier Hitler!"

ARBEITER

WÄHLT DEN FRONTSOLDATEN

HITLER!

106. Winning votes from farmers in East Prussia.

107. Hitler covered Germany by car and plane.

Christmas present. "Nothing will every come of my dreams." He had no hope left; his opponents were too powerful. "As soon as I am sure that everything is lost you know what I'll do, I was always determined to do it. I cannot accept defeat. I will stick to my word and end my life with a bullet."

At this bleak moment Hitler asked Erik Jan Hanussen to cast his horoscope. The famous seer presented a rhymed prediction to the Führer on New Year's Day, 1933. Hitler's power would begin in exactly thirty days.

On January 4 Hitler met secretly with Chancellor von Papen at the home of Baron Kurt von Schröder, one of a group of wealthy men who had recently petitioned Hindenburg to appoint him Chancellor. In the next few weeks there followed other secret meetings and deals with industrialists, military men, and right-wing political leaders. Each group thought it could use Hitler to smash the Reds and control the unions, and so the incredible occurred on January 30: Hitler, who had recently been repudiated by the German electorate, was made Chancellor of the Reich.

A few weeks later, a young Dutch member of "International Communists," a tiny splinter group which opposed Moscow policies, helped Hitler make the first giant step to dictatorship. Marinus van der Lubbe, in a protest against capitalism, set afire the Reichstag. Hitler used this one-man action as an excuse to invoke emergency powers to put down the Red revolution. The Cabinet approved the measure and President von Hindenburg signed the decree without comment.

On March 21 the new Reichstag opened in Potsdam. The ceremony, stage-managed by Goebbels, convinced those present—the military, the Junkers, and the monarchists—that Hitler was subservient to President von Hindenburg and would follow the Prussian ideal.

But two days later, at the first session of the Reichstag, Hitler made it clear that he was subservient to no one. SA and SS men patrolled Berlin's Kroll Opera House, temporary site of the Reichstag, and behind its stage hung a huge swastika flag as a reminder of who was going to be master

108. One of Hitler's favorite World War One heroes, pilot Ernst Udet, with the Crown Prince.

109. Prince August Wilhelm, popularly known as "Auwi," feared the spread of Communism, and his conversion influenced Prince Philip von Hessen, a nephew of the Kaiser and grandson of Queen Victoria, to join in support of Hitler.

of Germany. There was wild applause as Hitler strode up to the podium. He vowed to respect private property, give aid to peasants and the middle class, end unemployment, and promote peace with the world. All he needed was enactment of the Law for Alleviating the Distress of People and Reich. This enabling law would give him overriding although temporary authority in the land, but he made it sound moderate. The Social

Democrats protested but were outvoted 441 to 94, and the Nazis, with outstretched arms, triumphantly sang the "Horst Wessel Song." Democracy was overthrown in the German parliament with scarcely a protest.

This victory brought into the open a number of industrialists who had secretly supported Hitler. Now the steel magnate Krupp openly heiled acquaintances in the street. The bureaucrats stayed at their posts to keep the machinery of government running smoothly. Intellectual and literary figures began espousing the regeneration of Germany through Hitler. It was a revolution, but since on the surface almost bloodless, Germany received it without alarm. There was little resistance because Hitler kept within the law. He had won the temporary confidence of most Germans by an evolutionary policy, only gradually accumulating power in his own hands.

On April 1 Hitler instituted a boycott against the Jews. Storm troopers were posted before the doors of Jewish shops and offices. Jews were removed from all civil service posts and the number of Jews in higher institutions were reduced.

Hitler's personal popularity increased with every speech and public appearance. His birthday on April 20 was widely celebrated.

On May Day, Hitler expounded on the dignity of labor at a rally at Templehof airfield. The next morning the SA and SS, with the help of police, seized union offices throughout the nation. It was the end of organized labor.

The next month he took an even more important step. He outlawed the Social Democratic Party as "hostile to the nation and state." A few days later two other parties voluntarily disbanded, and Hitler proposed to his Cabinet that Germany become a one-party state. The measure passed without dissent. On Bastille Day, July 14, it became law. Germany, like the Soviet Union, was now controlled by a single party and that party by a single man.

The majority of the German people now supported Hitler. A street ruffian a few months earlier, he had been made respectable by the power and prestige of his office. The Führer's growing popularity was shown in the crowds that flocked to his birthplace. Their admiration was growing into a cult. Worshipers even journeyed by bus to honor the birthplace of his mother in Spital. They descended on the farmhouse where the boy Hitler had spent his summers. They climbed on the roof to take pictures, found their way in the courtyard to wash at the wooden trough as if it contained holy water, and chipped pieces from the large stones supporting the barn.

Hitler was so secure in the affections of his own people that he decided to present a similarly affable face to the world. That August he allowed Hanfstaengl, now his foreign press secretary, to publish a book of anti-Hitler caricatures from German and foreign magazines and newspapers. Entitled *Fact vs. Ink*, the jacket showed a good-natured Führer laughing indulgently at his critics. This kind of propanganda appalled

110. Hitler and Hanfstaengl arrive at Oberwiesenfeld, the Munich airport, near which Hitler will address a large crowd gathered in a vast tent: "He ran the gamut of emotions and a wave of frenzied enthusiasm swept the mass," Hanfstaengl's son Egon recalled. All shouted and applauded wildly as a single entity. Eleven-year-old Egon noticed one incongruous couple—a professor and a charwoman—leaving the tent "amid the tumultuous acclamation, talking together excitedly, fraternizing in fact."

Goebbels, but Hitler was swayed by Hanfstaengl's reasoning that the British and Americans would be impressed.

In October Hitler discarded his cautious approach to international politics. He announced on October 14 that Germany was withdrawing from the League of Nations and, calling a plebiscite for his action, cannily set it for November 12, the day after the anniversary of the Armistice. Hindenburg still regarded Hitler as a house painter and corporal, but on election eve, he finally identified himself with the Führer and

111. Checking the latest news.

112. A picnic lecture. Magda Goebbels is to Hitler's left.

113. Laughing with Adolf Wagner, Gauleiter of Bavaria.

broadcast an appeal to the nation to "show to the world that we have restored German unity and with God's help shall preserve it." It was an invocation that few patriots could resist, and the next day 95.1 per cent of the electorate approved Hitler's foreign policy. The mandate was so overwhelming that he was able, within weeks, to pass a law unifying party and state. Germany now stood on the threshold of totalitarianism.

114. Occasionally he could spend a few days at his modest villa, Haus Wachenfeld, on the Obersalzberg.

115. Tenant strike in Berlin. Reds join Nazis.

116. Depressed after his 1932 defeat, Hitler tried to find solace that December in his beloved Berchtesgaden.

117. Official proclamation of Hitler as Reichschancellor of Germany, 1933. President von Hindenburg's signature dwarfs Hitler's, and for several months Hitler remained in Hindenburg's shadow.

118. United States Nazis in the Yorkville section of New York City celebrate Hitler's great victory.

119. Hitler's Cabinet. From left to right, Seldte, Guertner, Goebbels, Elz von Rubenach, Hitler, Göring, Blomberg, Frick, Neurath, Schacht, Schwerin von Krosigk, unknown, Papen.

120. Hitler makes his first speech to the nation. February 1, 1933.

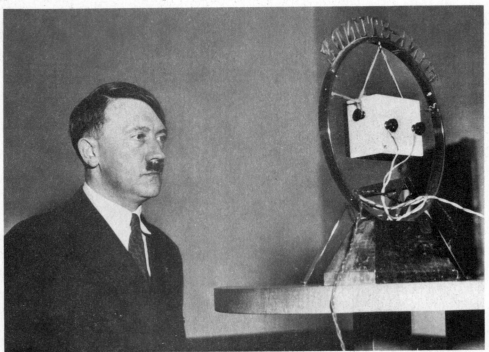

121. The Reichstag fire.

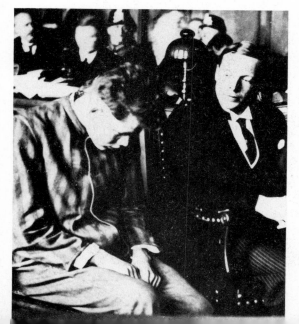

122. Marinus van der Lubbe on trial.

123. Hitler is still concerned as he listens to the results of the March 5 election. The Nazis received only 43.9 per cent of the votes, and it took those of his nationalist allies to give him a bare majority in the parliament.

124. Hindenburg and son drive to the Potsdam garrison church.

125. Blomberg, Hindenburg, Hitler, Göring, and Hindenburg's son, Oskar, honor the war dead a few days before the Potsdam ceremony.

126. Chancellor Hitler plays a secondary role during an address by Hindenburg at a youth convention in the Lustgarten in May.

127. Anti-Jewish action: "Germans! Don't buy from Jews!"

128. Hitler also feared that he was part Jewish and in 1931 had sent his private lawyer, Hans Frank, into Austria to check. Frank returned with the disconcerting report that Hitler's grandmother Schicklgruber had been "working for a Jewish family named Frankenberger when she gave birth to her son. And Frankenberger—this happened in the late 1830s—paid a paternity allowance on behalf of his nineteen-year-old son from the birth of the Schicklgruber woman's son until he was 14." Postwar research has tended to prove that there was little chance of Hitler's having had Jewish ancestry, but at the time he was badly shaken by Frank's report and lied to him in an attempt to discredit it.

129. Hitler honored with Goethe and Henry Ford—all nonsmokers, nondrinkers.

130. April 20, 1933: Happy Birthday!

131–132. Hands reach for the Führer.

133. On May 10 students, organized by Goebbels (once a novelist himself), burned more than 20,000 "subversive" books, including those of Remarque, Mann, Brecht, Hemingway, Proust, Zola, Upton Sinclair, and H. G. Wells. "The soul of the German people," Goebbels told the students, "can now express itself."

134. That summer Nazi mass marriages were staged: Fifty couples, all belonging to the militant "German Christian" group, parade through Berlin.

135. Braunau birthplace with banners.

136. Spital: "It was like a country fair," recalled a Hitler relative. "They painted swastikas on the cows and would parade around singing Hitler songs."

138. From a French language paper in Cairo, May 1933: "If strangers accuse us of barbarity, we will give you another turn of the screw!"

137. From *Der Wahr Jacob*, Berlin, November 1931: "They call Mr. Hitler the drummer. Drumming has long been known as the most primitive way to make oneself understood."

139. The year ends in triumph at Munich. Hitler and the Old Fighters follow the Blood Flag in a re-enactment of the march in 1923.

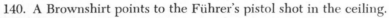

140. A Brownshirt points to the Führer's pistol shot in the ceiling.

141. Sister Pia, a heroine of the Putsch.

SIX

Year of Crises

1934

To counter a proposed alliance in the spring of 1934 between France and the Soviet Union, Hitler sought a strong ally. In June he set out for Italy to woo Mussolini—but with some reluctance. Hitler had been a hero-worshiper of Il Duce since his march on Rome. This, in fact, had inspired him to stage a march of his own which became the disastrous Beer Hall Putsch. While in prison in 1924, however, he had sent Göring to Italy to get a two-million-lire loan from the Fascists. But Mussolini had turned him down peremptorily on the grounds that the NSDAP was a minor party, and Hitler was still resentful.

Their historic meeting was doomed from the start. When Hitler stepped out of his plane at Lido airfield on June 14, he looked like a struggling salesman in his worn trench coat and blue serge suit. He was met by a Duce dressed in black shirt, jack boots, and glittering gold braid. Hitler acted like a schoolboy and didn't even know what to do with his fedora.

Their first conversation was a disaster, with Mussolini dominating the talk. Nor was Hitler favorably impressed by the Italian Navy when he saw sailors' washing flying from the masts. At their final meeting on a golf course, Il Duce was openly bored by Hitler's talk and the Führer left Venice stung by the realization that he had been not only snubbed by Mussolini but outmaneuvered diplomatically.

Upon Hitler's return home he was presented with a major crisis, the so-called Röhm Putsch. For some months Ernst Röhm, leader of the Brownshirts, had been demanding a military role for his men. The Army, naturally, opposed it. Secretly enemies of Röhm in the SS were already involved in a plot to destroy him. Himmler was then joined in the plot by Göring and Goebbels, both of whom were jealous of Röhm's growing power. They convinced Hitler that Röhm was about to stage a revolution, and so a bloody purge began, with many old scores being settled that had nothing to do with the so-called Putsch. Perhaps two hundred men—the exact number will never be known—were executed. Ironically, Röhm had no intention of revolting, and many of those murdered, including Gregor Strasser and Generals Kurt von Schleicher and Kurt von Bredow, had no connection with Röhm. The Nazis later made much of Röhm's homosexuality, but Hitler had known of this for several years. A man's private life was his own, he said. "But God help Röhm if he abuses young boys! Then he must go!"

The purge cost the NSDAP many of its most ardent members, the idealists of the SA. They were convinced that Röhm had merely attempted to bring Hitler back to the old ideals of National Socialism. "And here it was," recalled one of these men, "that Hitler really made his first true enemies, enemies in his own camp. For me and my friends, Hitler as a human being was finished."

Another crisis came a month later when Chancellor Engelbert Dollfuss of Austria was assassinated by Austrian Nazis. It was charged that Hitler had inspired the local Nazis, and he had to send Papen to Vienna to smooth over the affair. The shock of the Röhm purge, followed so quickly by that of the Dollfuss murder, affected Hindenburg. His health declined rapidly and soon he was confined to his bed. Now there was a crisis of a different nature. Who would succeed Hindenburg? Hitler made several trips to the Field Marshal's estate.

On August 2 Hitler's Cabinet passed a law combining the offices of President and Chancellor to become effective on the death of Hindenburg. Within the hour, he died on his spartan iron cot with the last words: "My Kaiser, my Fatherland." As a result of Hitler's legal maneuver, he now carried the title of Führer and Reich Chancellor. This meant he was also supreme commander of the armed forces. His first act was to summon General Werner von Blomberg, Minister of Defense, and the three commanders in chief of the armed forces. Hitler asked them to take an oath swearing before God to give their "unconditional obedience to Adolf Hitler, Führer of the Reich and its people, Supreme Commander of the Armed Forces." Before the end of the day, every officer and man in the land took the same oath of personal fealty. It was unprecedented, but there is no record of any officer having protested or even questioning the unique wording.

Twelve days later, the German people went to the polls, and almost 90 per cent voted their approval of Adolf Hitler as Hindenburg's successor.

That September Hitler's position was solidified at the Nuremberg Party Day Congress. He had selected Albert Speer as stage manager and Leni Riefenstahl as film maker. She accepted the assignment reluctantly on the grounds that she didn't know the difference between the SA and the SS. "That is why I want you to do it,'" said Hitler. "That will give it a fresh approach." She devised shots from planes, cranes, roller skates, and a tiny elevator attached to the tallest flagpole.

As the phenomenon of the Nuremberg rallies suggests, Hitler's appeal was, for many Germans, more than just political. "He is," Dr. Carl Jung observed at a later point in Hitler's life, "the first man to tell every German what he has been thinking and feeling all along in his unconscious about German fate, especially since the defeat in the World War, and the one characteristic which colors every German soul is the typical German inferiority complex, the complex of the younger brother, of the one who is always a bit late to the feast. Hitler's power is not political; it is *magic*." Of Hitler Freud said: "You cannot tell what a madman will do."

142. Hours after his humiliating visit with Mussolini, Hitler received another blow. Vice-chancellor von Papen delivered a speech at Marburg vigorously attacking Goebbels and the controlled press and then urging Hitler to break with Röhm and his so-called Second Revolution. Papen's assistant, who wrote the speech, will be murdered during the Röhm Putsch.

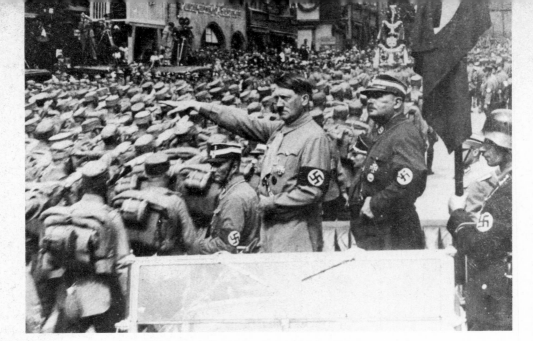

143. Hitler and Röhm, the closest of comrades, at the last Party Day.

144–45. Röhm at his Munich home. His mother agreed to this invasion of her privacy. "It is for my son," she said, "that the world may know him as he really is." To this day, Röhm's brother and his sister-in-law do not believe he was a homosexual.

146. The plot against Röhm had begun. Here he is flanked by Himmler, who initiated the scheme, and Hitler, who is not yet aware of it.

147. Goebbels (smiling, right) had entered the conspiracy.

148. Although by this time Hitler was under anti-Röhm pressure from all sides, Röhm still did not seem greatly worried about the rumors of a Göring-Goebbels-Himmler plot against him. "He had some feeling that there was something wrong," his sister-in-law recalled, "but still did not take it seriously. He never had any doubts whatsoever about Hitler."

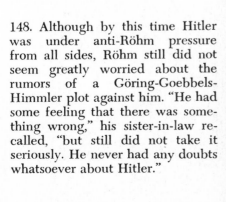

149. Assured that Röhm is a traitor (he actually was not), Hitler sent Sepp Dietrich, commander of his SS bodyguard, to Bad Wiessee, a lake resort south of Munich, to arrest Röhm and his group.

150. A little later Hitler decided to handle the matter in person. Here he is being briefed at the Munich airport. He would soon drive to Bad Wiessee and supervise the arrests.

151. General Blomberg (right) with Field Marshal August von Mackensen, hero of the Great War, who was one of the few officers to openly protest the assassinations of Generals von Schleicher and Bredow.

152. Dollfuss reviewing monarchist paratroops the year before his assassination.

153. One of the final meetings between Hitler and the failing Hindenburg.

154. August 1, 1934: Hitler's last visit to the Hindenburg estate. Oskar von Hindenburg escorted him to his father's bedside, telling his father that the Chancellor had one or two important matters to discuss. Hindenburg opened his eyes, stared at Hitler, and clamped his mouth shut.

155. The next day Hindenburg died.

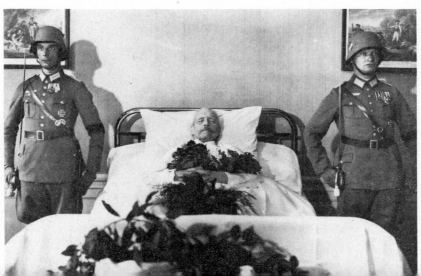

156. Hindenburg had wished to be buried near his estate, but Hitler insisted that burial take place at Tannenberg, scene of the Marshal's greatest triumph. Here Speer is making plans for a state funeral at the Tannenberg monument.

157. The body was placed on a catafalque in the center of the monument. Fires flamed from the sixty-foot towers. It reminded French Ambassador François-Poncet of a castle built by the Teutonic Knights.

158. Hitler relaxes with Eva (blonde) at Chiemsee, a lake not far from Berchtesgaden.

159. Eva rows.

160. By the fall of 1934 the Hitler movement had won wide acceptance. Here a Protestant rector blesses Nazi flags.

161. Hess, Speer, and Hitler.

162–63. Hitler with Leni Riefenstahl, and with Viktor Lutze who had succeeded Röhm as head of the SA.

164. Mock battle.

165. Hitler and Baldur von Schirach, the Reich youth leader, review the Hitler Jugend.

166. The SA and SS parade together. Months earlier, during the Röhm Putsch, the two groups had been fighting.

168. Aerial view of rally.

167. Speer's dramatic lighting effects.

SEVEN

War in Masquerade

1935–1936

The time had come at last to regain lost territories, and the first victory came on January 13, 1935, when the people of the Saar voted overwhelmingly to return to the Reich. On March 16 Hitler shocked the world by proclaiming universal military service and raising the peacetime army to 300,000 men. Hitler claimed that his intentions were purely defensive and his main enemy Communist Russia. A few days later he met with Sir John Simon and Anthony Eden to discuss disarmament. In June the British not only allowed Germany to fix her naval tonnage at 35 per cent of their own fleet but conceded a 45 per cent ratio for submarines. It was a notable diplomatic victory for Ribbentrop and Hitler.

Consequently Hitler's popularity at home that year increased.

The following year was even more successful. On March 7, 1936, against the advice of his generals, Hitler sent his troops into the demilitarized zone of the Rhineland. They had secret orders to retreat if challenged by French troops. But there was no resistance. Gemany had another bloodless victory, and no head of state in the world now enjoyed such popularity.

Two inner circles had formed around Hitler—one composed of top associates like Goebbels, Göring, Hess (and their wives), and another on a more personal level: the chauffeurs, secretaries, servants, and other intimates. This innermost circle, which included such disparate members as an architect, Speer, and a pilot, Hans Baur, also took in some of the younger military adjutants. A few belonged to both circles, most notably Martin Bormann, who had been working for Hess since the early days and now, as his representative in Berlin, was given the opportunity of assiduously devoting himself to the daily needs of the Führer. Although unknown to most Germans, the indefatigable Bormann had become Hitler's shadow.

Preoccupation with the international scene gave Hitler little time for his mistress, Eva Braun. In 1935 she became so despondent she swal-

169. Hitler visits Saarbrücken on March 1, 1935.

lowed twenty pills in a second attempt at suicide. She was found in a
coma by her sister, Ilse, and saved. After this Hitler was much more at-
tentive and brought Eva to his chalet on the Obersalzberg so often that
his half sister, Angela, the housekeeper of Haus Wachenfeld, became in-
censed. Angela referred to Eva as *die blöde Kuh* (the stupid cow) and
refused to shake hands. The relationship between Angela and Hitler became so strained that she gave up her post as housekeeper to get married. So, by 1936, Eva had become the undisputed mistress of Haus
Wachenfeld, which was already undergoing total reconstruction. As
official summer residence it had to be enlarged to accommodate high-
level diplomatic negotiations—and provide Eva with a bedroom, boudoir,
and bath adjoining Hitler's own room and studio. It also had a new
name, the Berghof.

Hitler welcomed many famous visitors to the Berghof and to the
Chancellery, but Eva would be confined to her quarters since their liaison was still a secret. She longed to meet Lloyd George, Admiral Horthy
of Hungary, King Carol of Romania, the Aga Khan, and such notables
and yet was forced to stay in her room like a child. She was particularly
disturbed, she confided to friends, when Hitler refused her pleas to meet
the Duchess of Windsor, since the two women, she thought, had so much
in common. She did console herself with the thrill of knowing that the
great of the world were coming from all over to honor her lover. This
knowledge made her "Back Street" existence endurable.

Overleaf: 170. Saar demonstration.

171. Disarmament conference. Afterward Hitler and Eden talked over their war-time experiences. They had fought opposite each other and together drew a map of the battle lines on the back of a dinner card.

172. Now when Hitler talks nearly all Germany seems to be listening: Goebbels, Milch, Darre, Elz von Rubenach, Blomberg, Guertner, and Seldte at the Reichstag.

173. Berliners gathered near outdoor radio speakers.

174. The Ribbentrops returning from the polls. In early 1936 Hitler had campaigned throughout Germany on the question of his seizure of the Rhineland. "What I have done," he told one audience, "I did according to my conscience, and to the best of my knowledge, filled with concern for my people, realizing the necessity of protecting its honor, in order to lead it again to a position of honor in this world. And should unnecessary sorrow or suffering ever come to my people because of my actions, then I beseech the Almighty God to punish me."

A week later the people went to the polls: 98.8 per cent voted for Hitler. (The poster to the right of the Ribbentrops reads: "The Führer gave us freedom and honor!")

175. French troops evacuating from the Rhineland.

THE HESSES

176. Bormann at wheel with Frau Hess; Hess on jump seat; in back Professor Karl Haushofer, the geopolitician, and Hildegard Fath, Hess's secretary.

177. Hess with his wife on a skiing holiday in the mid-1930s. He usually kept a stiff upper lip—to cover his buck teeth.

178. Athlete Hess takes off.

179. Professor Haushofer, Hess's mentor and friend. Frau Haushofer was Jewish and Hess protected her. Later one of the Haushofer sons became involved in the plot against Hitler and was executed.

180. Hess has just won the hazardous air race around the Zugspitze, Germany's highest peak, near Garmsich.

THE GOEBBELSES

181. One-pot dinner with the Führer.

182. Goebbels and his stepson.

183. Hitler greets his half sister, Angela, Magda Goebbels, and her son, Harald, by a previous marriage.

184. The Goebbelses with Winifred Wagner at Bayreuth.

THE GÖRINGS

185. Göring soon after the Great War.

186. Second marriage, to actress Emmy Sonnemann, in 1935. An irreverent flying comrade has just released two storks over the Evangelical Cathedral in Berlin. As the bride and groom leave the church a military band thunders out the march from *Lohengrin*.

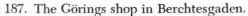
187. The Görings shop in Berchtesgaden.

188. Karin Hall, Göring's country estate near Berlin, was named after his first wife, Carin, but misspelled.

189. Rare photo of a pornographic table reported to be Göring's.

190. Göring on the Obersalzberg with a neighbor.

191. His chalet is in the background. Nearby were those of Hitler and Bormann.

192. Easter, 1935.

193. Eva's sister Gretl at the Niklaus Ball, December 1935.

194. Eva at the winter Olympic games in Garmisch, 1936.

195. Olympic hockey game. During the crucial game Hitler became too nervous to stay until the end and had to have someone give him a brief account later.

196. Hitler bought Eva a love nest in Munich after her second suicide attempt.

197. At her new home.

198. Mother Braun and daughters.

199. The Berghof, exterior.

200. Hitler's architectural sketch for the comprehensive alterations which would transform his Obersalzberg villa, Haus Wachenfeld (see photo ✠114), into "the Berghof." The traditional pitched roof design was part of his architectural credo: "the house with the flat roof," he wrote in 1924, "is oriental—oriental is Jewish—Jewish is bolshevistic."

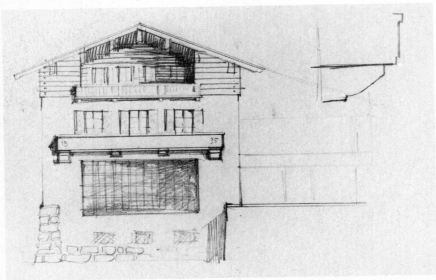

201. The Berghof, interior.

202. Eva's bedroom at the Berghof.

203. The passageway leading to it.

204. View of the Obersalzberg at the height of its development. Not shown are the homes of Bormann and Göring, which were behind the photographer's vantage point. The numbered buildings are identified as follows: "1. Post office off-limit area. 2. Gardening ground. 3. Quarter of drivers. 4. Grand garage. 5. House with gateway to 'off-limit area.' 6. Barrack, officers, and kitchen apart-

205–6. A view of the Berghof showing in the foreground the walkway Hitler would daily take down to the teahouse, a round stone building below.

ments. 7. Barrack, drill hall of the bodyguard. 8. Barrack square, with underground shooting ranges. 9. Barrack, dwelling house. 10. Hotel 'Platterhof.' 11. Dwelling house for the personnel of the Hotel Platterhof. 12. Intendancy of Obersalzberg. 13. Studio for architectural projecting. 14. Kindergarten house. 15. 'Berghof.' 16. Security Service of the Reich and Gestapo."

207–8. Hitler reading at the teahouse and dozing with Eva. Here he would drink apple-peel tea while Eva talked of plays and movies; the general conversation would usually be gay and superficial but occasionally Hitler would propagandize for vegetarianism, decry smoking and drinking, or expound the dangers of women using polluted make-up.

209–12. Five miles from the Berghof by a winding road, much of it blasted out of rock, was Hitler's mile-high mountain teahouse atop the Kehlstein. Visitors would drive up this road to an underground passage dug into the peak. At the end of the corridor was a copper-lined elevator, its shaft hacked out of solid rock. After a ride of about four hundred feet, it opened onto a gallery of Roman pillars. Beyond was an immense glassed-in circular hall. Great logs were burning in a huge open fireplace. On all sides extended such an immense panorama of mountains that visitors were given a sensation of being suspended in space.

213–14. Hitler and Eva with guests at the Kehlstein. After several visits the fantastic setting began to pall on Hitler because of its grandiosity. He also found the rarified air too difficult to breathe.

215. Receiving Lloyd George.

216. The Lindberghs visit Germany, here escorted by Col. Gustav Kästner, commandant of Staaken Field. Lindbergh was impressed by what he saw of German air strength. Later Göring presented him with the German Eagle, one of the highest German decorations, "by order of der Führer." In early 1939 Lindbergh wrote in his diary that Hitler held the future of Europe in his hands. "Much as I disapprove of many things Germany has done, I believe she has pursued the only consistent policy in Europe in recent years."

217. Hitler reminisces about the old days with a former war comrade, Ignaz Westenkirchner, and his family, while Amann, also a war comrade, and Hanfstaengl listen in.

218. Max Schmeling became a hero to Hitler in 1936 when he knocked out Joe Louis in the twelfth round—thus demonstrating the supremacy of the white race. Two years later Louis knocked out Schmeling in one round.

219. Hitler greets German Olympic stars.

220. The achievements of 1936 were highlighted for Hitler by the triumphant summer Olympics. Three Americans have just swept the decathlon but the crowd gives an enthusiastic "Heil, Hitler." Germany won the most gold medals (thirty-three), as well as the most silver and bronze, surprising everyone by beating the second-place Americans by fifty-seven points. Leni Riefenstahl recorded the victory in a two-part documentary, but most important for the Nazi regime were the favorable impressions of Hitler's Germany taken home by many of the visitors.

EIGHT

Tomorrow the World

1937–1938

On January 30, 1937, Hitler addressed the Reichstag to commemcrate his first four years in office. To the German people his achievements truly seemed impressive. He had defied tradition to expand production and curb unemployment. He was changing the face of the land with a network of *Autobahnen*, as well as developing a "People's Car" so compact and inexpensive that the average German could afford it. He envisaged other innovations for the future. In large cities there would be automated underground parking, traffic-free centers, parks and green areas, and strict pollution control. Antipollution devices were already installed in some factories in the Ruhr, and new plants were required to construct preventive devices to avoid pollution of the waters.

Unlike most Germans, though, Hitler had no use for the Zeppelin. He said it was against nature: "She has provided no bird with any sort of balloon, as she has done in the case of the fish. As far as I myself am concerned, I shall never consent to go up in a dirigible."

The welfare and training of youth were also given priority: Little children were taught absolute loyalty to the Führer and Greater Reich; older ones were required to attend work camps, with the rich laboring next to the poor.

While preparing the nation mentally and physically for the task of bringing Germany to "glory and prosperity," Hitler had managed in four years to raise the health standards to such a degree that many foreigners were impressed. Working conditions were also improved with more windows, less crowding, and better washrooms. Never before had the worker enjoyed such privileges. The "Strength Through Joy" program initiated by Robert Ley's Labor Front provided subsidized concerts, theater preformances, dances, films, adult education courses, and subsidized tourism. Now the humblest laborer and his family could travel aboard luxury liners for undreamed-of holidays.

Hitler's greatest achievement was perhaps his unification of the Ger-

221. Hitler at the auto show.

222. Hitler digs the first shovel of dirt for the *Autobahn* between Frankfurt and Darmstadt.

man nation, but this had been accomplished at the cost of civil liberties. This was not the only price paid for Hitler's program: He had lifted the nation out of depression by speeding up rearmament and thus forced Germany into a potentially disastrous situation.

Even so, if Hitler had died in 1937 he would have gone down as a great figure in German history. Throughout Europe he had millions of admirers. Gertrude Stein thought Hitler should get the Nobel Peace Prize. Shaw defended him, and so did Sven Hedin, the Swedish ex-

223. Little girls learning Nazi salute.

Mein Führer!

(Das Kind spricht:)

Ich kenne dich wohl und habe dich lieb
                         wie Vater und Mutter.
Ich will dir immer gehorsam sein
                         wie Vater und Mutter.
Und wenn ich groß bin, helfe ich dir
                         wie Vater und Mutter,
Und freuen sollst du dich an mir
                         wie Vater und Mutter!

224. From a Nazi children's coloring book: "My Führer!/I know you well and love you/like father and mother. I will always obey you/like father and mother. And when I grow up I will help you/like father and mother,/And you will be proud of me/like father and mother!"

225. Everyone works for the Third Reich. A labor camp for Hitler maidens who come from every walk of life.

226. Village children see movies for the first time at a traveling cinema theater sponsored by the "Strength Through Joy" program.

227. Léon Degrelle, head of the Belgian Rexist movement. He regarded himself as the spiritual son of Hitler.

plorer. Hitler also, by example, stimulated the growth of movements similiar to his own throughout Europe and even in the United States.

The people of Germany continued to pay homage and flocked to the Berghof whenever it was rumored that Hitler would be there.

On the brink of dictatorship, Hitler remained the artist and architect. Art and politics were to him inseparable. The architect he revered was Professor Paul Ludwig Troost. Perhaps his most memorable project for

228. A member of Sir Oswald Mosley's Blackshirts with the Brownshirts.

229–30. Hitler with some of the many admirers who came to see him at the Berghof, in candid photos taken by his chauffeur, Eric Kempka.

Hitler was a modern art museum for Munich, the Haus der Deutschen Kunst. Professor Troost died soon after the cornerstone was laid but his young widow carried on his work, and every time Hitler came to Munich he would visit her studio. A lady with a mind of her own, she expressed it forthrightly. But, to the surprise of his aides, Hitler did not resent Frau Troost's candor—except on one memorable occasion. For the grand opening of the Haus der Deutschen Kunst in the summer of 1937 an ambitious exhibition of German art was scheduled. The judges, including Frau Troost, selected a good many excellent modern paintings which Hitler considered degenerate. He and Frau Troost consequently had a violent argument at the museum just before opening day. She refused to back down. "And since you can't approve our selection and have a com-

231. To the right, Hitler greets an admirer gallantly. The two colorfully dressed youths, left, are apprentice carpenters from Hamburg.

pletely different opinion," she said, "I resign this moment as a member of the jury." They parted coolly but a few weeks later Hitler was back at the Troost studio as if nothing had happened.

On January 12, 1938, Field Marshal von Blomberg, the Minister of Defense, married his typist, with Göring and Hitler as witnesses. No sooner had the couple left on a honeymoon than it was revealed that the young Frau von Blomberg had been a prostitute. Hitler expressed shock and exclaimed, "If a German field marshal marries a whore, then anything in this world is possible!" Blomberg's fellow officers also demanded his resignation and it was expected that General Werner von Fritsch would succeed him. Then it was charged that Fritsch had been involved in homosexual acts. Hitler promptly ordered a full Gestapo investigation of the scandal and chose as the new army commander in chief General Walther von Brauchitsch, an open admirer although not a Nazi Party member.

With a more compliant Minister of Defense, Hitler summoned his Cabinet on February 4. He announced that he was reorganizing the Wehrmacht and had taken over personal command of the entire armed forces. It was the last time the Cabinet would ever meet and it was fitting that its members merely sat and approved. Just before midnight the German people were informed by radio of this momentous decision. They also learned that Blomberg and Fritsch had resigned, sixteen high-ranking

232. The wedding of Eva's friend Marion Schönemann to Herr Theissen, at the Berghof, August 1937. Kneeling near groom, Gretl Braun, Eva's sister. Standing, left to right, Heinrich Hoffmann, Frau Honni Morell, Erma Hoffmann, Eva Braun, Frau Dreesen (her husband owned the Hotel Dreesen), Dr. Morell, Herta Schneider (Eva's best friend), two unidentified men, and Hitler.

234. On May 7, 1937, Hitler's apprehensions became a reality. The *Hindenburg*'s explosion, which could have been sabotage, ended the epoch of giant rigid dirigibles.

generals had been dismissed, and that Hermann Göring had been promoted to Luftwaffe field marshal. The next morning the headlines of Hitler's newspaper, the *Völkischer Beobachter,* read:

STRONGEST CONCENTRATION OF ALL POWERS IN THE FÜHRER'S HANDS!

At last Hitler was the supreme dictator of the German Reich. Overriding objections of his generals, he marched into Austria.

Hitler's next goal was Czechoslovakia, which he regarded as a dagger aimed at the heart of Germany. All he needed was an excuse to invade and he had a ready-made one, Czechoslovakia's German minority. The 3,500,000 million people of the Sudetenland, inspired by the absorption of Austria, were now demanding a similar *Anschluss*. But Hitler was restrained by fear that France, England, and perhaps Russia would resist any invasion. Before facing such odds he wanted the blessing of his only ally, Italy, and on May 2, set out to get it.

233. The *Hindenburg* flies over the 1936 Nuremberg Party Day.

235. Frau Troost, Goebbels, Hitler, and Hess at the opening ceremonies for the Haus der Deutschen Kunst.

Hitler's threat to Czechoslovakia finally aroused England to action. Prime Minister Chamberlain flew to Munich to confer with Hitler at the Berghof and later in Bad Godesberg.

The problem was finally solved at the famous Munich Conference between Chamberlain, Hitler, Mussolini, and French Premier Daladier six days later. The Sudetenland was to be evacuated by the Czechs in four stages to begin on October 1.

The year ended with a violent attack on Jews—Crystal Night. It was sparked by the shooting of a minor German Foreign Office official in Paris on November 7, by a young Jew, Herschel Grynszpan, whose parents had been deported from Germany to Poland. He had gone to the embassy to assassinate the ambassador only to be sidetracked by Counselor Ernest von Rath. Himself an enemy of anti-Semites, Rath was being investigated by the Gestapo but it was he who took the bullets intended for his superior.

Rath's death was used as an excuse to ransack Jewish shops, burn synagogues, and commit murder. By official account thirty-six Jews were killed and another thirty-six seriously injured. But the figures, SS General Reinhard Heydrich himself admitted, "must have been exceeded considerably."

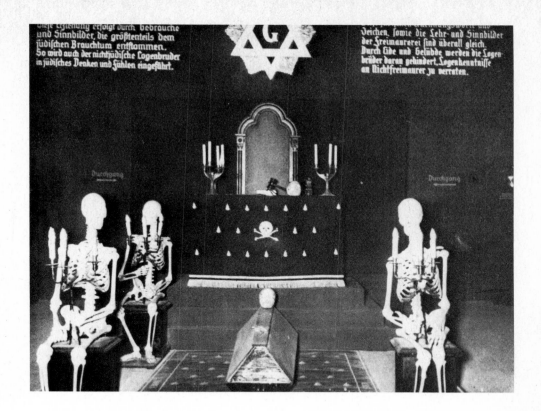

236. The "Eternal Jew" Exhibition also opened that year in Munich.

237. Arno Breker, one of Europe's leading sculptors, working on a bust of Speer in the style Hitler preferred.

238. "Anmut," by Breker.

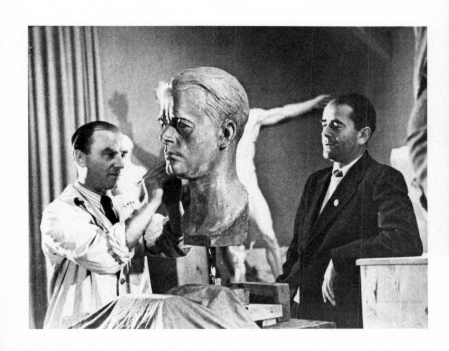

NAZI ARCHITECTURE

239. Speer's model of Berlin's proposed new center: Arch of Triumph with Great Domed Hall at far end.

240. Hitler dreamed of similar structures in his youth and made this sketch of a Great Domed Hall in 1925.

241. Hitler's sketch of a triumphal arch with domed hall visible in background to the left, also made in 1925.

242. March 1937 Hitler design for the pedestal to a monument.

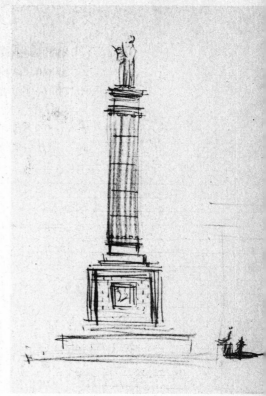

243. November 1942 Hitler sketch for a monument to composer Anton Bruckner in Linz.

244. The same year: sketch for bridge over the Elbe in Hamburg.

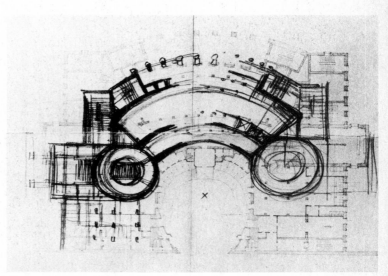

245. Rough Hitler sketch for a theater interior in Linz superimposed on plan.

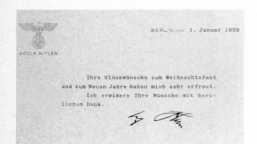

246. The Guests of the Führer. Eva between Hitler and the Bormanns.

247. Hitler's thank-you note for holiday greetings.

248. Hitler, Blomberg, and Fritsch. The end is near for both generals.

250. Austrian Prime Minister von Schuschnigg tried in vain to stop the Nazi take-over.

249. Blomberg, Hitler, Göring, and Goebbels at the horse show.

251. Enthusiastic crowds greet the German troops as they enter Vienna on March 14, 1938.

253. In Italy Hitler got what he came for: assurance that Czechoslovakia was not at all important to Mussolini, and tacit approval for Hitler's expansionist plans.

252. On March 16 Hitler gets a triumphant welcome in Berlin.

254. Eva celebrates Fasching that year with her mother (center) and sisters. She and Hitler were now living comfortably as man and wife, and with her position more stable, Eva could enjoy herself when he was busy with politics.

255. Eva en route to Italy with Frau Dreesen, wife of the owner of one of Hitler's favorite hotels, the Hotel Dreesen in Bad Godesberg.

256. On the bar at Tegernsee, where Röhm was arrested during the 1934 Putsch.

257. And relaxing during an office party at Hoffmann's photographic studio, where she had resumed work. It is doubtful whether Hitler would have approved her position on the floor, and certainly not her smoking. Not long after this he gave her an ultimatum: "Either give up smoking or me." She chose to give up smoking. To others in the family circle he had a standing offer of a gold watch for anyone who renounced tobacco.

258. At the Berghof, Goebbels entertains Eva, Speer, and others.

259. Candid shot of Hitler on the veranda of the Berghof.

260. Hitler and ordnance officer Max Wünsche visit a girls' school in Berchtesgaden.

261. Hitler with the Speer children. Eva takes a picture.

262. In Berlin Hitler attends the baptism of Edda Göring.

263. Hitler standing in limousine outside the Rheinhotel Dreesen.

264. Inside he assures Chamberlain that the Czech problem is "the last territorial demand" which he has to make in Europe.

265. The Führer is obviously in good spirits as he bids good-by to his guest—he has won the Sudetenland. Chamberlain was also pleased. Arriving in England, he announced that he had achieved peace with honor. "I believe it is peace in our time."

266. "The Game of Princes."

JEUX DE PRINCES

267. German troops enter the Sudetenland on October 1.

268. Two days later Hitler makes his triumphal entry.

269. Funeral service for diplomat Ernst von Rath, with Hitler in attendance.

270. That November, Hitler saying farewell to another guest. The year 1938 has been one of diplomatic triumph for him—diplomacy backed with the threat of overwhelming force.

NINE

The Road to War

1939–1940

The year 1939 began peacefully enough with the celebration of an ancient Teutonic ceremony at the Berghof. Molten lead was poured into a small basin of water and the shape it assumed supposedly determined the future.

On January 30 Hitler publicly hinted at his secret plan to exterminate Europe's Jews. "Today I shall act the prophet once again," he told the Reichstag. "If international Jewry inside and outside of Europe should succeed in thrusting the nations into a world war once again, then the result will not be the Bolshevization of the earth and with it the victory of Jewry, it will be the *annihilation of the Jewish race in Europe.*" Witnesses noted "long and vigorous applause."

That March Hitler made his move to take the rest of Czechoslovakia. First he summoned Monsignor Josef Tiso of Slovakia to Berlin and bullied him. The next evening, March 14, he called in President Emil Hacha of Czechoslovakia and also threatened him into submission. During the ordeal Hacha fainted. On March 15 Hitler occupied Czechoslovakia without bloodshed.

A week later came another conquest, with Hitler 'persuading' the Lithuanians to sign over to him the district of Memel.

Foreign diplomats correctly assumed Hitler's next target would be Poland. Soon, Polish Foreign Minister Josef Beck visited the Berghof. If he feared being browbeaten like Tiso, Hacha, and Austrian Chancellor Kurt von Schuschnigg, he was pleasantly surprised. There were no threats, only inducements. But Beck, as diplomatically as possible, refused even to consider the return of Danzig. Poland's plucky stand was rewarded that spring by a startling offer of military assistance from London in case of Nazi aggression. Beck accepted "without hesitation," and at last England was united and committed. There would be no more appeasement.

Hitler spent much of that summer at the Berghof, relaxing in preparation for his next political move. Eva was always nearby and took many pictures of the Führer and his visitors.

271. Pouring lead to read the future. "Hitler," recalled Ilse Braun, "did not seem satisfied with the results, for afterwards he sat down in an armchair, gazing dejectedly at the fire, and hardly spoke for the rest of the evening."

Hitler had agreed to let Stalin have the eastern half of Poland, which meant that the Soviet Union at least had been neutralized. Hitler was elated. Now he was free to proceed. Late that night he led his entourage onto the Berghof terrace. The sky in the north blazed wtih all the colors of the rainbow. It reminded Speer of the last act of *Götterdämmerung.* Hitler abruptly turned to his Luftwaffe adjutant. "Looks like a great deal of blood," he said. "This time we won't bring it off without violence."

On the morning of September 1, German artillery fire crashed down along the Polish-German border, followed by a massive attack of Nazi infantry and tanks. There was no formal declaration of war until late that morning when Hitler addressed the Reichstag at the Kroll Opera House. "I carry on this fight," he said, "no matter against whom, until the safety of the Reich and its rights are secured."

The Polish defenders were overwhelmed by a new form of warfare:

272. President Hacha of Czechoslovakia.

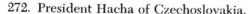

273. On March 15 the Nazis occupied Czechoslovakia without bloodshed.

Blitzkrieg! Lightning war. By the morning of September 5 the Polish Air Force was destroyed, and two days later most of Poland's thirty-five divisions were either routed or had surrendered.

Once Poland was conquered, Hitler began transforming it into a massive killing ground. He had already ordered Jews from the Reich massed in specific Polish cities having good rail connections. Object: "final solution, which will take some time," as Heydrich, head of the dreaded Security Service, told SS commanders on September 21. He was talking of the extermination of the Jews, already an open secret among many high-ranking party officials. These grisly preparations were augumented by a "house cleaning" of Polish intelligentsia, clergy, and nobility by five murder squads known as *Einsatzgruppen* (Special Action Groups). By midautumn of 1939, 3,500 intelligentsia were liquidated. "It is only in this manner," Hitler explained, "that we can acquire the vital territory which we need. After all, who today remembers the extermination of the Armenians." In addition to the urban terror campaign was the ruthless expulsion of 1,200,000 ordinary Poles from their ancestral homes; many of these people lost their lives in the resettlement from exposure to zero weather.

On the last day of September, Hitler went to Berlin and, in a speech at the Sport Palace, reminded the audience of his threat of annihilation to Jews if they should "start another" world war. "Some time ago the Jews laughed about my prophecies in Germany, too. I do not know whether they are still laughing today or whether they have stopped laughing already. I can only assure you even now; they will stop laughing everywhere. And I shall be proved right with these prophecies as well."

In November Hitler again returned to Munich for the annual commemoration of the Beer Hall Putsch. As he addressed the audience a

118

274. On March 24 Hitler made his triumphal entry into Memel.

bomb, hidden in a column just behind him, was ticking away. That afternoon Frau Troost had warned him of possible assassination and he decided to take an earlier train. Hitler hurried his speech and left the hall
ahead of time. Exactly eight minutes later the bomb exploded, killing
seven and wounding sixty-three, including Eva Braun's father. Eva arrived at the station just as the Führer's train was leaving and found an
air of carefree gaiety.

On March 18, 1940, Hitler met Mussolini at the Brenner Pass in a
snowstorm. He had come, he said, "simply to explain the situation" so Il
Duce could make his own decision. Without hesitation Mussolini agreed
to join Hitler in his war against the West. It began on April 7 with at-
tacks on Denmark and Norway.

Now the stage was set for the main invasion. On the morning of May
10 German troops flooded across the Belgian, Holland, and Luxembourg
borders. England and France, despite warnings, were caught by surprise.

275. Hitler was convinced that a
show of power would give him
Poland without war. The quixotic
Mussolini was persuaded to con-
clude the so-called Pact of Steel,
and his son-in-law, Count Galeazzo
Ciano, came to Berlin to sign it.
Foreign Minister Ribbentrop sits
to the right.

276. Eva, the self-styled "Rolleiflex Girl."

Hitler's unprecedented victory was followed by a diplomatic success, the signing of the Tripartite Pact with Japan and Italy in September. In it Japan agreed to recognize the leadership of Germany and Italy in the establishment of a new order in Europe as long as they recognized her new order in Asia.

Then came a series of setbacks: the loss of the bitter aerial Battle for Britain, the failure to mount Operation Sea Lion (the planned invasion of Britain), and two diplomatic reverses.

In early October Hitler met Mussolini again at the Brenner Pass and said his next goal was the root of the British Empire: Gibraltar. He was going to see Franco and get permission to transport German units across Spain to assault the Rock in an operation code-named Felix. Hitler complained that Franco was demanding too much grain and gasoline as their price for entry into the war against England. Franco, he said, was treating him "as if I were a little Jew who was haggling about the most precious possessions of mankind!" On October 23 he finally met the Caudillo at Hendaye, a French border town just below Biarritz.

For months Franco continued to stall Hitler, who finally, in disgust, abandoned the plan of capturing Gibraltar. Had Franco co-operated Hitler would have controlled the entire Mediterranean. Apart from the Caudillo's fear of aligning himself with a possible loser, there was a compelling motive for his decision to thwart Hitler: According to several sources—including the former British Ambassador to Spain, Sir Samuel Hoare—Franco was part Jewish.

On October 24, the day after his encounter with Franco, Hitler met with Marshal Henri Pétain, head of state of Vichy France, in Montoire. Once again he was frustrated: Pétain also, politely but firmly, refused to enter the war against England.

For Hitler it was a morose trip back to Germany. After his great victories in the West, the chief of a defeated power and the leader of a minor one were both refusing to be led into the crusade against England, and Hitler's own ally was stupidly endangering the Axis position in the Mediterranean to pursue personal glory on the battlefield. During the long train ride home the Führer railed at "deceiving" collaborators and ungrateful, unreliable friends.

277. Hitler watching the Rolleiflex Girl as she records Ciano's visit. The Berghof's famed picture window could be lowered into the wall below.

278. Göring, Edda, and pet lion cub.

279. Rare candid picture of the family circle relaxing in the Berghof's "beer hall."

280. In Berlin Hitler relished entertaining film, theater, and opera stars.

281. That August Hitler and Stalin shocked the world by making an alliance.

282.   WONDER HOW LONG THE HONEYMOON WILL LAST?

283. At the Berghof Hitler, flanked by Goebbels and Bormann, anxiously awaits word from Moscow. This picture was taken by Eva.

284. Hitler at the Reichstag on the morning of September 1, waiting to make his war speech.

285. "I will carry on this fight," he says, "no matter against whom, until the safety of the Reich and its rights are secured!"

286. Hitler watching his troops march into Poland.

287. After the battle of the Bzura, the Polish Army is completely annihilated. Caption to this photo in a Nazi propaganda book: "The Lord defeated them with horse, horseman and chariot!"

288. At Führer headquarters in Poland.

289. Hitler and General von Reichenau observe last phases of the battle for Warsaw through field glasses.

290. German troops goose-stepping through Warsaw after victory.

291. Polish Jews arrested after victory. Nazi caption: "Enemies of the German People."

292. Hitler's triumphal entry into Danzig on September 19. "Almighty God," he told a partisan crowd, "has now blessed our weapons."

293. Hitler speaking at the annual commemoration of the Beer Hall Putsch. "The fact that I left the Bürgerbräukeller earlier than usual," Hitler said afterward, "is a corroboration of Providence's intention to let me reach my goal." Wünsche, the ordnance office in charge of scheduling, stares at his chief from the front row.

294. The year ends as peacefully as it began. Hitler puts on a Christmas party for the children of Speer, Bormann, and others in the family circle.

295. Hitler takes time out to give the Ribbentrops a guided tour of the new Reich Chancellery.

296–97. He was planning another major conquest. In early 1940 in the old Reich Chancellery Hitler devised an invasion of the West. *Left,* Göring and Captain von Puttkamer, Hitler's naval adjutant, watching Hitler explain how to skirt the Maginot Line with tanks. Almost all his commanders opposed the unorthodox plan—which worked. *Right,* Keitl, Jodl, Schmundt (chief adjutant), and Puttkamer.

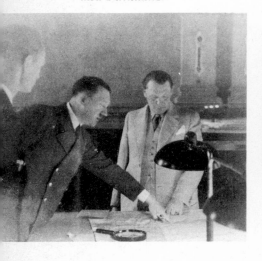

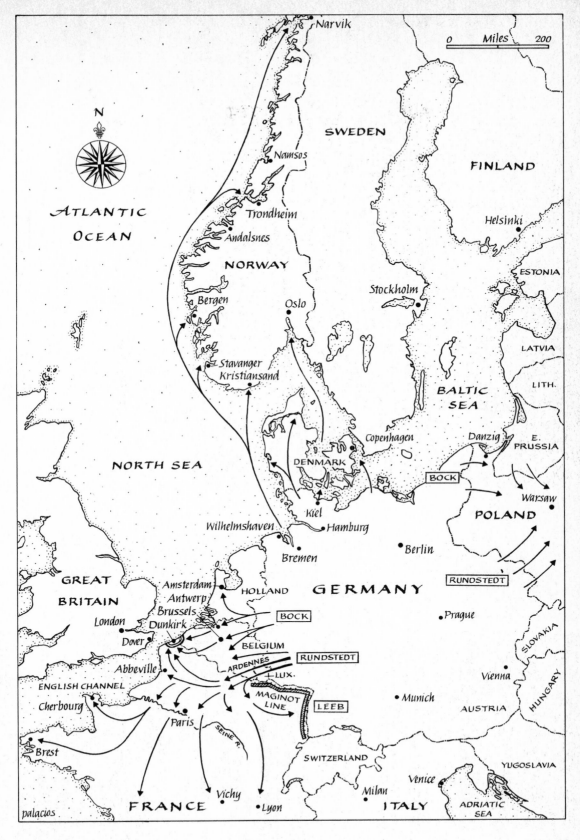

298. Victory in the west.

299. The fateful meeting at the Brenner Pass.

300. Nazi troops marching into Aalborg, Denmark.

301. The country falls with its navy never firing a shot and its land forces only managing to inflict twenty casualties on the invaders. But under occupation the Danes showed courage and saved their Jewish countrymen by transporting nearly all 6,500 of them to neutral Sweden. Here they cheer King Christian.

302. Hitler at his headquarters near the Holland-Belgian border, Rocky Nest, soon after launching his attack on the West.

303. The invasion is going well and Admiral Raeder brings up the possibility of invading England once France falls. Hitler is negative.

304. Following Hitler's plan, the German Blitz breaks through the French lines at Sedan and sweeps toward the English Channel—and Dunkirk.

305. German troops march into Dunkirk.

306. A French town destroyed.

307. A French column is caught on the bridge over l'Oise.

308. German troops parade down Avenue Foch in Paris, with the Arc de Triomphe in the background.

309–316. The jig that never was. Hitler's elation at news that France had surrendered was briefly filmed by Walter Frentz at Hitler's Belgium headquarters. The above frames (and there were no others, Frentz revealed to the author) were cleverly "looped" (repeated) by a Canadian film expert, making it appear that Hitler was executing a dance.

317. In the map room. Hitler hears more good news.

318. Hitler listens to a radio announcement of the Armistice at the Officers' Mess. The war with France is over.

321. Hitler meets Mussolini in Munich, June 19.

319. Sight-seeing in Paris.

320. Sentimental journey, June 1940. Hitler revisits his battlefields of 1914–18. "Never again trench warfare," he assures entourage.

322. The conqueror is welcomed home. July 1940. Note blackout hoods on the auto headlights.

323. From the balcony of the Reich Chancellery.

324. That September Hitler signs the Tripartite Pact with Japan and Italy. The Japanese bring gifts.

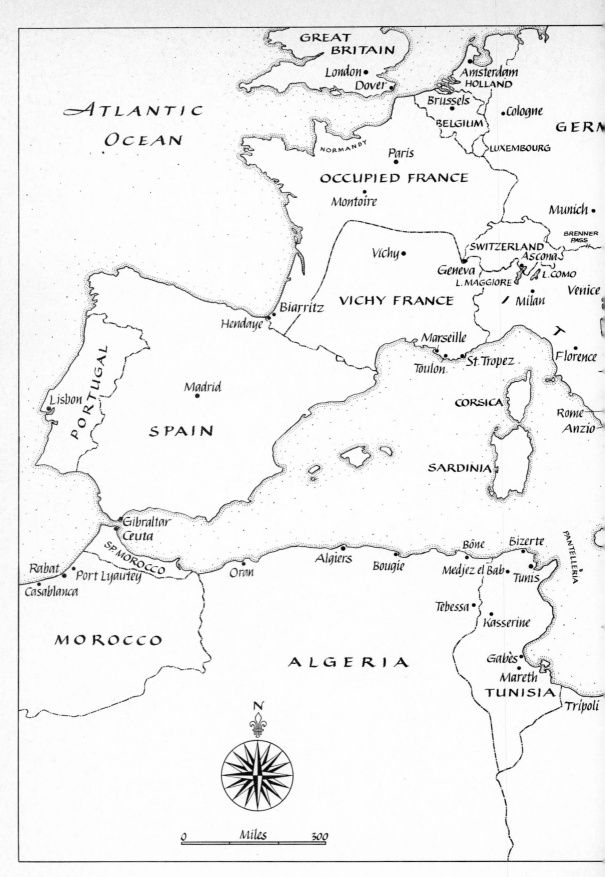

325. The Mediterranean.

326. The Battle
of Britain.

327. Göring, out of favor with the Führer after the loss of the Battle of Britain.

328. Franco's train arrived more than an hour late. "I'll have to use every trick I can," he told an adviser, "and this is one of them." At their meeting Franco avoided signing a treaty with Hitler and refused to accept Gibraltar as a present from foreign soldiers. That fortress, he insisted, must be taken by the Spaniards themselves. Hitler left Hendaye frustrated and enraged.

TEN

By Victory Undone

1940–1942

To the family circle, Hitler was a kindly father figure—a thoughtful employer who gave gold watches to those who ceased smoking, was sincerely interested in their welfare, and made at least one match between circle members. His relationship with Eva Braun had become more conjugal. Rather than separating them, the war brought them closer together, since he could now spend much more time at the Berghof. The routine there was strenuous, with luncheon served after 4 P.M. and dinner after 9, and most of Hitler's day filled with conferences. Later in the evening the guests would gather in the great hall where light refreshments would be served, and Hitler might play favorite records or lecture about the evils of tobacco, meat, or cosmetics. Sometimes the gathering did not break up until 4 in the morning.

After his failures with Franco, Pétain, and Mussolini, Hitler attempted to strengthen his ties with Stalin by drawing him into the Tripartite Pact. This scheme was the brain child of Ribbentrop, who saw an alliance of Germany, Italy, Japan, and the Soviet Union as the answer to European stability. Foreign Commissar Molotov promised to take the proposal back to Stalin but asked for so many concessions that Hitler was convinced that "sooner or later Stalin would abandon us and go over to the enemy." He decided irrevocably to do what he had talked about the last six months: invade Russia. He approved the plans in mid-December and gave the invasion a meaningful title: Operation Barbarossa (Red Beard) after Frederick I, the Holy Roman Emperor who had marched east in 1190 to take the Holy Land.

Late in March 1941 Hitler made a fatal decision. Concerned by the defeat of Italian troops in the Balkans, he decided to occupy that area. Only then, he said, would it be safe to launch Barbarossa. Twenty-nine German divisions were thrown into the Balkans campaign and within three weeks Yugoslavia was conquered and German tanks entered Athens. But of the huge German force only ten divisions saw action for

330. "Frettchen," Hansgeorg Schulze, Hitler's universally popular ordnance officer.

331. Eva snaps a smiling Sepp Dietrich, the commander of Leibstandarte SS Adolf Hitler—the bodyguard regiment. During the Röhm Putsch Dietrich had reluctantly presided over the executions of the top SA leaders.

329. Eva and Speer.

332. On the way to the teahouse. As usual Eva has her camera. The broadly smiling officer is Frettchen.

333. Hitler with Wolf.

334. A group walk in the spring of 1941.

335. Eva returned to Italy that summer. In Florence.

336. At Lake Garda in Italy.

337. On November 12, 1940, Foreign Commissar Molotov arrived in Berlin to talk of coalition.

338. Two faces of Adolf Hitler.

more than six days. A sledge hammer had been used to kill mosquitoes—and the opening of Operation Barbarossa was delayed for more than a month, a delay that would prove catastrophic.

On May 10 the security of Barbarossa seemed endangered when Rudolf Hess, Hitler's own deputy, flew to England in a quixotic effort to bring peace with England. It was a daring venture that ended in disaster for Hess. He was imprisoned by the English and reviled by the Nazis.

The day after learning about Hess, Hitler issued two repressive decrees. One declared that Russian civilians taking arms against the Wehrmacht in the coming invasion should be considered outlaws and shot without trial. The other empowered Himmler to carry out "special tasks which result from the struggle which has to be carried out between two opposing political systems." In plain words, Himmler was ordered to "cleanse" occupied Russian areas of Jews and other troublemakers by special SS murder squads, the *Einsatzgruppen.*

On the morning of June 22, 1941, Hitler finally launched Barbarossa. On that same day, 129 years before, Napoleon had crossed the Niemen River on his way to Moscow. Like Napoleon, Hitler advanced quickly on all fronts.

Millions of Russians were ready to greet Hitler as a liberator from the Stalinist terror, but Hitler, who from his youth considered Slavs as *Untermenschen,* listened to those advisers recommending harsh treatment of the conquered peoples—and turned them into bitter enemies. Following in the wake of the advancing German troops were four SS *Einsatzgruppen* of three thousand men each, whose mission was to prevent resistance by civilians. They were to round up and liquidate not only Bolshevik leaders but all Jews, as well as gypsies, "Asiatic inferiors," and "useless eaters," such as the deranged and incurable sick. The majority of *Einsatzgruppe* leaders were youngish intellectuals—a Protestant pastor, a physician, an opera singer, numerous lawyers—and it might be supposed

146

339–41. The Führer Train in the Balkans Campaign.

342. On April 20, 1941, the Führer's birthday, naval aide Puttkamer reports that he has been promoted to captain.

343. The train's cook presents Puttkamer with a ship made from a cucumber.

344. Bormann inspecting the train, which included a special car for the Führer's cow.

such men were unsuited for this work. On the contrary, they brought to the brutal task their considerable skills and training and became, despite qualms, efficient executioners. Most of the victims were Jews and the exterminations proceeded with cool calculation.

During that summer of 1941 covert preparations for the mass murder of Jews were also under way. Himmler summoned Rudolf Höss, commandant of the largest concentration camp in Poland, and gave him secret oral instructions. "He told me," Höss later testified, "something to the effect—I do not remember the exact words—that the Führer had given the order for the final solution of the Jewish question. We, the SS, must carry out that order. If it is not carried out now the Jews will later on destroy the German people." Himmler said he had chosen Höss's camp, since Auschwitz, strategically located near the border of Germany, afforded space for measures requiring isolation.

Until now the plans had been kept secret from Hitler's innermost circle—the secretaries, adjutants, servants, and personal staff. But that autumn the Führer began making open remarks during his evening table conversations. In mid-October he reminded his guests at the teahouse of his prophecy in the Reichstag that, if the Jews started a war, they would disappear from Europe. "That race of criminals has on its conscience the two million dead of the First World War, and now already hundreds and thousands more. Let nobody tell me that all the same we can't park them in the marshy parts of Russia. Who's worrying about our troops? It's not a bad idea, by the way, that public rumor attributes to us a plan to exterminate the Jews. Terror is a salutary thing."

345. Just before his flight, Hess and his son Wolf. The girl is Bormann's daughter. Hitler feared that Hess might have revealed the secret of Barbarossa to the British. He did not.

346. Two German soldiers amused at the hanging of Yugoslavian partisan.

The plan for Jewish extermination publicly rumored was soon to become fact. On May 1, 1942, Hitler left the eastern front to deliver a major speech to the Reichstag. He denounced Bolshevism as "the dictatorship of Jews" and labeled the Jew "a parasitic germ" who had to be dealt with ruthlessly. He demanded passage of a law granting him plenary powers. Every German was henceforth obliged to follow his personal orders—or suffer dire punishment. He was now officially above the law with the power of life and death. He had, in essence, appointed himself God's deputy and could do the Lord's work: wipe out the "Jewish vermin" and create a race of supermen.

By that spring six killing camps had been set up in Poland: Treblinka, Sobibor, Belzec, Lublin, Kulmhof, and Auschwitz. The first four gassed the Jews by engine-exhaust fumes, but Rudolf Höss, commandant of the huge complex near Auschwitz, thought this too "inefficient" and introduced to his camp a more lethal gas, hydrogen cyanide, marketed under the name of Zyklon B.

Against the advice of his generals Hitler ordered that the attack toward Moscow proceed on a wide rather than concentrated front. Panic

347. The swastika is raised over the Acropolis, with the Parthenon in background.

still swept the city and, at the Kremlin, Stalin had reputedly lost his nerve. Finally the Germans launched an all-out drive on the Soviet capital and came within sight of the city. But it was too late. Winter and the Red Army stopped the Nazis, and on December 6 Hitler admitted to General Alfred Jodl that "victory could no longer be achieved."

The following day the Japanese struck at Pearl Harbor. Four days later Hitler made another serious blunder: Instead of waiting for the United States to declare war on him, he convoked the Reichstag and said, "We will always strike first!"

The German retreat in the East threatened to degenerate into panicked flight by mid-December. Field Marshal von Brauchitsch, exhausted and depressed, wanted to continue the withdrawal but Hitler sent out a general order: "Stand fast, not one step back!" He fired Brauchitsch and took over personal command of the army.

He took time off from the Battle of Stalingrad to return to Munich and repeat once more his threat to exterminate the Jews of Europe. "People always laughed at me as a prophet," he told an enthusiastic audience at the Löwenbräukeller. "Of those who laughed then, *innumerable numbers* no longer laugh today, and those who laugh now will perhaps no longer laugh a short time from now. International Jewry will be recognized in its full demonic dangerousness; we National Socialists will see to that."

150

348. King Carol of Romania.

349. Admiral Horthy of Hungary.

350. Field Marshal Mannerheim of Finland.

351. Germany invades Russia: Panzer unit advances during the battle for Glosoff.

352. The German juggernaut advances along Russian highway.

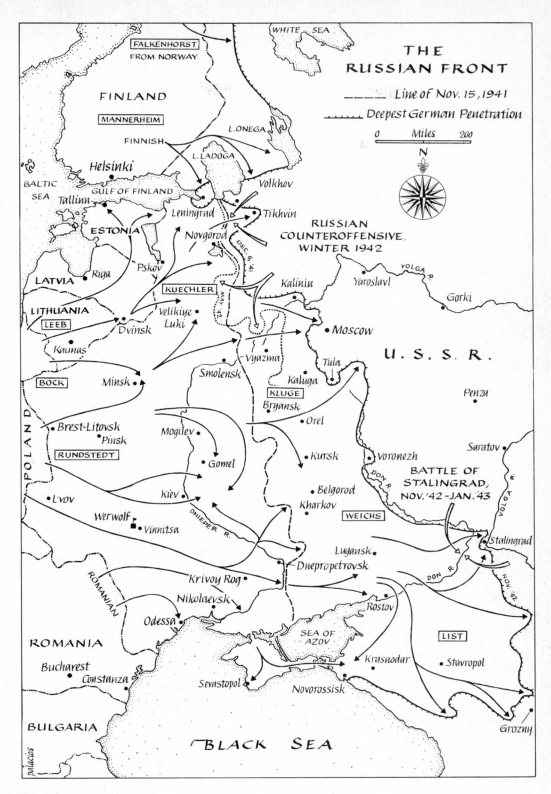

THE
RUSSIAN FRONT

_____ Line of Nov. 15, 1941
.... Deepest German Penetration

0   Miles   200

N

FALKENHORST
FROM NORWAY

FINLAND

MANNERHEIM

FINNISH

L. ONEGA

L. LADOGA

Helsinki

BALTIC
SEA

GULF OF FINLAND

Volkhov

Tallinn

Leningrad

Tikhvin

ESTONIA

Novgorod

RUSSIAN
COUNTEROFFENSIVE,
WINTER 1942

DEC. 6, '41

VOLGA R.

Riga

Pskov

Kalinin

Yaroslavl

Gorki

LATVIA

KUECHLER

MAY'42

LITHUANIA

LEEB

Velikiye
Luki

Moscow

U. S. S. R.

Dvinsk

Kaunas

Vyazma

Penza

Smolensk

Kaluga

Tula

BOCK

Minsk

KLUGE

Bryansk

Brest-Litovsk

Mogilev

Orel

Saratov

Pinsk

RUNDSTEDT

Gomel

Kursk

Voronezh

BATTLE OF
STALINGRAD,
NOV.'42 - JAN.'43

L'vov

Belgorod

DON R.

Werwolf

Vinnitsa

Kiev

Kharkov

WEICHS

DNIEPER R.

VOLGA R.

Lugansk

Stalingrad

Dnepropetrovsk

ROMANIAN

Krivoy Rog

DON R.

Nikolaevsk

Rostov

NOV.'42

Odessa

SEA OF
AZOV

LIST

ROMANIA

Krasnodar

Stavropol

Bucharest

Constanza

Sevastopol

Novorossisk

BULGARIA

Grozny

palacios

BLACK   SEA

353. The Russian Front.

354. Hitler's troops win land and, at first, people: Ukrainians greet soldiers from the Leibstandarte SS Adolf Hitler with bread, salt, and smiles.

355. Within a month of the invasion's start Hitler had vetoed plans for a conciliatory approach to the people of the conquered territory.

356. Russian victims of the *Einsatzgruppen*.

357. Improvised insignia for an SS jeep on the Russian front.

358. Soviet poster linking Hitler and Napoleon: "That's the way it was . . . That's the way it will be!"

359. Ribbentrop with Hitler at his East Prussian headquarters—*Wolfsschanze*, Wolf's Lair.

360. The Officers' Mess. "Photo" Hoffmann gives General Schmundt, Hitler's chief adjutant, a sausage for his birthday.

362. Adjutants cooling off.

361. A lake near Wolf's Lair, the Moyensee.

363. Mussolini also came to Wolf's Lair that August and went on a flight over Russian lines. Moments after this photo was taken, he insisted on taking the controls from pilot Baur. Hitler consented to his regret. Il Duce maneuvered the plane with boyish élan.

364. That summer Hitler was grieved to learn of the death in battle of Hansgeorg "Frettchen" Schulze. He went up to the front to console Schulze's brother, Richard, who was also a member of the elite Leibstandarte Division, and offered him his brother's former position as aide. Here, Richard and Frettchen shortly before the latter's death.

365. Hitler inspects new helicopter.

366. Early winter, 1941, on the Russian front: Germans take prisoners.

367. The Russian front, December 1941. German propaganda photo: "The Bolshevik Winter Offensive —a mass enemy suicide." In fact, the Red Army was on the verge of crushing the Wehrmacht.

368. The SS Division, Das Reich, nears the Moscow suburbs.

369. December 7, 1941. Pearl Harbor.

370. Hitler's aides and adjutants hold a Christmas party at Wolf's Lair.

371. On February 15, 1942, after the military reverses in Russia of November–December 1941, Hitler exhorts recent SS officer graduates to stem the Red tide and save civilization. Behind: Schaub and Richard Schulze. The latter was so moved he wanted to go back to the front. The young lieutenants, he recalled, jumped onto their seats and cheered in a spontaneous demonstration.

372. A few days later Hitler lost his Minister of Armaments, the famed engineer Fritz Todt, in a mysterious plane crash at Wolf's Lair. Todt was replaced by architect Speer.

373. Hitler trains Blondie to leap over barriers.

374. Schulze helps arrange the Führer's birthday reception.

375. Reinhard Heydrich, chief of the dreaded SD, had just been appointed Acting Protector of Bohemia and Moravia. On May 27 he was fatally wounded in a grenade attack by two British-trained Czechs. In retaliation more than 1,300 innocent Czechs, including all the male inhabitants of Lidice (the town itself was razed), were executed with the two assassins.

376. In July 1942 Hitler moved east to Werewolf, the new headquarters in the Ukraine, so he could personally direct the attack on Stalingrad. Birthday celebration that August for Bormann's secretary, Fräulein Wahlmann. From left to right, Schaub, Hewel, Fräulein Wahlmann, Bormann, Engel, Fräulein Fugger (another Bormann secretary), and Heinrich Heim, instructed by Bormann to note down surreptitiously Hitler's table conversations.

377. A month later the inner circle celebrates Below's birthday. From left to right, Below (legs crossed), Christa Schröder (Hitler's secretary), Dr. Brandt, Hewel, Albert Bormann, Schaub.

378. By the end of 1942 disaster has struck in Egypt, where Rommel faces total defeat.

379. Another winter begins on the eastern front, and Hitler (with Bormann, left, at the Werewolf headquarters) faces an even greater disaster in Stalingrad where the entire Sixth Army was surrounded and doomed.

380. Germans surrendering on the eastern front.

ELEVEN

Into the Abyss

1943–1944

The year 1943 began with the last death struggle of General Friedrich Paulus' army surrounded at Stalingrad. On January 24 Hitler's spirits were momentarily lifted by the startling announcement that Roosevelt had called for the unconditional surrender of the Axis at the conclusion of an Allied conference in Casablanca. (For some time the Germans believed Casablanca was the code name for the White House and that the conference had taken place in Washington.) By making any political settlement of the world conflict quite impossible, the President had handed Hitler an invaluable piece of propaganda for resistance to the end.

Isolated groups of Germans inside Stalingrad were already surrendering in considerable numbers, but General Paulus himself stood firm and on January 30 sent Hitler greetings on the anniversary of his assumption to power. "The swastika still flutters over Stalingrad," he said, and in a personal message informed the Führer that the son of his half sister Angela, Leo Raubal, was wounded. Should he be evacuated by air? The reply was negative: As a soldier he must remain with his comrades. Thus the brother of Hitler's one true love, Geli Raubal, was consigned to almost certain death.

In April Hitler and Mussolini met at the baroque Klessheim Castle near Salzburg. Hitler was shocked by Il Duce's sunken cheeks and pallid face. In their talks, Mussolini was disspirited. The trouble with Il Duce, concluded Hitler, was age; he was sixty and in poor health.

On July 25 Il Duce resigned and was placed under arrest and held prisoner in a hotel near the top of Gran Sasso, the loftiest peak in the Apennines a hundred miles from Rome. At Wolfsschanze Hitler decided to act drastically, dramatically—and rescue his ally. An attack up the steep, rocky slope would not only cost many casualties but give the guards time to kill Mussolini. Parachuting into such terrain was almost as risky and so it was agree to use gliders.

To carry off this piece of derring-do, Hitler chose a fellow Austrian, SS Captain Otto Skorzeny, a Viennese who stood six-foot-four. He bore deep scars on his face from the fourteen duels he had fought as a student and carried himself with the air of a fourteenth-century condottiere. Not only a bold man of action but a canny one, he led his 107 men to a brilliant success on September 12. After overpowering the guards, Skorzeny escaped with Mussolini in a small Fieseler-Storch plane. In the meantime Skorzeny's men escaped by cable car, with the only casualties ten men injured in a glider crash.

In the meantime, Hitler was carrying out his plan to exterminate the Jews. Under Himmler's supervision the work of the six killing centers reached the peak of efficiency by the fall of 1943. The thought of refusing the Führer's order to murder apparently occurred to few, if any, of the executioners. "I could only say *Jawohl*," Höss, commandant of Auschwitz, later confessed. "It didn't occur to me at all that I would be held responsible. Don't you see, we SS men were not supposed to think about these things; it never even occurred to us. . . . We were all so trained to obey orders, without even thinking, that the thought of disobeying an order would simply never have occurred to anybody, and somebody else would have done it just as well if I hadn't."

Himmler's task was to train his men to become hard but not hardened; to murder and yet remain noble knights. They were to be gentlemen, in fact, no matter how atrocious their mission. And with this in mind, Himmler summoned his SS generals to Posen on October 4, 1943. His primary purpose was to enlarge the circle of those privy to the extermination of the Jews. The truth of the Final Solution was leaking out and Hitler had decided to involve the party and the military in his crime. By making them, in effect, coconspirators, he would force them to fight on to the end. If worse came to worst he would take millions of Jews with him.

This was the first in a series of information lectures by Himmler that were to include many civilian leaders and Wehrmacht officers. The first was the most important, since he must convince the SS that the execution of this distasteful deed was not at variance with the highest principles of their knightly order. "Among ourselves it should be mentioned once, quite openly, but we will never speak of it publicly. I mean the evacuation of the Jews, the extermination of the Jewish race." It had been, he said, the most onerous, distasteful assignment the SS ever had. "In the final analysis, however, we can say that we have fulfilled this most difficult duty for the love of our people. And our spirit, our soul, our character have not suffered injury from it."

The Jews were not the only victims of Hitler's New Order. Millions of others, particularly in occupied Russia, had been shot, gassed, and beaten to death. Hitler's policy of oppression included the ruthless starvation of Soviet prisoners of war. Alfred Rosenberg, Reich Minister of the East, himself bore witness to this inhumanity in a scorching letter to

381. The unconditional surrender announcement was a surprise to everyone but Churchill, who had heard Roosevelt use the phrase the previous day at a private luncheon. Churchill had at first frowned, but then
broke into a grin and said, "Perfect! And I can just see how Goebbels
and the rest of them will squeal!"

Field Marshal Wilhelm Keitel. It charged that of the 3,600,000 Soviet
prisoners of war only a few hundred thousand were in good health. The
great majority had been starved or shot in a series of atrocities that,
charged Rosenberg, ignored "potential understanding."

Countless other Soviet prisoners, along with non-Jewish inmates of
concentration camps, were dying in a series of medical experiments:
some after lying naked in snow or icy water; some during high-altitude
tests; some as guinea pigs for mustard gas and poison bullets. Polish
women at the Ravensbrück camp were inflicted with gas gangrene
wounds; gypsies at Dachau and Buchenwald satisfied the curiosity of a
group of doctors who wanted to know how long human beings could live
on salt water.

The administration of occupied territories throughout Europe had also resulted in manifold executions as reprisals for acts of sabotage and rebellion. These were legalized by Hitler on Pearl Harbor Day under the odd but apt title, "Night and Fog Decree." It ordered that all people endangering German security, except those to be executed immediately, were to "vanish" without leaving a trace. Their families were to be told nothing of their fate.

By the fall of 1943 Hitler's New Order in Western Europe, which purported to be an amalgamation of states for the common good, was revealed in its true nature: a plunder economy. Faced with millions reluctant to become mere vassals, Hitler turned from persuasion to sheer force. Acts of work stoppage and sabotage were answered by enforced labor and the execution of innocent hostages. In Holland and France the death toll was more than 20,000. Legalized pillage had become common with boxcars of loot (including food, clothing, and art treasures) converging on the homeland from Norway, Holland, Belgium, Luxembourg, France, and Denmark. This did not include enormous occupation assessments. France alone was paying seven billion marks a year for membership in the New Order.

While Hitler still envisaged grandiose plans of conquest encompassing five continents, the last six months of 1943 saw his armies in the East steadily driven back, as much as 250 miles in some places, and to the south his Italian ally's sudden collapse. In one year the Wehrmacht had suffered 1,686,000 casualties.

"If Providence should actually deny us victory," Hitler told a gathering of senior officers in January 1944, "then you, my generals and admirals, must gather around me with upraised swords to fight to the last drop of blood for the honor of Germany!" But usually Hitler preached a message of hope. Any day, he assured his companions at the Berghof, the situation would change entirely. The Anglo-Saxons would eventually re-

382. The Germans retreat on the Neval front.

383. Depressed by the debacle at Stalingrad, Hitler decides to leave dreary Wolf's Lair for the Berghof. He poses with his chauffeur, Kempka.

alize their best interest lay with his anti-Bolshevist crusade. At other times he boasted that the Western Allies would destroy themselves in front of the Atlantic Wall.

As the Allies raced across France, a group of German officers was planning to assassinate Hitler. On July 20 a bomb exploded under a conference table where he was mapping strategy. Hitler was saved when at the last moment an aide, trying to get a better look at the situation map, moved the brief case containing the bomb away from him.

Crushed to discover that the plot involved a large number of his officers, Hitler took to his bed. That August while still recuperating, Hitler received more bad news: Paris had fallen to the Allies and Bulgaria had withdrawn from the war. A few days later Romania was overrun by the Red Army and Finland was on the verge of surrender.

October brought a further defection. Miklós Horthy, the Hungarian admiral without a navy and the nominal ruler of a kingdom without a king, sent envoys to Moscow to beg for armistice. Hitler learned of this and sent his favorite commando, Skorzeny, to Hungary to bring its leaders back into line. In a imaginative operation code-named Mickey Mouse Skorzney kidnaped Horthy's son Miki, wrapped him in a carpet (Skorzeny got the idea from Shaw's play *Caesar and Cleopatra*), and delivered him to the airport. Then with a single parachute battalion he captured the citadel where Admiral Horthy lived and ruled. It took an hour.

Soon afterward Skorzeny was given a new assignment by Hitler: subvert enemy operations in a coming offensive in the Ardennes that, Hitler believed, would split the Americans and British both militarily and politically. Skorzeny was to train men to masquerade as GIs and wreak havoc behind the American lines.

The Battle of the Bulge came close to success, but by New Year's Eve, 1944, it had clearly failed.

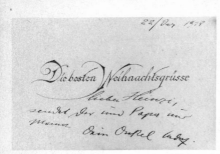

384. Life on the Obersalzberg agrees with the Führer. He poses with his secretary, Johanna Wolf, on her birthday.

385. He celebrates his own on April 20. Photographer Hoffmann holds a present, and Eva's sister Gretl looks on.

386. Hitler's new secretary, Gertraud "Traudl" Humps. He encouraged her to marry his valet, Hans Junge.

387. Hitler had three relatives on the Russian front: Leo Raubal son of his half sister, Angela: Heinz Hitler, son of his half brother, Alois, Jr.; and Hans Hitler, whose father was the Führer's first cousin. Hans escaped to Germany; both Leo and Heinz were captured. According to Stalin's daughter, the Germans proposed exchanging her brother Yasha for one of the prisoners (it could have been either Leo or Heinz). But Stalin told her, "I won't do it. War is war." Reportedly young Stalin was shot by the Germans. Heinz Hitler died in captivity but Geli's brother returned home in 1955. Pictured: a Christmas card from Hitler to Heinz, his favorite nephew.

388. Hitler and Eva with dogs.

389. Eva wearing her grandmother's wedding dress.

390. Hitler and Eva with Uschi Schneider, the daughter of Herta Schneider, Eva's best friend. The two Schneider girls were photographed so often with the couple that after war there were rumors that one of them was "Hitler's son."

391. Eva poses by a waterfall after swimming in the nude—a snapshot which would have infuriated the Führer.

392. Eva with Herta.

393. At Klessheim Castle, Mussolini shows silent doubt. During the conference Hitler compared himself favorably with Napoleon and at the luncheon table lectured his guests for an hour and forty minutes without interruption.

394. At the Berghof that July Hitler's three top adjutants—Engel, Schmundt, and Puttkamer—also look concerned. Hitler was about to set off for Italy for still another meeting with Il Duce. At this meeting near Feltre, their thirteenth, Mussolini fidgeted nervously as Hitler assailed the Italians for their defeatism.

395. Admiral Wagner, Göring, and Dönitz study map.

396. Escorted by Skorzeny, Mussolini was flown to Wolfsschanze, but upon landing the shattered dictator was reluctant to meet Hitler, and Skorzeny had to urge him to leave the plane.

397. "You have performed a military feat which will become part of history," Hitler told Skorzeny. "You have given me back my friend Mussolini." This one act of daring endeared Skorzeny to Hitler. The manner in which Mussolini had been rescued not only raised German spirits but also captured the imagination and admiration of much of the world, including their foes.

398. Ribbentrop escorts Mussolini at the Hitler headquarters.

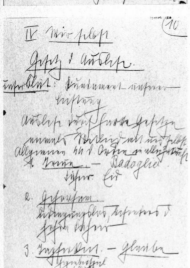

399. Pages from Himmler's outline for his October speech at Posen. Two days later he told a group of Gauleiters and Reichleiters, "The hard decision had to be taken—this people must disappear from the face of the earth." Himmler made some fifteen other speeches in the same vein to a wide range of audiences, including army and navy officers.

400. The Führer greets Himmler six days after the latter's first speech at Posen.

401. In the spring of that year, the Jews of the Warsaw Ghetto fought deportation to the death camps. The little Jewish army of 1,500 held out for four weeks until the last man was killed or wounded. SS General Stroop watches his troops burn the Ghetto.

402. Of the 56,065 who were rounded up, 7,000 were shot out of hand; 22,000 were sent to Treblinka and Lublin; the remainder to labor camps. The German losses were not heavy, but a severe blow had been dealt to Hitler's concept of "Jewish cowardice."

403. Nazi officials visit a concentration or killing camp. This photograph is notable for the resemblance of the man at the center to Hitler, and Himmler, right.

404. A few weeks before D-Day, Hitler and Mussolini say farewell—it would be their last—after conferring at Klessheim Castle. Moments later Mussolini confided to a diplomat that he had found Hitler's expectations for the war's outcome "devilishly optimistic!"

405. Field Marshal von Rundstedt inspects the defenses along the Atlantic Wall.

406. June 6, 1944: D-Day. Hitler was jubilant. "So, we're off!" he chuckled. "I am face to face with my real enemies!"

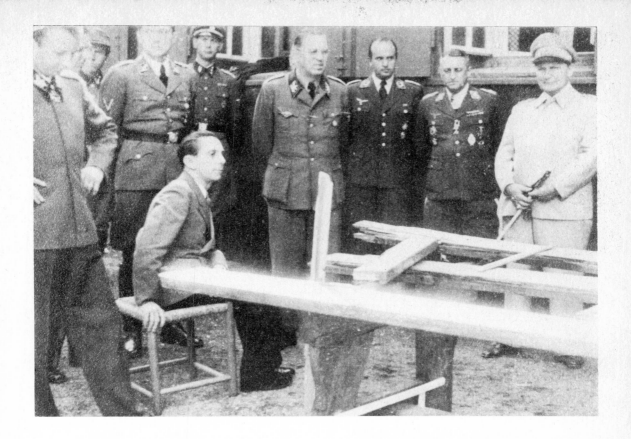

407. The bomb plot, July 20, 1944. Goebbels and Göring study wreckage of the conference table.

408. Major Otto Remer, promoted to major general by Hitler and given a division on the eastern front for his part in crushing the army bomb plot.

409. Hitler visits Puttkamer, who was injured in the blast.

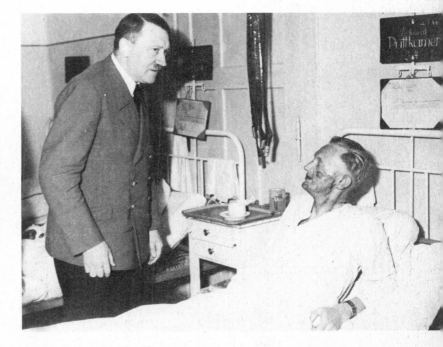

410. One of the few men Hitler now trusted was Dr. Erwin Giesing, who had treated him since the explosion. And Giesing, according to his diary, had once tried to kill Hitler, giving him a double dose of cocaine. Thinking he had killed the Führer, Giesing flew to Berlin only to learn that his attempt had failed and that no one was suspicious. The cocaine treatment was for a chronic headache Hitler suffered following the blast. Giesing persuaded Hitler to allow X rays of his skull to be taken. In 1977 Dr. C. W. Gehris, Jr., of Johns Hopkins Hospital commented that "the nasal septum in these X rays is fractured, consistent with sinusitis, which certainly sounds like the source of the headaches described, alleviated by cocainization."

411. Theo Morell, Hitler's chief doctor, is awarded a medal for his services to the Führer. Morell had been giving Hitler pills containing arsenic—through ignorance, not design. Dr. Giesing and other doctors in attendance exposed Morell's incompetence but Hitler would not listen. In 1945, however, he angrily dismissed Morell for suggesting that he take an injection of caffeine for his fatigue. "You will probably give me morphine!" Hitler shouted.

412. Joint funeral services in Budapest for the seven Hungarians and Germans who were killed during Operation Mickey Mouse. Skorzeny is at the far right.

413. Field Marshal Walter Model (right), Hitler's personal choice to command his last gamble, an offensive in the Ardennes, December 1944. Left, Bodenschatz; center, Luftwaffe General von Richtofen.

414. General Hasso von Manteuffel, (*above*) German pentathlon champion, whose tanks almost reached the Meuse River.

415. SS Colonel Peiper, whose tanks made the first deep break-through.

416. The New Year's party at Führer headquarters is a glum affair.

417. First the Americans are captured in great numbers.

418. Then the Germans.

TWELVE

The Last 100 Days of Adolf Hitler

1945

The personal leadership which had won Hitler such stunning victories early in the war now seemed to lead invariably to disaster. Himmler, with no military experience, was placed in command of an army group. Strategic withdrawals were forbidden, so that whole armies, including hundreds of thousands of men, were trapped behind enemy lines or annihilated. At almost every level National Socialist ineptitude or corruption was crippling government and industry. Meanwhile Hitler, who had taken on himself all responsibility for the conduct of the war and nation, was unwilling to see the situation in realistic terms, and veered between extremes of optimism and apocalyptic despair.

In choosing a successor Hitler had passed over Göring and Himmler, both of whom he considered disloyal for advocating surrender, to settle on Admiral Karl Dönitz. Realizing that the war was lost, the new German head of state set out to end hostilities as quickly as possible to prevent useless bloodshed. Himmler asked Dönitz to make him second man in the new government. "That is impossible," Dönitz said, "I have no job for you." The new Foreign Minister, Schwerin von Krosigk, suggested that Himmler take responsibility for the surrender of his SS troops, but instead he fled, poisoning himself after capture by the Allies two weeks later. Dönitz was unable to arrange a separate surrender on the western front, but in the forty-eight hours between the surrender's being signed and its taking effect thousands of German troops were able to make their way to western lines.

To the surprise of the world, Hitler's suicide a few days before the surrender brought an abrupt, absolute end to National Socialism. Without its only true leader, it burst like a bubble. There were no enclaves of fanatic followers bent on continuing Hitler's crusade; the feared Alpine Redoubt proved to be a chimera. What had appeared to be the most powerful and fearsome political force of the age had evaporated overnight. No other leader's death since Napoleon had so completely obliterated a regime.

419. American Secretary of State Stettinius proposes a toast at the end of the Yalta Conference in February, with Stalin, Roosevelt, Churchill, and Soviet Foreign Minister Molotov opposite. Conviction that a split in the alliance was imminent kept Nazi hopes alive.

420. The waiting room of the Führer bunker below the Reich Chancellery. Allied bombs had driven Hitler underground. Left edge, Dr. Morell; center, Hitler's former valet Krause and Admiral von Puttkamer.

421. Next to Bormann, the man Hitler saw most in these days was his favorite architect, Paul Giesler. They would spend many hours poring over illuminated wooden models of the new Linz, which would outrank Vienna as the jewel of Austria, or of a redesigned Munich (pictured). Hitler considered the Bavarian capital his true home: "Here I started my movement and here is my heart."

422. He visits the Oder front during the desperate days of mid-March. Hitler urged his commanders to contain the Russian drive on Berlin, promising that secret new wonder weapons would be ready momentarily.

423. On March 28 Chief of Staff Heinz Guderian, commander of the eastern front, angrily challenged Hitler's refusal to evacuate the army stranded in Kurland and was fired.

424. American soldiers climb the dragon's teeth tank obstacles of the Siegfried Line.

425. They captured books used in the public schools of Aachen during the Nazi regime.

426. East meets West. Cautious not to antagonize the Russians, Eisenhower held American forces back from Berlin and Prague, hampering Wehrmacht plans to surrender toward the West.

427–28. Many Germans are happy to surrender—at least to the Western allies.

429. Test pilot and ardent Nazi Hanna Reitsch flies with General Robert Ritter von Greim into besieged Berlin on April 26 and makes a forced landing on the broad avenue leading through the Brandenburg Gate. They urge Hitler to escape with them but he refuses.

430. On April 28 Hitler married Eva Braun. At left, their wedding certificate. Note errors: First, the date was smudged and then mistakenly altered to April 29; second, Eva started signing her maiden name before correcting herself so that a crossed out "B" precedes the "Hitler." After the ceremony Eva was radiant. She sent for the phonograph with its single record "Red Roses," and went out into the corridor to receive congratulations from the staff. Two days after saying their farewells to members of the inner circle, the couple secluded themselves in their private quarters. Eva took poison and Hitler shot himself in the right temple. Their bodies were carried to the garden of the Reich Chancellery and thoroughly cremated with gasoline.

431. The charred remains of Goebbels and his wife who after first poisoning their six youngest children had themselves shot by an SS orderly in the Chancellery garden. Himmler fled but took cyanide after capture.

432. Red flag is erected at the roof of the Reichstag.

433. Berlin is in ruins. The Reich Chancellery.

Overleaf: 434. Cologne in ruins.

SURRENDER

435. Three Hitler Youth, thrown into battle along with old men, are captured east of the Rhine.

436. German officer eating American C rations at Saarbrücken.

437. General von Trippelskirch and his aides.

438. A number of officers and civilians committed suicide rather than face defeat.

439. Field Marshal von Rundstedt.

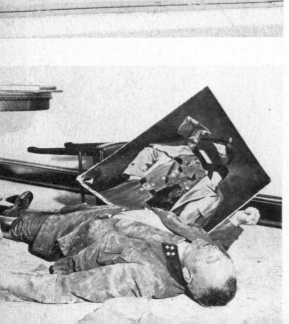

440. Endless lines are surrendering.

441. VICTORY . . . Eisenhower a few minutes after the first signing of the German surrender at Rheims, May 7.

442. AND DEFEAT . . . Field Marshal Keitel at the second and final surrender ceremony in Berlin, May 8.

HORRORS OF THE FINAL SOLUTION REVEALED

443. German civilians are forced to see the prisoner dead at Buchenwald. On February 13, 1945, while dictating his last testament to Martin Bormann, Hitler said: "I have fought the Jews with an open visor. I gave them a final warning when the war broke out. I left them in no doubt that they would not be spared this time, should they once more thrust the world into war—that the vermin in Europe would be exterminated once and for all. . . . I have lanced the Jewish abscess, like the others. For this, the future will be eternally grateful to us." On April 2: "the world will be eternally grateful to National Socialism that I have extinguished the Jews in Germany and Central Europe."

444. German girl forced to watch exhumation of bodies at Namering.

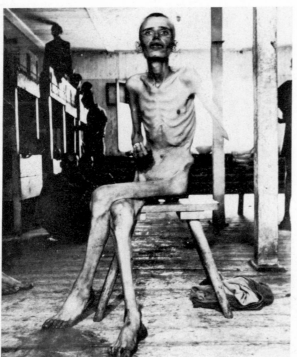

445. Slave laborers at Buchenwald.

446. Hungarian skeleton.

447. Crematoriums in German concentration camp at Weimar.

448. *"J'Accuse!"* A freed slave laborer points out a Nazi guard who brutally beat prisoners.

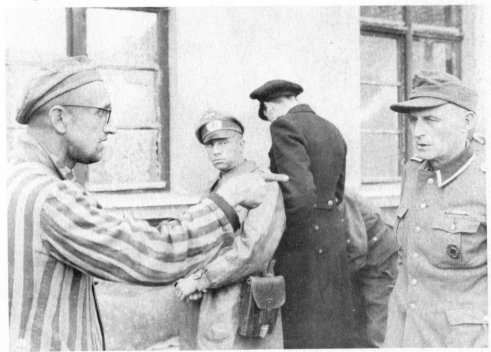

449. The Brandenburg Gate.

450. Allied soldiers at the emergency exit from Hitler's bunker, opening onto the blasted garden of the Reich Chancellery. Here the bodies of Hitler, Eva, and the Goebbelses were burned.

451. The picture window at the Berghof.

452. Hitler's tattered trousers from the July 20 bombing. They were kept in a U. S. Army vault for two years and then burned "to prevent their symbolic worship of what Hitler stood for."

453. Göring, Hess and Ribbentrop at the Nuremberg Trials. Of the twenty-eight major defendants only three (Schacht, Papen, and Fritzsche) were acquitted. Eight received long terms of imprisonment; the rest were sentenced to death. At 10:45 P.M., October 15, 1946, Göring cheated the hangman with a cyanide capsule. Two hours later the executions began.

454. When Hitler's SS adjutant, Otto Günsche (right), returned to West Germany after twelve years' imprisonment in the Soviet Union and East Germany, he was bewildered by the sight of young men with beards and long hair. "Dear friend," former Adjutant Schulze told him, "we have lost the war and all is now changed." Schulze took him to the Berghof. The remains of the building had been obliterated by the Americans. Everything looked different and it was difficult even to imagine where the long flight of steps leading up to the house had been. All trace of the most extraordinary figure in the history of the twentieth century had vanished—unlamented except by a faithful few.

Acknowledgments

This picture book could not have been compiled without the co-operation of numerous people in Germany, Austria, England, and the United States. Archives and libraries contributed many photographs: The National Archives, Still Picture Branch (Joe Thomas, William Leary, Deborah Gitomer, Paul White); The Library of Congress; The Imperial War Museum (Rose Coombs, Mike Willis): The Bayerisches Hauptstaatarchiv, Munich; the Bibliothek für Zeitgeschichte, Stuttgart (Dr. Jurgen Rohwer, Werner Haupt); and the Bundesarchiv, Koblenz.

Numerous agencies, organizations, and individuals also contributed to this book: The Department of the Army, Washington, D.C.; Central Military History Office, Department of the Army (Charles MacDonald, Marian Mc'Naughton); Munin-Verlag, Osnabruck, publishers of *Wenn alle Brüder Schweigen;* Max Wünsche; SS Major Otto Günsche, General Hasso von Manteuffel; SS Colonel Otto Skorzeny; Colonel Hans Ulrich Rudel; Colonel Edward Schaefer; Glen Sweeting; Monika and Richard Schulze-Kossens; Ben E. Swearingen; Harry Schulze-Wilde; Dr. Eleonore (Kandl) Weber; Edward Whalen; Dr. Walter Schultze; Nerin Gun; Dave Staton; Rogan Showalter; Jakob Tiefenthaler; Egon Hanfstaengl; Leni Riefenstahl; Rev. Bernard Strasser; Walter Frentz; General Walter Warlimont; and General Otto Remer.

Special thanks are due to Hildegard Fath for the Hess Family collection; Albert Speer for the Hitler sketches; Furmin Michel for his Göring and Schaub collection; Hans Hitler for the family pictures and documents; Wolfgang Glaser for his pictures of Hitlerland Today; Dr. Rudolph Binon for information regarding Dr. Bloch's cancer treatment of Frau Hitler; Erich Kempka for his candid photos of Hitler; Admiral Karl Jesko von Puttkamer for his Führer Headquarters collection; and Frau Herta Schneider for her Eva Braun albums. I would also like to thank my chief research assistant in Germany, Karola Gillich; Edward Weiss; and my Doubleday editors: Carolyn Blakemore, Ken McCormick, and

John Stillman. Finally, my greatest benefactor has been the United States Government which gave me the pick of hundreds of thousands of photographs from 279 captured Nazi albums. At the Library of Congress there are the 47 personal albums of Hermann Göring which go back to his career as a fighter pilot in World War I. At the National Archives are three magnificent collections: the 33 personal albums of Eva Braun, Hitler's mistress of some thirteen years and wife of less than two days; the 68 personal albums of Joachim von Ribbentrop, Hitler's Foreign Minister; and the 131 albums of Heinrich Hoffmann, Hitler's personal photographer from 1923 until the end of the Third Reich. Thousands of these photographs have never been published outside of Hitler's Germany. Hundreds have never been published anywhere.

CREDITS

Photographs identified solely by reference number are from the National Archives.

1. No credit.
2. Dr. Eleonore (Kandl) Weber.
3. Library of Congress.
4. Hans Hitler.
5. Library of Congress.
6. Hans Hitler.
7. Hoffmann.
8. Bundesarchiv.
9. No credit.
10. Palacios, Doubleday.
11. No credit.
12. Schulze-Wilde.
13. Schulze-Wilde.
14. Schulze-Wilde.
15. Toland.
16. Schulze-Wilde.
17. 242-HB-590.
18. Library of Congress.
19. Schulze-Wilde.
20. U. S. Army.
21. Toland.
22. No credit.
23. Bundesarchiv.
24. Toland.
25. Toland.
26. U. S. Army.
27. U. S. Army 32239.
28. U. S. Army 1076.
29. U. S. Army 1081.
30. Bundesarchiv ABC-3373.
31. Bundesarchiv.
32. No credit.
33. U. S. Army.
34. Bernhard Strasser.
35. Toland.
36. Bibliothek für Zeitgeschichte.
37. 242-HB-9027.
38. Festschrift.
39. Bundesarchiv.
40. Bundesarchiv.
41. No credit.
42. 242-HMA-632.
43. 242-HMA-1008.
44. 242-HMA-003.
45. Library of Congress.
46. 242-HB-18499.
47. 242-HB-2274.
48. 242-HMA-2400.
49. Hauptstaadt Archiv.
50. U. S. Army.
51. Imperial War Museum.
52. National Archives.
53. Imperial War Museum.
54. National Archives.
55. 242-HMA-2733.
56. 242-HMA-2766.
57. 242-HMA-2438A.
58. 242-HMA-2374.
59. National Archives.
60. Library of Congress.
61. No credit.
62. Hans Hitler.
63. National Archives.
64. Schulze-Wilde.
65. Rogan Showalter.
66. Imperial War Museum.
67. Library of Congress.
68. Hanfstaengl.
69. No credit.
70. U. S. Army.
71. U. S. Army.
72. 242-HAR-2-30B.

73. 242-HMC-3803.
74. Firmin Michel Collection.
75. Library of Congress.
76. 242-HAP-1928-17C.
77. 242-HAP-1928-11A.
78. 242-HAP-1928-11C.
79. 242-HF-304.
80. G. Sweeting.
81. 242-HB-2887.
82. National Archives.
83. 242-HF-309.
84. 242-HB-4066B.
85. Schulze-Wilde.
86. 306-NT-865G-7.
87. Toland.
88. Hans Hitler.
89. Hans Hitler.
90. Dave Staton.
91. Library of Congress.
92. 242-EB-24-4.
93. 242-EB-24-5.
94. 242-EB-31-26A.
95. 242-EB-24-6B.
96. 242-EB-11-40A.
97. 242-EB-31-45B.
98. 242-EB-33-27A.
99. 242-EB-5-45.
100. 242-EB-24-13A.
101. 242-EB-1-45B.
102. 242-EB-1-43E.
103. Imperial War Museum.
104. 306-NT-112-458.
105. Library of Congress.
106. National Archives.
107. 242-HB-1121.
108. 242-HB-5167.
109. 242-HB-49.
110. Stadtarchiv, Munich.
111. No credit.
112. U. S. Army.
113. U. S. Army.
114. Hans Hitler.
115. Bundesarchiv.
116. 242-EB-28-6C.
117. U. S. Army.
118. 306-NT-865-6.
119. 242-HB-3835.
120. 242-HB-2747.
121. 306-NT-176413C.
122. 306-NT-864-20.
123. 242-HB-2748.
124. 306-NT-865-10.
125. 306-NT-176664.
126. 242-HB-1171.

127. 306-NT-178018C.
128. 242-HB-1877a.
129. 242-HB-998.
130. 242-HB-1019.
131. 242-HB-67.
132. 242-EB-23-32A.
133. 242-HB-1339.
134. 306-NT-870-8.
135. No credit.
136. Toland.
137. Hanfstaengl.
138. Hanfstaengl.
139. 306-NT-865-R-1.
140. Stadtarchiv, Munich.
141. Ben Swearingen.
142. 242-HB-7069.
143. 242-HB-2506.
144. 306-NT-340-WW-3.
145. 306-NT-340-WW-1.
146. 242-HB-4925.
147. 242-5564A.
148. 242-HB-3849.
149. 242-HB-3851.
150. 306-NT-395-52.
151. 242-HB-6694.
152. 305-NT-969-30.
153. 242-HB-6862-a1.
154. 242-HB-6677.
155. 242-HB-7385.
156. 242-HB-7421.
157. 242-HB-7494.
158. 242-EB-29-8A.
159. 242-EB-1-33D.
160. G. Sweeting.
161. 242-HB-7313A8.
162. 242-HB-7675.
163. 242-HB-7677.
164. 242-HB-8199a509.
165. 242-HB-8199a152.
166. 242-HB-8199a261.
167. Speer Archiv.
168. 242-HB-8199a43.
169. 306-NT-870-11.
170. 242-HB-7727, 242-HB-7736.
171. 242-JRA-2-5.
172. 242-HB-6978a18.
173. 242-HB-6978a13.
174. 242-HB-19418.
175. 306-NT-870-9.
176. Fath.
177. Fath.
178. Fath.
179. Fath.
180. Fath.

181. Hanfstaengl.
182. 242-HB-2.
183. 242-HB-129.
184. 242-HB-21857.
185. Firmin Michel Collection.
186. Library of Congress.
187. Library of Congress.
188. 242-HB-31674-43.
189. Firmin Michel Collection.
190. Library of Congress.
191. Library of Congress.
192. 242-EB-9-25.
193. 242-EB-1-171B.
194. 242-EB-1-36A.
195. 242-EB-1-37D.
196. 242-EB-2-11A.
197. Fr. Schneider.
198. 242-EB-1-41D.
199. Kempka.
200. Speer Archiv.
201. No credit.
202. 242-EB-12-12A.
203. 242-EB-12-2.
204. E. Baumann.
205. 242-EB-11-11A.
206. Frentz.
207. 242-EB-6-13C.
208. 242-EB-22-33B.
209. 242-EB-11-12A.
210. 242-EB-11-12B.
211. 242-EB-11-19A.
212. 242-EB-11-13B.
213. 242-EB-11-40B.
214. U. S. Army.
215. 242-JRA-11-29.
216. 242-HB-21919-3.
217. 242-HB-3528.
218. 242-HB-21299-1.
219. 242-HB-22280-1.
220. 208-AA-2030-3.
221. 242-HB-4825.
222. 242-HB-2769.
223. 208-N-39828.
224. National Archives.
225. 242-HB-2193.
226. 208-AA-203G-8.
227. Degrelle.
228. 306-NT-865-2.
229. Kempka.
230. Kempka.
231. Kempka.
232. U. S. Army.
233. 306-NT-865K-12.
234. 80-G-410205.

235. Library of Congress.
236. 306-NT-865N-1.
237. Breker.
238. Breker.
239. Speer Archiv.
240. Speer Archiv.
241. Speer Archiv.
242. Speer Archiv.
243. Speer Archiv.
244. Speer Archiv.
245. Speer Archiv.
246. 242-EB-6-7.
247. 242-EB-3-2.
248. 242-HB-6250-1.
249. 242-HB-3877.
250. 306-NT-969-18.
251. 306-NT-969-3.
252. 306-NT-969-33.
253. 242-JRB-1-75.
254. 242-EB-4-41B.
255. 242-EB-5-2D.
256. 242-EB-2-41E.
257. 242-EB-4-43B.
258. 242-EB-28-12D.
259. Wünsche.
260. Wünsche.
261. 242-EB-28-26B.
262. U. S. Army 585 662.
263. Imperial War Museum.
264. 306-NT-948E.
265. 306-NT-865c-3.
266. Library of Congress.
267. 242-GAP-303K-1.
268. 242-JRB-7-8.
269. 242-JRB-8-5.
270. 242-JRB-28-41F.
271. 242-EB-6-4.
272. 306-NT-128917.
273. 306-NT-129057C.
274. 306-NT-182760.
275. 242-JRB-20-29.
276. 242-EB-6-11B.
277. 242-EB-6-28.
278. Library of Congress.
279. Firmin Michel Collection.
280. Firmin Michel Collection.
281. 242-JRB-26-38.
282. Library of Congress.
283. 242-EB-6-41C.
284. 242-JRB-27-51.
285. 306-NT-1222E.
286. Imperial War Museum.
287. G. Sweeting.
288. 242-JRB-28-9.

289. 131-NO-2-100.
290. G. Sweeting.
291. G. Sweeting.
292. 306-NT-132A-A-7.
293. Bibliothek für Zeitgeschichte.
294. 242-EB-8-5c.
295. 242-JRB-41-23.
296. Puttkamer.
297. Puttkamer.
298. Palacios, Doubleday.
299. 242-JRB-41-27.
300. 242-GAP-17A-6.
301. 242-GAP-17CC-2.
302. Puttkamer.
303. Puttkamer.
304. 242-GAP-61B-2.
305. G. Sweeting.
306. G. Sweeting.
307. G. Sweeting.
308. G. Sweeting.
309. Transit Film Munich.
310. Transit Film, Munich.
311. Transit Film, Munich.
312. Transit Film, Munich.
313. Transit Film, Munich.
314. Transit Film, Munich.
315. Transit Film, Munich.
316. Transit Film, Munich.
317. Bibliothek für Zeitgeschichte.
318. Puttkamer.
319. National Archives.
320. Puttkamer.
321. 242-JRB-37-13.
322. 242-EB-7-47.
323. U. S. Army.
324. 242-HB-22250-1.
325. Palacios, Doubleday.
326. 306-NT-2743V.
327. Firmin Michel.
328. 242-JRB-47-29.
329. 242-EB-27-166.
330. 242-EB-13-2C.
331. 242-EB-11-5C.
332. 242-EB-27-15E.
333. 242-EB-13-36B.
334. 242-EB-13-1.
335. 242-EB-3-40B.
336. 242-EB-15-13C.
337. Library of Congress.
338. Puttkamer.
339. 242-HB-46581-7.
340. 242-HB-46581-17.
341. 242-HB-46581-27.
342. Puttkamer.

343. Puttkamer.
344. Firmin Michel Collection.
345. Fath.
346. Library of Congress.
347. G. Sweeting.
348. 242-JRB-9-39.
349. 242-HB-61900-224.
350. 242-HB-48400-183.
351. 200(S)-GT-173.
352. 242-GAV-96.
353. Palacios, Doubleday.
354. 242-GAV-106B.
355. 242-GAV-43B.
356. 242-SS-11-21-18.
357. 242-SS-11-32-39.
358. 200(S)-G-104.
359. U. S. Army.
360. Puttkamer.
361. Puttkamer.
362. Puttkamer.
363. Puttkamer.
364. Schulze; also in National
     Archives, 242-EB-13-7.
365. 242-HB-48400-411.
366. 242-SS-10-101-6.
367. G. Sweeting.
368. Munin Verlag.
369. U. S. Army.
370. Puttkamer.
371. Schulze.
372. Puttkamer.
373. Puttkamer.
374. 242-EB-14-2A.
375. 242-HBA-5948.
376. Puttkamer.
377. Puttkamer.
378. U. S. Army.
379. 242-HB-48400-5300.
380. 306-NT-1334-12.
381. U. S. Army.
382. 306-NT-1334-14.
383. 242-HB-48400-89.
384. 242-EB-11-24.
385. 242-EB-13-25.
386. Gertraud Junge.
387. Hans Hitler.
388. 242-EB-14-7A.
389. 242-EB-25-53.
390. 242-EB-13-40A.
391. No credit.
392. 242-EB-11-29.
393. 242-HB-48400-641.
394. Puttkamer.
395. Puttkamer.

396. Tiefenthaler.
397. 242-HB-48400-932.
398. 242-HB-48400-926.
399. National Archives.
400. U. S. Army.
401. 238-NT-289.
402. 238-NT-298.
403. National Archives.
404. U. S. Army.
405. U. S. Army.
406. U. S. Army.
407. Puttkamer.
408. Remer.
409. Puttkamer.
410. Schulze.
411. 242-HB-61900-172.
412. Skorzeny.
413. U. S. Army.
414. Manteuffel.
415. Peiper.
416. Puttkamer.
417. U. S. Army.
418. U. S. Army.
419. U. S. Army.
420. Puttkamer.
421. Frentz.
422. Bibliothek für Zeitgeschichte.
423. 200(S)-GT-64.
424. U. S. Army.
425. U. S. Army.

426. U. S. Army.
427. U. S. Army.
428. U. S. Army.
429. 242-HB-222494-18.
430. Dwight D. Eisenhower Library.
431. Sovfoto.
432. Sovfoto.
433. Firmin Michel Collection.
434. 239-RC-18-1.
435. U. S. Army 204587.
436. 208-YE-145.
437. U. S. Army 205637.
438. 208-YE-148.
439. U. S. Army 207633.
440. U. S. Army 207207.
441. Culver Pictures.
442. U. S. Army 206291.
443. U. S. Army 203472.
444. 208-YE-1B-12.
445. Signal Corps, U. S. Army
446. 208-AA-12764.
447. Signal Corps, U. S. Army
448. U. S. Army 203466.
449. U. S. Army 210303.
450. 208-PU-932-23.
451. 208-PU-932-22.
452. U. S. Army 304-534.
453. 306-NT-1378A-6.
454. Monika Schulze-Kossens.

COLOR SECTION

I. U. S. Army.
II. U. S. Army.
III. U. S. Army.
IV. Toland.
V. Toland.
VI. U. S. Army.
VII. Toland.
VIII. U. S. Army.
IX. Toland.
X. Toland.
XI. U. S. Army.